Robert Florio

MW01286149

Life! It Must Be a Comedy
An Autobiography by Robert Florio

Some of the names in this true story were changed to protect the names of individuals.

White Rhino Production
A Robert Florio Trade Mark TM
"The crap you actually want to buy."

FIRST EDITION, 2010

Life! It Must Be a Comedy
An Autobiography by Robert Florio

Quotation: Robert Frost
Quotation: Linkin Park

Cover design: by Robert Florio

Photos: Personal

ISBN-1452833508
EAN-13 9781452833507

Manufactured in the United States of America

TABLE OF CONTENTS

...Earth...

Robert Matthew Florio

Mother: Elena Florio

Father: Ubaldo Florio

March 2, 1982 A.D.

United States of America
Maryland
Glen Burnie

"I don't have to see to believe..."
(Robert Florio)

Life!

It Must Be a Comedy

An Autobiography by Robert Florio

Chapter 1
The Awakening

I had no fear as a child. There was no challenge I wouldn't face, no obstacle I could not see myself defeating. I was a seven-year-old boy with a fast mouth, a crew cut, flashing orange shorts and a hand-me-down overly-used favorite T-shirt. I was the toughest kid in the neighborhood. Even though my two older brothers Adriano and Carlo were bigger than me and stood up for me, I held my own weight against anyone.

I can see myself waking up in my twin bunk bed with the sheets softly brushing over my legs, my hand on the pillow with little feathers poking through slightly, feeling a little itchy. Mom yells at me to get up.

Robert get up! Are you going to sleep all day? I hear her Italian accent echo through the house.

I hear my father's shiny black leather work shoes stomp down the hallway and from my parent's bedroom next to mine. I dread hearing him getting ready for church. My brothers and I are dragged out of the house and always the last family to arrive,

Come on, come on, come on! Let's go, let's go, let's go! Get up, get up, get up! Dad says in his melodious Italian accent.

My older brothers and their friends in the neighborhood are already up, ready to have fun on the new skateboard ramp in the front yard. I walk on the cold wood floor of my bedroom, down the hallway.

Life! It Must Be A Comedy

My two-story, split foyer house, the coolest house on the street, was built by my father and his brother I never met, who passed away. The front facing is redbrick. There's a long patio stretching the width of the house with old-style Italian masonry blocks between brick pillars making railings all the way around the patio.

I eat a bowl of Rice Crispies loaded with enough sugar at the bottom my spoon almost stands up in it. It grinds as I scrape the bottom of the wooden cereal bowl. I somberly rub my eyes waiting to wake up, sitting at that kitchen bar-like tabletop. The yellow wooden laminate countertops and dark wood cabinets hanging above the counter top made a U-shape around my kitchen. I sat down on the tall wooden bar stool with gray and white knitted fabric, soft cushion and a small backing. My bare legs stick to the protective plastic over the fabric, a comfortable reminder it's my home. I grab an apple from the refrigerator, and grab my overly worn-out Air Walk high tops with some duct tape holding them together. I tie them extra tight for super strength, thinking it will make me run faster and stronger. I look at myself in the bathroom mirror, making sure the two zigzags my dad cut into my hair are still looking cool. There seems to be an unwelcome echo and heightened sensitivity of some sort, disturbing sounds disrupting everything that is perfect. I see a white haze fade in and out.

The sensation of what I'm going to do is something amazing because I'm the best and nobody else can do it. I grab my skateboard with large yellow and orange offset wheels and matching grip tape on top, with sticker's right in the middle where the emblem is smooth, fresh and brand new. My wheels are broken in, but still fast. My brother Carlo picked out my first professional skateboard, just like Tony Hawk's. My new grip tape gives me the footing I need. I smell freshly sprayed WD40 in the ball bearings and feel residue leaking around the wheels.

I hear the playful rattling of the backstop fence in the field in front of my house where we play baseball. I can't wait to begin. With my skateboard and gear, my confidence level is higher than anyone's. I'm running down the wooden steps over the foyer at the bottom, the brown smooth ceramic tiles dad did himself. I can hear the railing dividing the living room from the steps rattling and the picture frames of my family, chattering from the vibration that I make racing down the wooden steps. My hand slaps the white aluminum screen door and with

2

lightning speed I burst onto the porch, jumping all three steps into the front yard, running straight to the street, slapping down my skateboard.

My brothers and my friends from the neighborhood are messing with the brand-new six-foot vert plywood ramp my brothers built for jumping. Carlo is teaching me to bend my knees with the curve of the ramp, just like he taught me to ride the four-foot plywood halfpipe in our backyard. Carlo is my coach and the source of my confidence that I can ride any ramp my brothers can. We ride the vert dreaming of daring ourselves to jump it. I watch Adrian riding up the ramp and then turning around right when he gets to the top. I duplicate and repeat everything anyone else does.

I'm not going to jump it. I'm not stupid. I already broke my elbow jumping the ramp at the firehouse, Carlo says.

One of Carlo's friends Andy, always had bright ideas but he's never brave enough or talented enough to go through with them.

I could jump this thing, Andy *says* really boisterously like a tough guy, but no one ever takes him seriously, causing more trouble than accomplishment.

Yeah right! Your fat ass couldn't jump anything, Adrian snaps back.

With a voice of confidence, like a tiny glimmering stone shining brighter than all the larger stones, like the little engine that could kick butt I know, *I could*!

I know I can jump this thing, I say without any hesitation, claiming my turn.

Carlo is quick to tell me not to do it because he doesn't want me to get hurt. But I know that his confidence in me was strong. If anyone knows I can do it, it is Carlo, and Adrian.

No! I'm not going to let you get hurt, Carlo is usually quick to protect me, but this time he is the one that says *OK*.

I can do this. I remember what you told me, I tell Carlo. I quickly rehearse: *Make sure to bend your knees with the curve of the ramp and keep your balance in the air with your feet evenly spread apart. Yeah, I know man.*

This is the moment I am waiting for. I was born to do this. As my brothers and friends sit around trying to be cool skateboard guys, showing off their eighties fashions, I decide to give it my best. The tape is holding strong and my shoes feel very tight. I'm completely in the zone and I'm skating down Pine Road. I make a right and go down to the next street at the end of Linden Road. Now I'm completely on the other side of the field. I can't see my house, I only have to go straight and fast and remember what I was told.

I have to remember who I am. It's a little white and hazy now and it seems to be in slow motion, but I must remember it. Familiar sounds echoing, the beating of my heart and heightened sense of awareness appear fuzzy, but I can see myself taking off. My breathing is cool. I get in my stride and push off with my left foot, going faster and faster down Linden Road. Everything is perfect. Thinking about that left turn coming up, keeping my balance and speed, avoiding the bumpy little rocks, passing by houses, making sure I don't stomp my wheel and fall on the rocks below. I make the turn, I see the ramp. I am lining up on the right side of the road. I hear them all yelling, getting louder, and cheering me on.

The wheels racing over the pavement is getting louder, that familiar sound of skateboard rumbling through the neighborhood. Each push faster and faster. My mind is only on this ramp, bending with the curve and being the best. I am the athlete I was born to be and nothing is going to change that. This is my future, I know I'm going to be great. It's the last push and the first thump to get my balance. Seamlessly the ramp and my wheels connect.

It's absolutely quiet now, my wheels, my feet, my knees, and my hands are all one. My balance is perfect. I'm at the top of the ramp, faster than I've ever gone. I'm soaring, bent over in a streamlined position one hand forward, the other hand back, right foot forward left foot back. Everyone is looking up to me, as I leave the ramp. I'm almost to the middle of my property, like a moment frozen in time, soaring through the air. The wind is racing by my face. Everything is getting louder. The cheering is now brought back from its quiet gasp of anxious observation. Everything is in real time now. I'm launched five feet above the ramp and fifteen feet away… I landed it!

(Off a different three foot ramp)

Life! It Must Be A Comedy

Disconnected from myself, daydreaming, my eyes are wide open. I lie on my back with my head on a pillow, staring at the ceiling. The memories of who I was crashing over me. Everything has changed. I no longer have any control. I'm not the best and I'm not the strongest after all. My body will never be the same. The bed mechanically rotates me side-to-side. I'm in a dark, cold and lonely room. Outside the door, people talk in a completely foreign language. They have authority over my life now. My breathing is irregular. I don't know when my next breath will come. The echoing beeps that monitor my life haunt every familiar memory I have. Knowing someone somewhere is faintly protecting me is the only hope I have that someone might come to help me. Faith might see me through this. I have nothing else.

Jesus loves me this I know for the Bible tells me so, I keep repeating to myself, hoping I will be saved.

This is not the way my future was supposed to be. My memory of who I am from my birth until now is the only comfort I have. I am horrified by what I have lost, what I have left behind. To survive I'm going to have is to discover who I am again. My sedated dreams feel intoxicated, but my waking hours are as surreal, forcing me to run back in to those dreams and memories. My hope comes as a prayer.

If I close my eyes and concentrate hard enough maybe I can see the future. I cannot let my life be for nothing. I know I am supposed to be special. If only I had something else no one possessed. If I can get control back again (in a way I can not yet imagine) then I might be able to live.

I can find my way if you let me God. I need You now God. Give me something that makes me the best again. Help me find out who I'm supposed to be and give me something, a gift, something in my power to control. I can't see or imagine anything being possible right now, but I believe what is waiting for me will make me the best at something in the world again. I don't know what that is, but please give it to me when I'm ready. Next to the window which reveals a wall and the sky, I see a recent picture of me and my dog as I finish my prayer.

6

Chapter 2
The Quest

Life! It Must Be A Comedy

From an early age it is easy to predict who you are going to become by favorite hobbies, interests, and adventures. My life certainly didn't lack any adventures. In pre-K a photograph was taken of me kneeling in long khaki pants and white T-shirt, with my middle finger in my mouth, biting my nails, while balancing myself on some sort of wooden beam stair-stepping obstacle course on the playground. When asked my favorite at school I replied:

I like paint and blocks and sand.

Little did I know that those activities would become my serum for life, the building blocks for success, rewards and re-discovery of who I am and want to become.

My best early childhood friend was Jared. We were inseparable. We were both born in March 1982. We liked to pretend we were born on the same day but my birthday was March second. We felt like brothers.

Life! It Must Be A Comedy

We were born in the same hospital and lay side-by-side in the baby viewing area when our parents would come look at us.

It wasn't true, but it sure felt like it was. We often got into fights and pulled each other's hair thinking whoever pulled the most was the toughest. Jared had blond hair and was only slightly taller and always a little more intelligent because he was interested in school. His parents made their kids do their homework, where I felt free as a bird outside playing. It was rooted in adventure and being the bravest, toughest and

most successful of my friends. One particular day in kindergarten Jared and I were playing together after a session of painting and then a nap. I woke up in a tired state surrounded by other five year olds, some of which became my best friends throughout most of my childhood, not to mention the girls I had early crushes on. It was a typical kindergarten class but in a small unordinary school. I would peek out the doors and look all the way down one hall to the other side of the school. It was

9

Life! It Must Be A Comedy

Solley Elementary School on Solley Road. The same school my brothers and sister attended. Often I was peeking down the hall, yelling toward my brother and my next-door neighbors in their classes at the end of the day, ready to run to the buses, I found myself teasing the girls I had crushes on and staring at my kindergarten teacher who I had a crush on too.

While lying on the carpeted floor at the front of the class room and chalkboard, I woke up from a nap. I often stared out the window at the playground. I felt a little extra curious and mischievous. I never really played doctor with other little girls. I just figured out what I wanted to find out. I started walking around the room with my scissors with Jared by my side. Clumsily, but on purpose, I stumbled into a girl I had a crush on and dropped my scissors.

Oh no! I dropped my scissors...I'll get them, Jared and I would say acting out the part as we fell on the ground to get them.

While trying to be funny lying on our backs, we chose precisely where to fall? Near the middle of the room, under girls wearing dresses, we found the answers to our questions. We carefully dropped them near the cute girls. Anywhere between the building blocks at the back and the classroom tables at the front of class, we were guaranteed to get some action. The middle of the room was usually the best place for most of the traffic where we would repeat this antic time and time again staring and giggling to ourselves and high-fiving each other. It still amazes me that we were never caught. On one particular trip to the zoo Jared's mother captured a photograph of Shelly, a blond cute girl with pigtails, Jared and me hugging with big smiles. We all grew up in the same neighborhood. We were having the time of our lives. Shelly and Jared were always the smartest kids in my class, and in many ways that photograph showed the kid and spirit of joy that I was.

I was always getting away with something I wasn't supposed to be doing or pushing my curiosity to its limit. I climbed the tallest tree in my front yard to its highest point to escape. This tree divided the property line, but more on our side than our next-door neighbors. Not that it would have stopped me. On one particular trip to the zoo Jared's mother captured a photograph of Shelly, a blond cute girl with pigtails, Jared and myself with big smiles hugging. We were having the time of our lives.

It was a nice perch to sit on. Here my adventures and curiosity piqued for the very first time. I had a girlfriend in kindergarten and a climbing partner. I didn't know much about girls except they were very pretty and I always knew how to charm them. At the top of this tree Desiree and I were like two lovebirds pecking at each other. Her house was behind mine. The garden my father created was a perfect place for us to jump corners of our property over the fence to hang out. This tree was a very tall tree and lined up directly with the garden and I could see her house and right into the front window of my houses living room.

My brothers were quick to tease me when they discovered our secret hiding place. My crush lasted through fourth grade. I wasn't always sweetest to her. Desiree often reminded me of the time when I hit her over the head with a plastic shovel. That was just my way of saying I liked her. When I was at home with my family I always knew how to get my way. Whether having my sister stand up for me, starting fights, running to my mother, at a very young age I knew how to outwit my older brothers. I often got scared of the dark and found myself in my parent's bedroom sleeping right in between them. As a youngster building a hard crust of toughness and a courageous reputation, I was also a gentle lion cub, falling asleep on the couch with my head on my mother's lap, being carried to bed.

I shared bunk beds with Adrian. Carlo had the room attached to ours directly across from my parent's bedroom which faced the backyard. With such close proximity, it was hard to get away with anything without mom screaming her lungs out, coming at us with a wooden spoon. Helen had the basement bedroom directly to the right at the bottom of the steps. The basement was a repository for our junk and toys. My father's parents lived down the hall in the basement. They were very old and didn't speak much English, mostly spoke Italian. That part of the house was the most frightening to me. I didn't spend much time there. Helen had one wall painted purple with a brass railing daybed. Sometimes I would sleepwalk. Other times late at night I would run to her bedroom to snuggle up with her. At a very early age my sister became a source of comfort and protection.

One night, I was sleep walking down the hall in my green frog suit that was zippered all the up, with white canvas like grip on the feet, but very soft fabric on the outside. My eyes were barely open and I found myself passing the bathroom on my left. Fortunately I missed the stairs to my right and walked right into the kitchen. The floor was slightly cool, with the blue square patterns cracked looking tile. The first silver bumper separating the tile from the wood floors made a clicking noise. I heard my sister talking on the phone. I thought she was my mother for a moment.

Mommy pick me up, I said almost like a whimper as she picked me up and rested my head on her shoulder my legs wrapped around and fell asleep.

In first-grade I started to get braver and no longer cried at the bus stop. My fears of school turned into unwillingness to learn and stubbornness toward anyone trying to get me to do something I did not want to do. Clowning around by saying things to other students while sitting behind them was my expertise. I was willing to fight anyone who didn't agree with me or said anything against me. The first-grade teacher was Miss Frasier, who used to smoke in the bathroom in the corner of the first-grade classroom. My brothers and I didn't have any respect for her doing that. I had the advantage of knowing about the teachers they had before I did. Besides not paying attention in class, recess became the time to establish dominance over my class mates.

As a seven-year-old in second grade I was drawing in textbooks. My curiosity about girls was growing. The whole class was shown a projected drawing of male and female body parts. It was very strange and emotionally confusing. We were all giggling, but horrified repeating the names of the body parts after the teacher pointed to them. With these images and words burned in my mind, it was the only topic I was interested in. Adrian is three years older so second grade was the last year we were in the same school together. Carlo is three years older than Adrian and it is the same with my sister being older than Carlo. Adrian was making his own bad reputation for me to follow. Our school allowed the excellent students to advance and the ones who were behind to stay behind. The system never allowed kids like me to catch up.

Third grade was the time in my life that highlighted, sports, art, and skating. My potential was starting to shine. Boundaries, limits and discipline still did not dictate my life as an eight-year-old. Freedom of expression showed up even more in my personality and my physical abilities.

Since both my mother and father are from Italy they didn't have the best English and educated background to reinforce school for me and my brothers. Helen was much more studious, graduating from a private high school. In 1990 my sister was eighteen years old and getting married. I was the ring boy so I got to ride in the limo with her and her best friend and stood pretty close to her, along with Carlo who was one of the ushers. She married a very tall, stiff-hearted man who swept her off her feet but made her life a living hell. He was always a jerk and never friendly to my parents or respectful by the way he would talk or act. Dick would completely shut himself out and away from us. My sister should have known from his name that he was trouble and would also cheat on her.

So, now just my brothers and I would be in the backyard skating on our new ramp. With dad's help we built a twenty feet wide by four feet high plywood half pipe. You could hear us dropping in from the coping metal poles, to grind on up and down like thunder as the wheels rolled over the joints, up and down the vert. Carlo had his hair half-spiked on top and the other half came to the side in a long mullet inspired by the hit Batman film starring Michael Keaton. Carlo's skateboard had clear grip tape over his favorite stickers with Batman's symbol in the middle. He wore black skater gloves with finger cut outs, a helmet, and elbow and knee pads. We all had Airwalk high tops. Carlo wore short washed stone jeans and Tony Hawk T-shirts. I dressed just like him or like Adrian. Adrian had washed denim short jeans or

Skids. We always wore our helmet and pads and dad was always reinforcing safety. My parents always said we looked a lot alike, especially in our baby pictures, almost like twins. While I wasn't the tallest, we both were thin and lean. I would tease Adrian a little bit because I thought he was a little bit too heavy. I'd also tease him about his red hair, cautious not to call him "*fat boy*" too many times and I got punished with titty twisters or punched in the arm or leg. Adrian and I were the toughest, always fighting back, while Carlo was calmer and smarter, shy and always making accurate predictions. Adrian had a larger nose than me, a more protruding forehead and a huge smile. He was always the ladies' man, especially with our three next-door neighbor girls. Their brother Robert and I had a lot in common even though he was three years younger than me and could not skateboard. We'd jump over each other's fences, play house, cops and robbers, cars and tunnels in his sandbox with a pool in the middle for playing horseshoes or playing wiffle ball.

My mom and dad kept rabbits and ducks in the backyard next to the shed. A great big grapevine covered the fenced off animal pen. There was a homemade punching bag too hanging in the center. I loved teasing our ducks Rosie and Cindy. Rosie the big white male would chase me up and down the ramp and bite my belly button. Our house sat on three quarters of an acre, much longer than it is wide. There were many tall trees toward the back of the yard and an above ground blue swimming pool. Our poll had a white railing around it and a small deck with green turf carpet and a large stepladder that we had to pull down. We never went in it much because it was too much work to clean being next to the pear tree and under the giant tree in the middle of the yard. We had one great giant tree splitting at the base making two trees in the middle of our back yard. I always stepped on the sticker balls that fell from it. My parents decorated it with a little garden and bricks circling it.

Dad spent most of his time in the garden which consumed a large part of our yard. He grew a forest of tomatoes, peppers, squash, cucumbers and green zucchini going all the way up one of the tall trees at the back. My father always jokingly called us one of his squash, or *cucoch* whenever we did something stupid. My parents also spoke in Italian when they didn't want us to know what they were saying, in order to direct our behavior.

Life! It Must Be A Comedy

Cucoch! I should've left you in the garden. You weren't ripe yet to pick, dad would say. His favorite time to reflect on something we did was always at dinner time, as we all sat together joking around and trying to avoid my mother's wooden spatula slapping our heads. She always sat closest to the stove and with one reach grabbed her favorite tool and smacked or through whatever she could to reach at us.

The garden was on one side of our yard, the half pipe on the other in the far back. I could sense Italian in my blood, meditating on the big fig trees growing bushy. They were obstacles when walking between the half pipe and the garden. The tall fence side of the yard was fortified so our skateboards would not fly over. This neighbor often started arguments with my father and my brothers since the first day we moved in. To avoid any communication, my father planted huge bushes to create a barrier. The opposite side of our yard was wide open until that neighbor put up a long wooden fence.   When my brothers and I weren't skateboarding we'd be swimming. I got teased that a shark was in the pool and my brothers wouldn't let me get out. Kicking and screaming at the top of my lungs, I'd fight for respect one way or another. My yard also provided a maze of gymnastics, a metal swing set, extreme sports, and kept us occupied into the dark hours of the night. No one looked for us, covered in dirt running around the yard between the houses. We stayed out until all our friends went home. Then, we looked for a flashlight so we could stay out even longer.

Every shadow and every adventure was a training ground. It was all I knew. Lessons came the hard way. Something or someone was always getting in the way of what I wanted, but between those hard times, I felt pretty good. I soon found myself literally running into something, or should I say…someone.

Chapter 3
Coming of Age

It takes many footsteps and discoveries to find one's way in the world, to become a man who does great things, who becomes a hero. Sometimes, I stumbled and fell in. I learned to pick myself up and put my life back together. Growing up accident prone my creativity and energy sometimes caused me to trip on obstacles. Like the day when I got the most identifiable feature on my face. A scar slanting up toward my nose is two inches long on my left cheek. It helped mold my physical impression of my visual self in the world. It makes me look handsome and a little bit dangerous and mysterious.

I ran down the hallway in my house as a young six -year-old growing into a seven year-old boy. My legs were strong. I got that scar one afternoon after running out of my bedroom at the end of the hall in nothing but boxer shorts, a T-shirt, and one sock. My skinny little body came running down the hall with lightning speed. I was gliding, my toes barely touching the ground. My mother was carrying a huge oval-shaped white porcelain dish of her incredible pasta. She was taking the pasta to the downstairs kitchen refrigerator. My head was at the same level as the hot runny red pasta sauce. Mom made the best lasagna with the most flavorful spicy sauce and perfect al dente noodles. I was always a picky eater, but her pasta was irresistible.

In that instant my universe was smashed. My face and pasta were one. I was completely numb to anything happening. I ran right through her hands and right through the posta dish. She yelled and threw her head and arms back and up in the air as the pasta dish went soaring through the air near the ceiling, crashing down. With my mother screaming after me, I ran into the kitchen at the end of the hallway and hid behind the oval brown wood dining table. That is where I would shield myself from her. My mom tried to catch me but I would always match her moves, going the opposite direction if I could get away.

Robert stop! my mother was screaming.

I was afraid for my life, not knowing why she was screaming at me. I was completely covered in sauce from head to neck and all over my face and shirt and on my hands. While I was scared, I licked my lips and tasted delicious sauce and flicked a few pieces of spaghetti noodle off my shoulder. Hiding frantically and confused, I was just scared of the yelling. Completely filled with adrenaline, to my surprise what I heard next forever defined a moment in my life.

Robert stop! Don't touch the walls! My mother screamed while pointing at me.

She grabbed me and brought me to the bathroom, wiped my cheek with a kitchen towel, and held my head so tight I could not get out of her grasp. She's worried I have a huge cut on my face. I was barely tall enough to see over the green marble bathroom sink to the bottom of the three door medicine cabinet mirror to see. It opened up three ways to see everything creating the deep skin gash. My cheek looked like a lip spreading open.

Mommy am I going to die? I asked, horrified.

She drove me to North Arundel Hospital where we sat surprised that we had to wait. There was not much blood, so it wasn't extremely deep. It did not cut all the way through my cheek or damage any nerves. The doctors put me under anesthesia using eighteen stitches and plastic surgery. Waking up from the anesthesia in the middle of the procedure I started kicking and screaming. I might have punched the doctor. They put me under again and I woke up with a chic full of black little stitches.

As I grew, I had more scars due to my athletic ability and my attitude. I was ready to join my brothers in the backyard for a skateboarding session. I had my Airwalks shoes, knee and elbow pads and my bright orange helmet with extra thick padding which made my head look like a mushroom. My white shirt sleeves were cut off all the way up past the armpit. My black gloves had the redlining cut off at the knuckles just like my brother's. I had my brand-new skateboard Carlo helped pick out for me at Christmas. It was perfect for me and it had a little cartoon kid with dreadlocks and overall jeans on. He had a slingshot in one hand and a stressed out cat he fiercely gripped in his other hand, holding it by the tail. Not only did the skateboard represent me but Carlo felt it would give me good balance with its extra long tail for jumping. This image became rooted in my mind and childhood dreams. Carlo even drew it with black magic marker on one of the walls of his bedroom.

I was waiting impatiently sitting at the bottom of the steps while my dad was looking for his work boots and tools. He was always wearing his high heeled yellow work boots with steel toes, white T-shirt with a V-neck, long and a gold necklace with a cross in the middle where his black chest hairs curled up. His thick black mustache went all the way around his smile, edge to edge. He was a happy tough guy with a downward frown. I grab my skateboard by the truck and we walked out to the yard to meet my brothers and their friends.

Waiting for me was my new best friend. A puppy I named Fluffy. He was barking at the back glass door waiting to come in the house and always ready to chase us up and down the skateboard ramp. He was a black lab, long-haired shepherd and schnauzer mix. I adored that dog attaching to him emotionally in a very strong way. He was the cutest dog with a white tipped tail, a white patch on his chest and white tips on his polls. I would put my nose up to his soft nose with thick hair at his cheeks, along with a little curly tail and a white tip on the end. His ears would come straight up and the very tip would always flop forward. Parking with his high-pitched yelp wagging his tail furiously he was always starved for attention and the most hardheaded horny dog. I didn't have a strong understanding for caring for him, but I understood what love was.

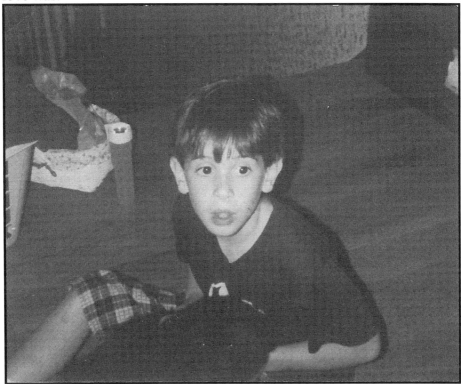

He was just a puppy but to me a little brother, a best friend and we were kindred souls. We always want my mother saying, *In Italy dogs are always outside dogs and rarely ever pets.* Surprisingly my mother brought home this little puppy but swore it would only be an outside dog. That would soon change. He was the only puppy in a litter that looked like him and the only one that approach my mother when she got him. He chose us.

Come on dad what are you doing? Let's go already. I impatiently called.

All right hold your horses. Geez, are you running a race or something? My dad said funnily with his accent.

Hey! I'll race you to the backyard! I challenged my dad all the time to a race.

OK, when we get outside, line it up, said my dad who was always quick to accept a challenge as soon as he stopped what he was doing.

Come on Fluffy, let's go. I would try to tell fluffy what to do but he rarely listened. Not once would he not run after me when I fell and tried to jump on me.

We get out the backdoor closed the sliding glass and got ready set to race. I always felt like I could keep up but my dad's legs were strong and extremely fast. He always sucked in his lips under that big thick mustache, holding his breath. The bond we have in some way is a lot closer than my other brother's because I'm still the baby. I was always hanging off my dad.

You all better not bring dirt in the house when you're done. My mother yelled from the kitchen upstairs.

Hey dad when are we going to play catch? I was always asking my dad.

OK, you are playing with your skateboard. I have to do some work in the garden. When I'm finished. Maybe later, my dad said always giving me the chance. I wouldn't forget and always hold him to it. On that warm summer day the sun was going down late past 8:30 p.m. I would wait for it to set, playing outside using up every bit of day light.

Adrian, Carlo, myself and a few friends started ripping up the half pipe, and skating it like we wanted to be professionals. Our neighbor friends across the field and down near the beach lived closer to the water that nearly surrounded our entire neighborhood like a peninsula. Andy and Sammy were brothers and not very agile on skateboards because they were significantly overweight, but they always ran their mouths. Andy was Carlo's age and Sammy was closer to Adrian's age. One of Carlo's closest friend in the neighborhood was Ron. They were equally matched in ability on the board always challenging each other. Jason was there sometimes. He was a good friend who went to karate classes with us, a master of videogames like Atari and Nintendo. He always had the next best thing and every Wrestle Mania action figure with accessories and had to prove he was better. His mother Mrs. Grindy was my mom's best friend. Our families often got together for very delicious and memorable dinners.

Life! It Must Be A Comedy

The ramp was still fresh. With Carlo and Ron holding each one of my hands, Carlo coached me through, making sure I'd stay balanced and bend my knees. I connected the back trucks and planted my left foot on the tail of the board, ready to go down as I held their hands. I was nervous and scared but Carlo was giving me confidence that once I did it once I'd always be able. I was ready on top of that four foot wide deck, the fig tree branches piercing through somehow supporting me because they've always been there. Freshly painted green water dripping pattern on the top of the ramp vert was staring at me also as if waiting for me to crash or ride its vert.

You're not going to fall we've got you. Just keep your feet where I told you and try to keep your balance forward, bending your knees with the ramp, Carlo coaxed me.

No! I'm going to fall, I told him. *You better catch me or I'm going to be pissed.*

Come on Robert don't be a baby, Adrian teased me so I would do it.

Shut up fat boy! I screamed out to Adrian, scared I'd have some kind of punch coming my way for saying it.

Come on Robert boy! You can do it. Vemuz, andiamo, forza, dad yelled from inside the garden. Looking back, I can see his head just popping out above the thick tomato plants.

I leaned forward, holding their hands tightly, going down the first drop very quickly, but my front foot started to come up and I started leaning back too much. My butt barely scraped the ramp. Sliding down on my skateboard my skateboard went shooting straight to the other side of the ramp, up over the coping, hitting the high back plywood. The wheels on my new skateboard where extra fast, and Carlo had tightened the trucks just right for me. I got up speed, ran up the edge pulling up, got handed my skateboard and I planted my foot for one more try. I was psyched, but it was just my first time, and I was ready for my second.

I was still scared that I would fall, but more determined since I had the feel of it. With dad cheering me on, two trusted hands holding me, and one more word of encouragement from Carlo I was confident.

See, I got you. Now do it. Once you get this you're going to be skating up and down this ramp like a professional, better than all of us and jumping ramps, Carlo said with an extra forceful breath of confidence and impatience.

Okay, I'm going to do it. Ready? I asked proudly.

Andy, get out of my way man! I shouted as he skated right across my path.

Feet firmly planted, I slowly started to drop in, my force and momentum magnetically glued to the vert this time. My hands grasped tightly, my focus and balance on the board and ramp. The hands supporting me let go. The four-foot tall mountain no longer held any fear for me, so I completely let go and shot fast and straight, approaching the other side of the ramp all by myself.

That's it, now bend! Carlo shouted as I approached with more speed than ever before.

I sped toward the vert, going up to the left and as I got to the top of the metal coping a grinded my trucks across doing a 50-50 grind, going halfway across the other side of the ramp. I came down gently on an angle parallel to the ramp down to the other side, perfectly zooming past everyone. Carlo's voice was ecstatic as was everyone else's. They were cheering me on with astonishment and disbelief as I showed everyone up.

Life! It Must Be A Comedy

Did you see that? I did it! Hey dad, I did it! I shouted and slapped hands while everyone else stood in amazement, witnessing the birth of a phenomenal professional skateboarder.

I'm often with my brothers and friends, skateboarding that ramp, as the wheels go over the plywood, risking splinters, sounding off the thunder of our noise. Adrian broke his ankle and arm, but injuries never stopped us from playing together. We skated that ramp, drinking my mom's freshly made ice tea. I would always get more sugar to make my drinks as sweet as possible. We also had great times playing laser tag or playing wiffle ball with little Robert. I was skating around the neighborhood, finding jumps and grinds, and neighbors yelling at us for being on their property. The good times never ended stealing fresh plywood at any new house construction. We were like ninjas, scurrying away, careful to balance the wood on our skateboards, rumbling down the street, never getting caught.

At night we heard my mother's call, loud and clear, demanding that we *come home right now*, shouted out like a siren all our names. We could be three streets away, across the field, in Andy's backyard playing laser tag, in the trails dividing his house, near Lombardi Circle. We would still hear her call or, her special whistle, loud and clear, a very high pitch stretched-out whistle, followed by a very low pitch stretched-out whistle.

Adrian, Carlo, Robert! Come home right now! Her demand calling us in from trouble.

Or, she called us Alvin, Simon and Theodore. The chipmunks were definitely an accurate description. I was always the instigator, the one to push everyone on to the next stage, like Alvin. Carlo was the smart one, only guiding us to do the right thing or making the safer decision, like Simon. Theodore had to be Adrian because compared to Carlo and me he was the one that was heavier and just a little bit slower on the skateboard.

My mother was just starting to become a businesswoman, no longer home all the time babysitting, no longer relying on cleaning other people's houses. Most of the time she wore long T-shirt like a nightgown with black afro hair and huge bug-eye 1980s pink and black glasses. All that was starting to change, with her new job as a Mary Kay cosmetics consultant. Her cooking was from her experience in Italy. She was taught by her mother to create the best pizza anyone ever had.

27

For three boys, so courageous and full of energy, we had a great heritage passed down to us. I always wondered if I'd get any taller, but that was the only worry I had about facing my opponents. My mother was four-eleven and very petite, fast to crack a wooden spoon over my head for doing something wrong or to yell at me in Italian to sit in the corner and do my torturous phonics, learning to read, which I didn't really like.

I could always run to my dad, a man who spoke softly but carried a very big stick. My dad was not tall either at five-three. He had considerably thinning brown hair on top, clean-cut in the back. My dad's most famous characteristic was his thick, dark mustache. It made it seem like he was grimacing. He also had thick sideburns down below his ears. He had powerful arms from lifting weights, but the skinniest white legs, rarely getting sun all those years, wearing pants to work and in the garden or backyard. It was the genes passed down from his father, Papa Carlo, which included the strong Florio physique. It didn't slow either of us down. My father always worked from nine a.m. until eight p.m. at the barbershop with my Uncle Sandro, except Wednesdays and Sundays. My father and mother were great role models, hard workers and very devoted to their families. Still there was a lot of unwillingness on my part and my brothers' to embrace that old-school way of thinking and living. Instead we tried our own challenges and life situations. Somehow learning the hard way might quickly become a Florio trade mark. Parental rules were blocked by our stubbornness and our own decisions. No one felt freer than me, learning from my brothers' mistakes, but ready to make my own. I did not think anything bad would happen. I didn't stop to think what might happen next. My curiosity and energy were bound to get me into some kind of trouble.

Chapter 4
The Little Pieces

By the time I was eight years old, baseball became my passion. I attempted football for a few years a little bit later. The front yard of my house was the greatest place to grow up. From my porch I could see the creek that surrounded my entire neighborhood. There was also a local beach across the field and down a couple blocks, where kids hung out, experimented with everything. My brothers would start fires, girls and boys would go there to make out, fish, crab and swim. One road led down to a boat ramp and a very heavy metal chain connected by two bars on each side kept anyone out. Community members would use a key to unlock it.

The baseball field wasn't exactly built to be a baseball field. It was more of a hangout place for neighborhood troublemakers. My parents felt the brunt of the trouble, mostly for being different. Somehow it's amusing to be Italian, but my family was always ready to fight back. My sister was not so much affected, but even with Carlo the older boys were relentless. It was my turn to stand, and rise over those guys. It was my turn to be in control of those older trouble maker's younger brothers, and their family members because I was tough now. The roles finally reversed. It was a perfect match. I was going to stand up for my family and create a definite Florio reputation (along with Adrian) -- not to be messed with.

Much of this took place on the field. For a baseball field right field was completely missing, only a slope past first base meeting up

30

with the road. We always had to chase the ball down the hill and onto the curved road, up the hill in the overgrown shrubs on both sides of that street. My brothers and I build forts in the tall overgrown area in right field. People in the neighborhood would volunteer to cut the field grass, especially one man with a giant red tractor. Mr. Jones, the old faithful man across the field was out there every week on his tractor. The backstop was directly in front of my driveway. There was a swing set out in center field with a tall metal slide facing my house, a sliding poll on the other side, and three rubber swings with medal chains. The old metal merry-go-round was my favorite, to watch the neighborhood spin around me. We would climb to the edge of the beam holding up the swings and draw all over the wood. Late at night people would go there to sit on the huge thick wooden planks and swing through the night, creaking and cracking. Making the first and second level to hang out, do what ever and mostly at night seeing people making out.

Life! It Must Be a Comedy

My next-door neighbor Robert Cherry was three years younger than me. With the same name he was always like a little brother. He was the youngest of four siblings. His father was Robert Cherry Sr. and his sisters all had different fathers. I had a serious crush on the oldest, Stephanie. She had great beautiful big brown eyes, with something different about her more provocative with brunette hair. Tina the second oldest, was very tall and lanky with red hair. She was always the quietest of the three girls, but had a great friendly funny smile. The third oldest and a few years older than Robert was Crystal. Crystal was only one year older than me. I occasionally flirted with her but she always beat me up. Feisty and boyish and sometimes speaking with a lisp, Crystal always came out fighting and ready to talk back. With long straight brown hair and carrying a heavy step my curiosity and attraction was always scared off in intimidation. I used to call her Crystal pistol. Playing in the sand box, playing guns, or playing baseball or whiffle ball in our backyards was fun. Our mothers would always call us and we both would always respond together. Robert looked just like his dad. He had a great smile with a dimple, a freckled nose and slightly droopy eyes and a crew cut of dirty blonde hair. His head always seem to be bigger than other kids our age. He had a great personality always, smiling, and always quick to stand up for his sisters, even with me. Robert was always Robert. A boy with a great heart.

Robert! Shouted my mother.

What!? We both would turn around and shout back simultaneously.

It would go back and forth with his mother Barbara too. Standing at the front door halfway leaning out the screen door holding on to the handle and yelling. Checking up on us, quick to poke either of their heads back in.

Not you. The other Robert, our mothers would say.

We were always on the same team when it was time to play or pick teammates for seven innings of baseball. When anyone was playing on the field, I would always grab my glove to play with the big kids and their fathers or friends. My swing was very natural. They thought I wasn't going to make a hit because I was so small, but I crushed it over their heads, running, making it to first base. It was the same with football or any other sport I played. I was the littlest one out there. I would be given the ball and I would run right between their legs and make touchdowns. No one could touch me. I was fast and agile and very smart and made all the right moves.

I would play any ball game in the field all day, in between running around the neighborhood with my friends and chasing after girls that I liked. I was a typical boy showing my interest in a girl by slapping her on the butt or throwing eggs at her.

I always waited for my dad to get home right around 7:30 to 8:00 p.m. As a barber my dad worked very hard. I didn't see him all day except for Wednesday and Sunday. When he came home he was usually tired from standing all day, hardly eating anything, trying to make that extra buck. I dragged him onto the field to play baseball with me. We would play for a few hours in the summertime, even when the sun was almost completely gone. We had only one streetlight between my house and my neighbor's house, barely lighting up the field. He was usually always hungry for pasta my mother had prepared. My mother would be standing on the front porch, telling him to go eat. I was right behind him as he walked around all the cars, checking the locks, making sure the locks and windows were closed. It was a ritual for him to sit in the car for a couple minutes, finally shutting off the engine and hearing me nagging him to play catch. The old blue Ford station wagon was baby blue with tons of junk and debris, cables, tackle box and blanket in the back. The cold fake leather upholstery always seemed uncomfortable, but it was my dad most reliable car that he could not do without. The maroon family station wagon was always kept cleaner. My brothers and my sister all have their first experience learning to drive in the baby blue station wagon. The heat was slow to warm up and it was not very pretty and kind of run down, but my dad loved it.

Dad, want to play catch? I would say running up to him as soon as he got out of the car and was locking the doors.

Life! It Must Be a Comedy

Hi son. Oh, I just got home I'm hungry, Dad told me.

Come on, I've got everything. Let's play catch for a little while. Please? I would beg him.

We'll see, Dad would reply as usual.

Oh come on, it's going to get dark soon. Please! I wouldn't give up asking.

All right. Go get the gloves. Mannagia! You're not going to leave me alone. Let's play, my dad said, giving in, being funny, and saying a few words in Italian.

Yes! Do you want to play catch or hit me the ball or be the catcher? Usually I gave the option.

H.Y.S.L.-1993

Life! It Must Be a Comedy

Running in the house, I grabbed the gloves and bat and favorite balls under the steps, jumping over Fluffy who would sit at the bottom of the steps. Holding as many things as I could including my catcher's mitt to practice pitching, I would run straight outside throwing my dad his glove and running out to the field. Dad would hit me grounders while I played shortstop, emulating Cal Ripken. He'd hit me pop flies and I'd catch almost every one of them. The field was uneven and the ball would bounce up after being hit, taking a tricky bounce into my glove. Our lopsided field kept me on my toes. My favorite was my Easton gray aluminum baseball bat, as well as practice pitching. Dad told me I had a natural curve which would go up and down and then up again right into his glove. He was amazed. We played till it was nearly too dark to see the ball. My mother would wait impatiently, lean out the front door with her famous, high/low pitch whistle and we knew dinner was ready. If I was ever lost that whistle got me home.

Some people are visited by angels or think they have scene a ghost. Some people feel they are chosen for some reason, but they don't know for what, that they are special and they don't know why they are singled out. Once, as a child I was visited by something. I don't know exactly what it was. It's still a mystery, but it was extraordinary and it was real. It made me feel like I was one in a million and somehow whatever my future held I would be guided and helped to find out who I am and what my purpose in life might be.

One morning very early I got up from my bed. Being both a heavy and light sleeper, I was never up that early. The day before, Adrian and I were shooting a bow and arrows into a large stuffed cardboard box at the back of the yard. It had a bull's-eye painted on it. I didn't take too many turns, afraid I might mess up. I was an excellent marksman. I could match my brother on any target, standing anywhere from thirty feet to sixty feet away. It was the same when I would practice pitching. My arm and abilities were very accurate.

I woke up the next morning with an uncontrollable desire leading me, like a zombie, to my brother's room. I grabbed the bow and arrow to practice in the backyard. Everyone was still sleeping. Without any fear, I had the chance to use this time to myself and not have my brother take it from me. It was a relatively warm morning. The sun had just hit its horizon point, where it's still rising but the workday had not started. The weather was calm and there was no breeze in the air.

Life! It Must Be a Comedy

About fifty feet from the target I shot a couple arrows. For no particular reason, barefooted, only wearing a T-shirt and shorts, I walked toward the far left corner of my yard. I set my aim toward the tree fort my brothers and I built. It was six feet tall in the far left corner of my yard, around five tall trees and up against the fence. It was draped in old green carpet like fake Astro Turf. Inside the fort was all dirt floors and fluffy would dig big holes and lay inside to cool off on hot days. I've always been afraid to go near that tree fort by myself, but that day I was drawn in by something led blindly from my fears. Behind the fort was a five foot rusted metal garden fence with 6 inch squares, making it impossible for someone to go in the fort from the other side, without monstrously jumping on top through the giant hole square we've built in the roof. There was only two entrances, both near the back cut in the carpet and walls reinforced by some wood planks. The walls were fortified, nailed to two by four wood planks even at the bottom of the fort, keeping it from moving with the wind. Adding to the mystique of our fun house, but a place I would always be afraid of alone was the fact that the wood where only 1 yard away. The only way I wasn't afraid to go in there was if I wasn't by myself, or when the neighbors, Stephanie and Robert, would play house with me. What I experienced next was a one in a million opportunity.

I stopped about twenty feet facing its corner. I aimed at the tree in front of the fort. I pulled back holding my aim for the center of the tree bark, at eye level, then released. It streamed straight and fast with a determined purpose. The arrow firmly lodged itself perfectly in the center of the tree. I walked up slowly, as motion slowed down and time became more like a dream. I leaned over slightly, grabbed the end of the arrow when something caught my attention. I was frozen in fear instantly. Seconds felt like minutes, when I realized what I had done. I was still as a statue and the wind was completely still, with no sound. It revealed itself to me, what looked like fingers piercing the far edge of the carpet wall. The curtain slowly pulled open. The carpet moved from my left to right held open. The fingers had claws and were like a scaly green texture I've never seen before. Standing there was a tall creature. I was face to face with the source and purpose of my abnormal behavior. I was brought out in my trance, to stand beside an entity trying to show me something I did not understand or was ready for. I did not know then, but my life later would put me in that same position to stand alone, and figure out something I would not be ready for, but not able to run away from. It was my calling.

Between the figure and me was a tall, skinny, young tree with leaves and a chain link fence. It was blending slightly with the object standing directly in front of me. Stuck in my fear, the tall, athletic, green human-like creature stared at me with big round eyes and a flat nose frowning at me. There was a connection I knew was not normal. Standing there frozen, facing the horror of realizing I was vulnerable, afraid I could not understand. My body stopped, but my mind started moving forward as I realized I was in danger. I knew what I had done and it was something I could never get myself to do alone ever. I snapped out of my haze, and everything sped up in desperation. I immediately saw things clearly. I knew I had to run away.

With my hands still on the arrow, clenched tightly, I stood straight up and ran with my lightning fast legs, screaming at the top of my lungs *AHHH!* I reached the sliding glass doors in seconds, with Olympic strength and speed, opening the door and closing it behind me. The adrenaline in my system gave me extra strength because that door was always hard to open and very hard to close. I reached Carlo's bedroom downstairs and started pounding on his door to wake him up. I was afraid to look over my shoulder, feeling like I was caught in some horror film. I barged through Carlo's door and out of breath tried to speak with tears of fear.

There's a monster! Or some alien or something; I don't know what but I saw it and I'm scared! Carlo please you have to believe me, I frantically pleaded for his help.

What! Where? Are you sure? Okay, I believe you... gezz, Carlo said irritated and half awake.

In the backyard I was shooting my bow and arrow and I shot at the tree in front of the fort. Something like a tall green monster was looking right at me and opened up the curtain and just stood there. I couldn't move. I'm so scared. You have to believe me. If I describe it can you draw it at least? I said.

I was sounding so crazy it startled Adrian and he came running downstairs, pushing me around for waking him up but I quickly explained hysterically and he started to listen. We were all freaked out and afraid to go outside. I called Jared and told him to come over. I needed someone to see what I was talking about and told him that I just saw a monster and I needed him to be my proof. When Jared arrived we were all ready to walk out to the backyard with the drawing and holding bats. In this frantic moment I thought to grab a camera, but remembered I did not know how to use it with the giant rectangular flash. I was worried enough to get everyone's attention so I decided to go without it. I was the only one willing to take the time and grab what I needed to document my proof, but working not to lose my eyewitnesses. I had to abandon my photo plans as we walked outside together.

We slowly approached the fort and by this time the sun was in full force lighting the path, awaiting some dark secret that could still be behind the curtain. Standing outside the entrance we hesitated to walk in. I was very hot headed and grabbed my baseball bat very tightly in both hands as we tiptoed one after another. I followed Carlo first than walked in behind him. Carlo spun around a couple of times and apparently didn't see anything. We examined the entire fort but as soon as I walked in I saw an object or a shape on the floor. The object was exactly where the creature would have been standing like a very smooth bump in the dirt. Immediately I pointed it out and seeing this thing suddenly everyone became startled. It was some sort of evidence left behind, a symbol or a footprint. This perfectly smooth, rounded mound shape of an egg, about two feet long and one foot wide. It looked as if someone molded rich dark soil with perfect craftsmanship. It would have taken a good amount of time for someone or something to make this form. It felt like it was a parting gift, a symbol or a message to figure out.

In the very center of the shape was a footprint going the same direction as the mound. It was a very thin but elongated peanut shape about ten inches long and about two or three inches wide and much narrower in the center. This elongated peanut shape looked like a footprint, but without any toe marks. Everyone was tingling with suspense trying to make sense of what I saw. We inspected the area vigorously again, trying to keep Fluffy away from the area so he didn't dig it up. The shape was quickly ruled out by all of us to be anything my dog could have done. With the mounds detail, smooth surface flawlessly crafted and perfectly centered footprint in the middle, there was only one explanation. More than anything, it was an alien.

My brothers and friends still remember this event and I hope they carry the memories as proof. Even at my birthday sleepovers my friends were teasing, hoping to be given an opportunity to see what I saw. This event shaped the person I am today. I cannot say exactly what it was I saw. There are other people all across the country and the world with similar encounters. I don't know how this encounter affected my future path directly or indirectly. I do know it is undeniable what I saw and what I felt.

Dirt Mound Foot Impression With Perfect Form
Robert Florio's Alien Encounter

1 Foot

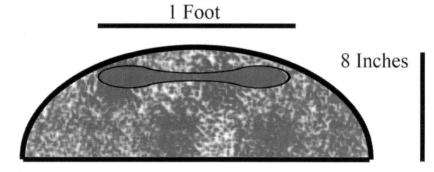

8 Inches

Side View

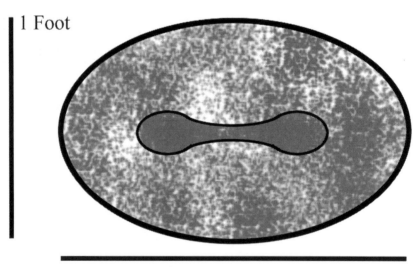

1 Foot

2 Feet

Top View

Life! It Must Be a Comedy

Someone in this encounter was trying to tell me something. I only wish I knew how to understand alien, if that was some kind of message. In my perfect little world I did not know my life might not be guided by my own actions. Maybe I am being watched more by the God I believe in. I was always running toward my dreams and away from my fears. Becoming a teenager soon proved that I would have to run even faster. There were no more places to hide. The roads I chose were starting to get narrower and disappearing, until there were none left. I would have to survive by fighting everything and everyone that got in my way. My purpose is very different and unfamiliar, but will come with innocent judgment of the unknown. I held on to what I could control. I felt some great providence approaching.

Chapter 5
Hell Boy

I was yanked out of public school and put into a private one. My path was beginning to become dictated, pushing me toward the unknown. The last day of fourth grade. I was swinging through the monkey bars, fast and strong. I would fly through the air grabbing at the third one, hoping to land on my feet when I got to the end. I was showing off. When I got to the end a classmate was in my way so I kicked him in the face and he fell through the air and landed on soft sand. I yelled at him to watch out, but it was too late.

Chris came after me furiously ready to strike back. He tried to kick my face and I ducked under. Sand went everywhere. I was the bad boy everyone was afraid of, the toughest kid. Chris knew he was in trouble, but kept fighting back. I chased him intently trying to explain that it was an accident, but he didn't listen. I wanted to teach him a lesson. We ran around the monkey bars and swings set. I chased him across the blacktop. Chris was hiding behind the second-grade teacher. I watched him hide trying to tell on me, as if I was the one that did something wrong. I clenched my fist visualizing one punch to knock him on his butt. I was filled with rage and lessons from karate class. Chris started stuttering. The anger and determination surged through me like an adrenaline rush as time slowed and I focused my punch.

*He, he, he, t*he boy stuttered.

I leaned in with my left foot and followed through with my right arm in a tight slow motion. I struck him right across the cheek as hard as I could. My fist sunk into his cheek, as his lips puckered and all my stress was relieved at once. I shut him up in the middle of his sentence. His body flew off the ground. He landed hard on his butt.

We both sat in the lobby in the front entrance of the school, reprimanded, while Chris held ice packs to his face. We ignored each other after that but still hung out a few times in the neighborhood. I punched my way through many doors, but finally I had to leave my friends.

After the joy of summer's freedom, it was time to enter another institution. It was another penitentiary or holding cell to hold me down. A new strange and unfamiliar school year started. This place was meant to teach me and help me grow, but I fought because it was a strange Baptist private school, Calvary. I had to wear the same long gray dress pants and white button up short sleeve or long-sleeved dressy shirt and a tie. I hated dressing like that. I only had one pair of pants, so if they were dirty my whole day was uncomfortable. I felt like a wild thing, in a God-teaching, God-fearing environment. A showdown was inevitable. Mr. Grindel was a good teacher who collected Pepsi bottles. He was short and chubby, with salt-and-pepper hair. He was someone who had great authority and really cared. He showed me the side of teachers I had never seen before. I felt out of place, surrounded by a bunch of prick, know-it-all, goody-two-shoes kids. I didn't have anything in common with them. I did not have a reputation there. I participated, learned and had a decent grade of a C average, something I'd never had.

I would sing the Bible-related songs lined up with the kids in front of the class. I actually had a good voice. I walked on the carpeted hallway in a very small building separate from the church. I used to go down to the high grass, close to the highway during recess and throw stones over the giant barrier sound wall hoping to hit some of the cars on the freeway. A few of the kids would collect praying mantises and bring them into class, putting them in the glass five-gallon fish aquarium. I participated in the marathon run we had to raise money for the school. I outran everyone, making the most laps on the big oval by the woods. Running made me feel like I was running away. I could run in that circle forever, as if I had some place to go. The church was connected by a gravel stone parking lot. It was all brick, classic for Baptist churches in that area. During chapel, I had a timeout punishment in the pews while the rest of the class was singing. I ducked down behind them and made puppets with my hands to get the kids to laugh. I made the tips of my fingers look like people kicking each other, body slamming each other, and even eating each other. The music teacher put her hands on her hips and told me to *stand up right now*. She was very mad, but trying to hold back her own laughter. I guess the school didn't get very many kids that didn't listen and tried to set their own rules.

Do you think you're being funny? she asked.

Come on. Yes. Look, it's funny, I honestly tried to explain.

I had a confrontation with another Italian boy. It was during library class. I realized I didn't have as much power over other kids like I had in public school. He didn't back down or seem afraid. I felt evenly matched. He was my mirror-image. I was shocked staring at who I have become. I was helpless, in a place I did not belong. I begged my mother to let me go back to public school where my friends were. I promised I would be good. My grades were improving. My fifth grade teacher told my mother not to let me go back because I was doing much better in the private school.

I wasn't a bad boy when playing baseball in a league. I felt comfortable taking directions from my coach welcoming any recommendations or critiques about improving my performance. I was in my element, thriving in my natural habitat. I felt so free. Holding the ball in my hands was a symbol of strength. I could put my hand on that ball and make it do whatever I wanted. I showed talent running as fast as I could, making my own decisions, taking a hit, stealing a base, throwing a punch in karate, tackling someone in football, kicking a ball fast and accurately down a soccer field. My abilities shined brighter and better. I was happy to be myself in these environments where I excelled.

I grew up playing soccer with my friend Jared and his younger brother in the Harundale Leagues. It was only a twenty-minute drive from my house past North Arundel Hospital. I got anxious after going down that exit ramp. I saw the church at the intersection, then quickly to the right we made another left turn. The school was on the right and the fields in the distance. The butterflies would rise in my stomach, a familiar feeling every time I approached a field. It was performance anxiety. I wanted to hide in the car, but as soon as I opened the door and I stood up and looked at the field, I knew where I belonged. Seeing the other players dressed up in soccer or baseball gear, I felt energized and felt strong, like I was in control and this was my destiny. After a couple years of soccer, I was frustrated that I never made the All-Star league, even though Jared and I were the best on the team and his father was the coach. Jerod's younger brother Jonathan was always the goalie and those two always made the All-Star league. I remember being strong and confident kicking the ball in a game from one end of the field, down the middle straight to the goal, kicking between seven or eight other opponents. I kicked high and strong as if it were slow motion and my path was clear. I knew exactly where my feet needed to go and if I needed to kick out of a crowd, I would land a striking blow. I felt Jared and I were always a team passing to each other, but I could never seem to score a goal. I'd lineup for the kick, the ball would hit the post on the left and ricochet like a pinball. I kicked so hard the ball ricocheted inside the net hitting one post then the second post three or five times. It never went in, after all that effort.

I joined the bronco baseball league when I was ten years old. I could see teenagers playing on the larger baseball field behind mine. I always wanted to be with them. They were intimidating. I was finally playing baseball, learning to catch with my free McDonald's plastic Orioles glove. That glove was very symbolic to me. Even though I felt like a star athlete practicing and playing with friends in my front yard, I wasn't strong or tough enough to make it in the older league. I didn't have the right equipment. Playing left field, wearing my oversized red, yellow and blue 1990s coat, I started to cry, feeling completely vulnerable. My coach Mr. Marley came running toward me. He wore skintight blue shorts and a tucked in T-shirt that had the number 14 on the back. With his trimmed mustache and very skinny, tall physique, I felt a sense of responsibility to help us win. My glove was so stiff I couldn't catch anything. I think I was his favorite player because I was the number fourteen each year. He walked up to me just trying to figure out what I was so upset about. The wind was a little chilly even though it was a clear day. My hand felt cold inside the glove. I could barely open or squeeze to catch pop flies. A pop fly came at me and the ball bounced right off the edge of my glove. I needed something better to catch with. Mr. Marley always walked with one hand in the back of his pocket and his head leaning down a little bit. He walked up to me to say something and he kneeled down on one knee.

*Robert what's going on why are you so upset? h*e asked.

It's my glove---I can't open it to catch anything, I told him. My eyes started to water.

That's all right. You can get a new glove. For now, you can use this one. All right? Mr. Marley said to console me.

I could hear my dad in the stands yelling for me to keep my chin up. I knew this was a really silly thing to be upset about, but I wanted to be the best. I was supposed to be like Cal Ripken. The glove I grew up with and had the Orioles logo was supposed to be my strength. I had time on my side, never thinking it could run out.

Mr. Marley patted me on the back and walked back to our third-base dugout. I felt a little bit better about myself and I finished the game. I don't think many balls came my direction. I could not wait to get older and stronger and hit the ball harder and run faster. All I had was time on my hands and to learn as I developed my talent. When I purchased my new leather glove it was so soft and flexible with open netting. I tied the knots off every once in awhile when they loosened. It was big, like an extension of my arm. It gave me an extra boost in height to reach up higher than before. I was able to catching the ball cleanly. I cherished this glove forever. I knew it was going to take me through my preprofessional training. I still had my sights set on that field where the teenagers played in the pony leagues. I had to wait till I was at least thirteen years old.

Life! It Must Be a Comedy

I got my wish after begging my mother and I was back in the public school system starting sixth grade. I thought my friends would remember me, but I quickly found I'd never really had any. I had all the answers on the baseball field, but not in a public school. They always tried telling my parents I had a learning disability. I was put in classes where most of the kids caused trouble. George Fox Middle School became my playground. It was a very large brick building right down the street from the middle schooler's hang out, the roller skating rink. I rarely went there. I didn't like the place. I felt like it was for geeks and nerds, even though the cool kids hung out there for girls. I did enjoy racing at the rink and always tried to be the fastest to show off.

I was disconnected from my friends I grew up with in the public school. The local bully Annie, was shorter than me, and he had a shaved head. His older brother in the eighth grade would back him up. Annie would bully over other friends of mine who were double his height. My boisterous and strong attitude no longer made them feel afraid. I was not in control.

49

Life! It Must Be a Comedy

I thought I had to project dominance and goof off to be funny so I could avoid any serious school work and restrictions. When it was my turn to prove that I was tough, I looked to my previous friends and to tell the rest of the kids who I was. Instead they acted like they didn't know me. I had to prove I was still that same bad kid, depending on the way I walked, the words I said, my actions and the way I dressed. My transition from private school back to public school was almost completed.

So I had to look for the only friends I thought I still had. I turned to my old gang reuniting my good friends from elementary school. The small group of buddies I left behind. I thought my friends would always support me forever. There was no way they would ever abandon me now or in the future. I rounded up my friends, Jared, Jeff, Jimmy and Dan. Jared was the tall, blond and smart one. Jeff was a little shorter than me, race car driven, quiet more book smart than me with brown hair and his eyebrows always went up when he smiled. Jeff would give me a look like I was crazy sometimes, but he always followed along. Jimmy was tall as Jeff, nervous with blond hair, skinny and the first to point out when something was wrong. Dan was taller than me, had blond hair and skinny, very smart and knows a little bit about everything, especially hockey. He mostly kept to himself. Our candle was quickly flamed and we were reunited. I chose to sit all the way at the back of the lunchroom to the far left closest to the street. It was where I felt like if any of us wanted to escape, I could run out the doors behind me if I ever wanted to. Windows wrapped around the lunchroom and we could clearly see the parking lot where all the buses picked up the kids. The floors were classic white and blue ceramic square tiles. The walls where a light blue wash and echoed our footsteps. Two large double led to that lunchroom. My favorite area was the snack area to buy junk food.

My mother always signed me up for the ticket program for lunch. I never used it and always asked for a dollar anyway. I always felt too embarrassed to use it in front of my friends. Though I did sneak the ticket for a second meal. In elementary school I loved cafeteria rice crispies for breakfast with chocolate milk on them. In middle school I used my money for two bags of large chocolate chip cookies. I dunked those cookies in chocolate milk and that was my lunch almost every day. We'd all talk like old times. Usually I was trying to make a fool of myself. I respected my friends and never talked bad about them.

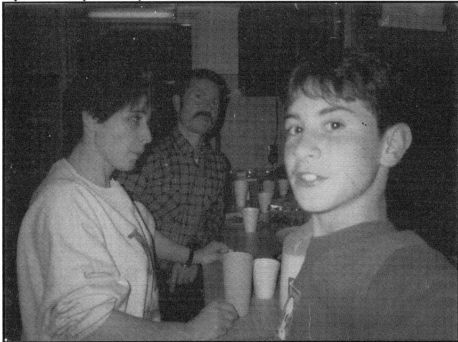

I had classes with all the trouble making kids. My friends chose to be a lot smarter than me so we were never in any classes together. I never liked being in the bad classes, but I could never survive all the homework in the good classes. My life was divided and upside down. I managed to keep us together in a pack during lunch. The friends I had left were my only source of stability, so I held onto them. I did not know too many people in the lunch line, but one day the kids who were popular in my grade were recognized me as a contender. They tested me, but I had to put up with the beating for now. Deep inside I still felt discontented. I could not find peace. There was a storm conflicting in my mind about good and doing good, but I had no control over the rules and boundaries I didn't like. I stumbled into a trend I thought I'd ever get out of.

I was always in the principal's office for something. My status was finally upgraded. I was late to class or I was caught skipping class. I pushed other people around in the hallways, showed off in class, or talked to other students. When asked to turn in work, I simply ignored the teacher. I moved forward like an untamed dog, cute on the outside but doing whatever I wanted. The school bus ride was time to flirt with girls like Megan, the snobby brunette and Kristen the know-it-all blonde. They were the two prettiest girls in my class. I always had a crush on them both. They were best friends. My naughty ways progressed since my technique in kindergarten when Jared and I used to look under their dresses. I could never impress them with any of my antics. Megan went out with me a couple of times and she was my first real attempt at a kiss when I was twelve. We were behind Kristen's house on the water and hiding behind her shed while our friends from the neighborhood, Jones who was one grade under me, had dark hair, Jimmy, Kristen and Stella stood on the other side nagging us on. My good friend Jimmy and Stella were cousins. Stella was tall, with blond hair and was one grade above me. It was awkward and our teeth touched. It was exciting but not what I thought after all these years thinking about kissing her. Our kiss lasted for five seconds. Afterwards Megan wouldn't talk to me the rest of the night. I tried to move my tongue but I didn't know what to do. I was told I should move my tongue in circles but I was more worried about her braces. I quickly got expelled from the school bus for disrespecting the driver, and I punched a kid with glasses for running is mouth.

One day a few of the other kids from my grade, Leslie and John, bet me $2.50 in quarters to kiss Kristen. I started walking toward Kristen. I sat next to her and stared at her cheek. Extremely nervous I leaned over pushing away her long arm strength pushing me away. I kissed her right on her cheek. The next morning I was called to the principal's office. He was shaking his head giggling at such a simple little thing like a kiss. I could only imagine that Kristen's parents were really upset about me kissing her on the bus the day before. With regret in his voice his hands were forced to suspend me. The principal had to suspend me. I welcomed my suspension, a couple of days off of school. My dad wasn't happy. I didn't care much.

Part of me was a little bit sad when I got in trouble. Sometimes I truly could not help when I got in trouble. With my reputation it wasn't easy for anyone to believe me though. I could not figure out how to open my combination spinlock so I was always late for my math class. I tried to explain to my teacher who always insisted I was lying. I finally got the hang of it. Down every road I traveled I found obstacles and a way to push down the barriers. Sometimes the monsters guarding all of the doors and gateways of my path I met head on. I had some consequences for my actions and sooner or later that year one of my gatekeepers where going to catch up to me.

I skipped class with Marky, my old elementary school friend and partner in all of our deficiency classes. Usually he took credit for my artwork when we had to use art to tell our stories, words were too complicated for some reason. It was the seventh-grade wing of school where we came out of the bathrooms. As soon as we walked down the steps we walked into two older boys in eighth grade coming up the steps toward us. The older boy had a shaved head. He grabbed me by my chest and I turned around with my back facing down the steps. His friend with the dark hair and the jeans started spitting out threats that didn't make any sense. I didn't understand why they were on a mission after me. He grabbed me tight. I used one of my karate moves on him. Holding me by both sides of my shirt collar, I clenched my fist down at my side. Coming upward with a swooping action straight together between his forearms I broke through, pulling apart the grip he had on me. Richard and I took off running fast as we could down both flights of steps dashing around turns. We burst out the door straight to the dirt path between the buildings, when his arm grabbed me by the back and I was pinned. I knew I couldn't run forever and when the boy with a shaved head and his friend came out those doors right after me, I heard undying words from Marky's mouth. Richard yelled my last name. Richard always called me by my last name growing up. I never liked him for that and he never entered the pack of my other friends. I was surprised Marky kept up with me because he was always fat.

Get him Florio! Marky yelled with his lisp and slur.

I was ready to fight. Standing in a ready position standing on top of the little concrete platform outside the door the shaved head boy came at me. The boy was standing a little bit higher than me and stepped forward. Marky kept yelling for me to kick his butt. As quickly as he grabbed me, suddenly the boys became afraid and let go. As this boy started a step backward both him and his friend started telling me how lucky I was.

Your last name is Florio? the shaved head boy said.

Are you related to Adriano Florio? the shaved head boy said.

Yeah! He's my brother, I quickly shouted.

I was lucky I had a brother. Adrian went to the same school and instilled fear in that boy. I now had my own little reputation I was starting to build. Neither that boy or his younger brother ever messed with me ever again. That was the first time I ever thanked Marky for yelling my name. The older boy was sent after me when his younger brother, the little kid with a shaved head and a big mouth, decided he did not like me stepping on his turf.

I rumbled and tumbled through summer after I finished sixth grade. I was twelve years old, escaping reality playing the Nintendo NES. Some of my favorite games were Earthworm Jim by Shiny Entertainment along with Super Mario Brothers, F Zero, and Nintendo Bazooka Gun. My fingers would streamline like playing an instrument, fast and accurate, connecting the signals from my brain through my spinal cord with precision. These were stored on top of and underneath my grandparent's old coffee table. The gaming units managed to work on their television, a thirty -year-old twenty-seven inch television with turning knobs. My brothers and I often retreated to the old living room of my grandparents once they both were in nursing homes.

My brothers and I started to develop a much stranger and experienced personalities. It was no longer normal frustration over being teased or picked on by my brothers or getting in trouble for spilling the milk. All of our lives started to change the older we got. I could always bury my frustrations and found solitude playing my favorite videogames. Earthworm Jim was my favorite escape and most difficult challenge. The character Jim and I were traversing similar paths and we had more in common than I knew.

Jeff and I created a strong friendship carried over from elementary school, and now the only two from our pack, we became friends fast. We challenged each other in all sports, and we even got in trouble together. We were becoming like brothers, nothing could separate us like friends forever. Life started changing but Jeff and I made a promise to always be there for each other. Every weekend Jeff and I would take our dirt bikes from my house to his. We raced through the trails near power lines leading up to BG&E Electric in the woods near my house. We also ran in and out of Jeff's house made from two trailers. There was a track in a patch of abandoned properties behind a truck lot next to his house. Jeff's house was right across the border from Anne Arundel County where I lived and Baltimore City where he lived. Fort Smallwood Road was a bridging road from my house to Jeff's. We'd pass industrial buildings, gas stations, bars, a few old beaten up houses, company storage facilities, and J's Auto sales, were Jeff grew up on a large piece of property. Everyday I could hear the cars on the Beltway 695, smell the city trash dump across the highway. Jeff's father, grandfather and uncle had their own little car mechanic shop where they also sold cars, old beaten cars that needed fixing. Jeff's mother was never around because she left when he was very young so it was just him, his dad, and his younger brother Buzz. We often played in the four foot above ground circular swimming pool in the middle of the property. Jeff's house was up against the fence right next to a truck lot, shaking the house every night and every morning. His grandparents' house was on the other side of the swimming pool facing the mechanic shop. There was a little parking lot and next to it his grandfather's long speedboat, The Power Plant, sat always covered up. There were four houses in the back of the property but the newest little house closest to Jeff's trailer seemed to always be vacant. In the far back portion of the vacant property, beyond the little forested area, was a long one-way railroad track. We would follow it sometimes but couldn't walk far, because the Coast Guard training facility was on the other side of the tracks.

I had a used PW80 Yamaha with a purple cushion seat and a freshly raised rear axle lifted by two steel plates Jeff's dad helped me fix up. Jeff and his little brother rode around on little PW fifty until Jeff finally bought a bigger Yamaha one hundred. The sounds of my two-stroke winding out through its three gears and Jeff's new-four stroke was great. It was the sound of freedom. Side-by-side we were like a friendship of horsepower throughout our neighborhoods, maxing out our speed limit at forty mph. I would wear my tightly-fit pointed-nose-front blue helmet with a face mask and he would race down the road with his oversize round red and white-pointed mask helmet. We were enjoying all of the leisure's of adolescence, gaining whatever experience came from that, to put forth in the real world. We never believed in the real world. We were both running away from it.

When we were not riding our dirt bikes we were playing laser tag with Jeff's youngest uncle Jeremiah, who went to school with Adrian. When we were at my house we would always play baseball or football, hitting golf balls trying to reach the neighbors' houses. We both knew the trails in our backyards like pros. We would race through them, get dirty and hit the jumps, feeling power and speed at our control. All of Jeff's uncles shared the same family traits. Jeff's uncles shared the responsibilities as mechanics in the shop. Jeff and I never let our imaginations stop us, as we even started snowboarding at the local resort, Whitetail. On hot summer days we would be swimming or watching rented movies or playing video games on his Sega. On chilly days, snowing or raining, we'd also make up games, shooting each other with Nerf darts or suiting up for the closest hill to snowboard or sled down.

We were both in the exploratory stage in our lives, as we started experimenting with cigarettes and trying to get his uncle or someone else I knew to give us a joint. My body was developing just a little bit faster and we would show off our muscles all the time to each other and have weightlifting sessions. We didn't always get along and when we occasionally disagreed I always made sure I came out on top to act stronger. We thought we were untouchable. No one was catching us when we snuck around our neighborhoods looking for trouble or smoking a couple of cigarettes or lighting a joint. We were captivated by our own little world that we were in control of. Jeff and I would get into as many activities as we could. Jeff's father worried about our safety. I always assured Jeff if anything were to happen, I joked around with Jeff trying to be serious, that everything would be fine. I cared about my friend and as much trouble as we got into I certainly had no realization of any particular kind of injury. That was the last thing on our minds. We just wanted to be free.

The first drag of a cigarette for me was a natural experience. I remember Andy, now at the age of thirteen, given me one of his cigarettes. He asked me if I would try it. I was hanging out in my neighborhood, the far end of Lombardi Circle, at the local beach. I skateboard down the street on to Lombardi Circle. I gained speed where the road started sloping down and I cruised on my own, drifting. I cut into the property where my brothers cut the grass of Mr. Cluster on the waterfront, and through the U-shaped driveway. I cut through the fence and exited on my skateboard keeping my speed, out the other side of the driveway. I kept my balance and went under the chain, down the boat ramp into the beach. One of the neighbor kids lived on the corner in the old busted up little house overlooking the water at the beach, who I often got in arguments with. The right side of the ramp was a summer home, but they were rarely ever home. I would sled ride down their backyard hill trying to avoid landing in the water. There was an old abandoned aluminum shed next to the road at the bottom of the neighbor's yard with the summer home. I passed the old wooden fence that bordered the rest of the street from the shed down to the water next to the summer house property. The road got bumpier before getting closer to the grass forcing me to jump off and walk.

I walked around with a view of the other neighborhood kids and was mostly curious about what was going on as everyone sat around the low wooden bench in the middle. Some kids were playing on the peer at the end of the peninsula like beach. There were two sides of sand and waves to play on as the water surrounded us crashing all around. The grass was sometimes not cut by the neighbors, but there wasn't much supervision especially at night. It was the perfect place to hang out for getting in trouble. Far out into the creek to the left was a draw bridge and past that was the Bay. I went down there to relax and stare at all the other waterfront houses, their boats, peers, watching the boats go by. Each house was fairly away from the water level, almost fifteen feet off of the water on grassy hills sloping straight down, a very serious incline. While I was "down the beach" like we used to say it, I saw, Andy, Adrian, Len a couple of Adrian's friends from the neighborhood, and my childhood friend from elementary school Jimmy. We were all being teased to try a cigarette. Adrian wasn't there to supervise me, mostly interested in getting in his own trouble, and fishing at his favorite fishing hole at the end of the man-made peer of rocks that were thrown in the water.

Hey Robert want to take a drag? Andy said teasing.

No I don't think so, leave me alone idiot, I shouted back

Andy was always teasing, jumping around, and like a pervert flirting like he was a girl, even with his own brother. Andy was obsessed with sexuality, and getting other people to fall for his stupid tricks. This was my chance to show I was tough to my brother's friends and all the older kids in the neighborhood. I always tried to be the coolest of anyone in the neighborhood, so if I did this, it would just be one more thing that established me as the bad boy. I found another way to manipulate and gain control. The challenges were getting tougher and I could not rely on simple antics and pleasures anymore to find where I was safe and free. Adrian didn't have that problem at all, being older than me. I didn't really have any rivals and he'd already established his dominance amongst friends. Carlo almost completely shied away from everyone, probably the only smart one who actually saw what the kind of people in our neighborhood were capable of. Carlo more introverted almost entirely more than Adrian and I. I knew I actually wanted to try a cigarette but I did not know that this would be my first time. I gave in to the demand to see what kind of reaction I would get and whether or not it would work. I was very nervous and the first inhalation happened almost naturally as I was being praised for being a natural. My eyes started to tear up and I started to choke but I took deep and long inhalations almost like a pro. Being the talented kid that I was I ask held in everything I tried to keep up with everyone and anyone but I did not know I was on the wrong path that my talent should have been used in a better direction. I caught myself in the exact same situation when I was eight years old trying to show everyone that I was better than the rest that I could do something no one else would do and that I could do it better for my first time. Except for this time it's not a skateboard ramp and it's not something that would build me up. This time it could potentially tear me down. If I was to control my world then I had to conform and step up to all the challenges, or else I was not ready to give in to my fears of the unknown and what I might have to do to stop whatever it was, waiting for me. The situation I was in was not glamorous as compared to my first of many confrontations that I met head-on to prove myself. I knew it was the wrong thing to do. My decision was made, so I could be the best or I thought I was. I did not know that I was trying to be the best in the worst way.

Yeah I'll do it, I said

Danm, look, he's doing it. He's a natural. Look! Robert, show us how you inhale and how it exhales just like it should look, Andy shouted with admiration.

Jeff and I continued exploration. We both passed our first time inhaling, and whatever challenges came next we were both matching each other's quest for discovering freedom. We became the strongest of best friends. Out of all of the gang in elementary school, Jeff and I were the only ones still together. We were matched in ferocity and brothers from another mother, but we did not look alike. Jeff had hazel green eyes and slightly bad vision, while I had brown eyes and perfect vision. I tried to always look kind of sharp but at the same time grungy, with a hoodie, jean shorts, kind of baggy below the knees, hanging below my waist and my boxers showing. Jeff usually had the same fashion but dressed more grunge. We both would wear our No Fear baseball hats black-and-white plaid on top and plaid bill. The inside of my hat said "rules were meant to be broken," which became our unofficial motto.

Jeff had a long metal chain hanging down his side past his knees, connected to his wallet. I always had a T-shirt on with some sort of skateboarding logo and one T-shirt layered over the other. I mostly had a shaved head growing up with some style cut around. I never thought Jeff ever cut his hair from the youngest grade together, until a long time. It always grew wild and long. Jeff didn't have a growth spurt yet and I was always taller than him, even though I considered myself to be the shortest kid in class. In my growing troubled times I tried to pick up skateboarding again. The style had changed and the skateboards now had a tail on both ends. Something did not feel right, my brothers were not there to join me. I still tried to pick up where my brothers left off but now it was the new school of skateboards. There were long and skinny skateboards with tiny little wheels. All the kids skating dressed in dark clothing and very grungy. I tried to hold onto my past, when I felt the most safe and innocent, but as much as I tried, without my brothers skating it wasn't the same. I didn't understand the trend anymore.

Jeff and I were inseparable now that we were a little older. We were a pair with my shaved head, next to his long black hair past his ears. Jeff changed, just a little better from the dirt ball days. In our class group pictures, I sometimes would tease Jeff with his two canine teeth that protruded higher on his gums, more than normal, and me with my two front teeth like a rabbit. I've always had problems with my teeth, in and out of the dentist from an early age for cavities and metal caps on my molars. My mother spent extra on my teeth, more than my brothers. I gave my mother hell every way I could, from the wallet, the attitude, and being accident prone. It wasn't until the beginning of middle school that I just started realizing who I could become. Still I never faced the reality.

Everything about me was growing, and my muscles were finally starting to catch up to my expectations. I was preparing for my seventh-grade year. The way that I prepared was to build myself up against peer pressure as the strongest kid, as the toughest mentally. I certainly ignored all the academics, only concentrating on how I could make school be fun and how I would survive another year in hell. I was even more determined to create my own freedom and rules like never before. As every grade approached now, the older I was getting, I felt like I had more knowledge against the system to benefit me. Seventh-grade was my proving ground. Even though I feared it and knew I was walking into something new, I was tested and my resolve was purged in the fire, strengthened like steel in attitude and will. I was the same Robert I built my reputation around, and this time entering with an established reputation, ready to face all challenges. I would be the popular kid, entering the same middle school, with a new year of confrontations ready to be me and break all the rules.

Life! It Must Be a Comedy

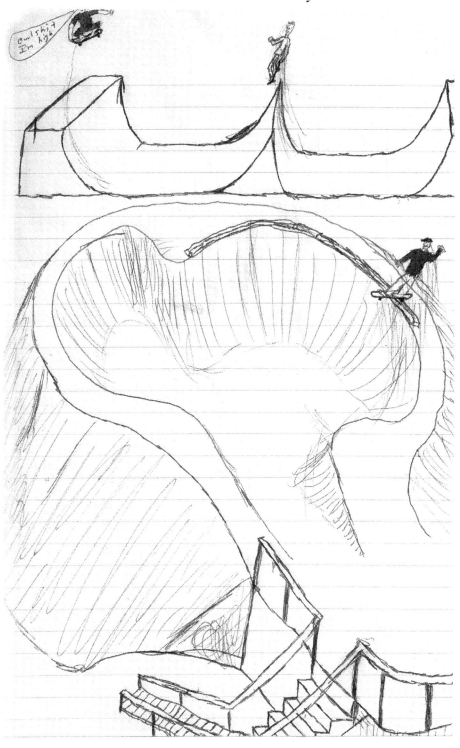

Chapter 6
Beginnings Aren't So Simple

I was on the school bus again ready to start seventh grade at George Fox middle school. It was the beginning of a new chapter in a year of my life. I waited for the school bus with my next-door neighbors and friends from the neighborhood. The morning walk to the bus stop was a brisk and misty early morning. From the start I was walking with a chip on my shoulder. I sat at the very back of the bus, ready to establish myself as a new contender, as the person to be reckoned with. I had a fresh and stronger perspective of myself, as others view me to be dominant and strong. Eyes would look away and hands turned the other direction as I approached. School had become a competition, not of my artistic or athletic abilities so much but now, back in public school again, my second year in middle school, I knew this time it would be how I expected it to be. Seventh grade was intensely different than sixth-grade. The storm that started clustering in my mind started becoming a reality in the actions of my decisions. I had shaved my head but oddly enough, I was afraid to show myself in class, so I wore a bandana. I should not have shaved my head the day before the first day of school, because I set myself up to be in a less confident state of mind. I pleaded with the guidance counselor to let me wear my bandanna as some passing eighth-graders let me know that I hadn't reached the status I thought I had yet. They yelled, teasing me to take that thing off.

I got through the first month and a half of seventh-grade, and my armor wasn't damaged but I was ready to be expelled at any time for the rest of the year. My parents always threatened to me put in military school but that never fazed me. I continued to mouth off on the bus, punching kids who disagreed with me, and standing up for friends when the school bus driver was arguing with them for what seemed to be ridiculous infractions. I had three suspensions from the bus expelled from it within a month. My dad was extremely mad having to drive me to school. I did not know my parents were planning something, so I just continued acting up in classes, avoiding homework, talking back to teachers, pushing students, talking during class and goofing around, just doing whatever I wanted. I was never doing what I was supposed to be doing. Because of my grades, I was again placed in the classes with the troublemaking kids. All the smart kids were placed in better classes with students who actually wanted to learn. For the second year in a row I was not in classes with any of my close friends that I ate lunch with. We were all still eating lunch together at the exact same spot during lunch. Things were not going exactly the way I hoped with my popularity level in this larger group of kids than elementary school. I kept skipping classes and getting suspended from school almost every week.

There were two other boys I particularly enjoyed getting in trouble with. In home economics I met Jason who had failed eighth-grade and repeated seventh-grade and Chris who was in my grade. We got along famously. We sat in the corner playing around with baking equipment and flirting with the girls. When the teacher told us to be quiet or listen to instructions we completely phased him out. I was the one looked at to dare someone and come up with other great ideas. Giggling, getting some laughs from the other classmates was how we felt successful. All our talents, abilities, and willpower were channeled into goofing off. In music class together, when I asked for a pass to go to the bathroom and was denied, I got fed up and got even louder and disruptive. My teacher finally stood in front of me and wrote a pass to the principal. I acted like it was my pass to do whatever I wanted. Instead I used it as my pass to use the bathroom. I snatched the piece of paper from the teacher, said goodbye to my classmates, and walked out of the room all the way down to the end of the hallway. I played around in the bathroom for almost ten minutes. Instead of going to the principal I decided to return to class and act like I never heard a word he said, and that I was returning my bathroom pass. I thought it would be extremely funny if I acted like I actually got what I asked for. I saw an opportunity and created my own passage. When I showed up in the class my two classmates who seemed to be cheering me on were silent with disbelief that I totally disregarded when I was told to do. I felt I had to establish myself in front of everyone, especially Jason and Chris who could spread the word about my reputation faster. This was my opportunity to get the respect I wanted. My teacher was furious, asking me what I thought I was doing. This time I did go to the principal's office.

What do you think you are doing? my teacher said.

What do you mean? You gave me a pass to go to the bathroom so I was in the bathroom, I said laughing.

You think you're funny don't you? This time it's for real. Take yourself to the principal's office and don't come back, my teacher said.

I looked at my classmates, feeling almost no remorse. I gladly took the pass and walked myself down to the principal's office. I was not surprised to hear what the principal said. I was suspended for a couple of days and threatened that my next suspension would be an expulsion. I had a lot of free time on my hands when I was home and my parents let me have it, punishing me by taking the front wheel off of my dirt bike. My dad kept it in his barbershop for a couple of months. My dad worked every day of the week except for Wednesday and Sunday from eight a.m. to seven p.m. At least I did not have to face him too often during the day. That also meant I didn't get too much of an opportunity to plead for my freedom, to get back my dirt bike wheel.

Only one and a half months had passed and I was already facing expulsion. While I was sitting in history class one day goofing off with the other classmates something started to happen. A very fat student sitting in front of me said something about my hair so we got up in front of each other like we were going to fight, but only stared each other down, intensely. He was making fun of my hair, but looking at his head, he had the same haircut. We both sat down and I suddenly became quiet, feeling alone and not having any friends. Nobody was there supporting me. It was an empty feeling. Sitting in that very quiet moment in my mind, the other students swarming around in laughter and noise, I got out a piece of paper and a pencil and I tried to listen to what the teacher was saying and writing on the blackboard about a homework assignment. It was the only moment I remember actually trying to learn. I couldn't think because there was so much noise and distraction going on. All of the students were trying to fight with each other, overtaking the environment. I don't know how the teacher got through to anyone. Only the people in the front row actually had a chance, as well as those who were actually listening.

As I began to write down what was on the board I could not make sense of what I was writing or why I was writing. I started to feel like I was missing out on something. The experience I got back in fifth grade, actually learning and having someone show me the way one-on-one, at that private school was great. I couldn't believe I started to actually miss it. At that exact moment of my realization I had a sort of transformation in my mind. I was trying to fight to keep that moment, but I did not have the support or anyone to turn to. I was a faint light in stormy water in the middle of the ocean, feeling like my ship was sinking and I was the only one who could save myself. I did not feel I had a chance for rescue. I was trying to wake up and swim for my life, but the waves kept getting higher as I was drowning. Though I would not have said it out loud, I needed someone to pluck me out of the water.

Shortly after, a student brought a note from the principal's office, about me, and handed it to the teacher. I watched the student carry the note past me, instinctively from experience, I saw my lifeline hoping for a message that was reaching for me. The teacher read it and then looked up at me slowly, pointed at me and yelled across the room. The teacher handed me the note. I collected my things and was sent to the front office, where my mother was waiting for me to take me home. I could barely hear what she was saying. Other than my own perspective, it was the first time I felt the distraction and hurdles the teacher had to work with. I felt a sudden shock bringing me back to life, figuratively, floating in my cold storming ocean, sending me into hypothermic shock.

I had a sinking feeling inside as I looked for some ability to rescue myself. My mother was waiting for me in the school office.

Life! It Must Be a Comedy

Mom was taking me out of public school to look for a private school for me to excel again. I did not like that and fought every school she took me to. The glimmering part of me looked for a sign of hope. It was not going to come from my own willpower. I was trying to listen, but I continued to fight the system, feeling trapped, still struggling for freedom. The wild animal in me was still feeling caged, even though my mother tried to put me in the right environment. Before a school would accept me and my parents' money I had to audition.

I went from school to school doing interviews. I acted with disgust and complete disrespect for the authority figures questioning me. When I was asked a question I was negative, hoping I would not get in. It was no arguing with my mother or my father, they were determined in their plan. I had a couple of week trials, but most immediately rejected me. I did not even last the first days. Hellen completed her high school education at a private school, but when I showed up at her own school I was not as nice or as eager. Most of the private schools for which I interviewed had about one hundred students and one-on-one education. Little did my mother know that I thrived in small groups which made it easier to establish my dominance quickly.

I had a bad attitude when I was interviewing with one particular principal. My mother and I were sitting in red leather seats in his office. He sat in his chair behind his desk, questioning me. My mother was slapping me on the back of the head, telling me to sit up straight. She always told me to walk straight going down the road because I walked with an attitude and a hop in my step like I was a bad boy. The room was very dark and just like every other principal's office I had seen. I immediately went into defensive mode.

So Robert why should we accept you into this school... Why do you want to be here? the principal asked me.

I don't want to be here! I said with strong attitude and a chuckling shout.

Just like that I was out, off to another school, and then another. I spent some whole days in a few classes, ending back in the principal's office being asked if I thought school was just for studying the weather. Most of the schools my mom took me to were Baptist. They had very strict rules, even their dress code, which I thought was ridiculous, because the kids were already in uniforms. I promised my mother that I would be good if she let me return to public school. It was a lie. I only wanted to be back with friends and feel that sense of control again. That choice of leaving private school once before caused me to relapse much more, making me struggle tenfold to find my place again.

One school gave me a three-week trial working at my own pace. I had to read books, do my own studying, take the test in the back of the book and progress as fast as I wanted. I refused to do any work sitting in my wall desk attached but divided by a piece of plywood two and a half feet high. I had to raise an American flag if I wanted someone to come over for help. There was also a Maryland State flag in the black little holder on a black plastic pole. The shelf above all of our desks was high enough over our heads for the teachers to see our flags, but I just sat there picking away at the wall in front of me. I dug a hole deeper and deeper into the side of the dividing wall, trying to peek at the classmate next to me. Sitting there with my Forty-Niners Starter coat, extra-large, over my seventh grade frame of one hundred and five pounds of lean muscle and athletic tone, the hoodie sported back, wearing it like I was a cool guy everywhere I went.

My pants hung past my butt crack ending at my black penny loafers. My clothes didn't change much from school to school, usually blue or gray dress pants and a blue or gray button up long-sleeve or short-sleeved shirt and a blue tie. I got a kick out of goofing off at lunchtime, taking all the dares to throw food at someone or yell something at someone. Classmates turned their heads and laughed getting me much popularity with the older kids and impressing the older girls quickly. Trying to play basketball in the parking lot during lunchtime was the only time I probably paid attention to what was going on. I didn't do any work in my books. So many teachers, so many times told me to do my work. I was always in the principal's office by my three-week of probation. At the end of the three weeks, I got up and walked out of the building and started walking down the road close to the intersection where Wal-Mart was, not too far away. Carlo was working there at the time in the animal section taking care of the fish, becoming a fish expert, even bring back his favorite Jack Dempsey and Red Devil fishes. He placed them in huge fifty gallon tanks in his bedroom downstairs. They started to stink like someone relieved themselves. Fed up, hoping that somehow I was taking control of my own life on my own two legs, walking with confidence out the front door of the school down the long pavement, walking down the hill of the driveway, I was above the highway where I could see down to the intersection. I stopped when I got to the end of the property at the beginning of the driveway, paused for a moment, and just took a deep breath and I turned around. I walked right back confidently. I felt like I was in control since no one even saw me leave. I walked back into the lobby where the hallway led to the principal's office.

I was stopped by my teacher who looked at me oddly. I thought for sure I was caught and was going to be kicked out immediately. She started to question me asking me whether or not I walked out that door and where I just been. Of course I lied to her, played it off as if I was always right there. She knew I was up to no good.

Where did you just go? my teacher asked.

What do you mean? I was right here the whole time, I explained.

That did not go very well so she grabbed me by the arm and walked me back to class. While sitting at my desk I heard another yell by my teacher to start doing my work or else. I continued to ignore her completely, phased out, even though I knew there was some consequence that was going to be very hard. Even if I wanted to respond, my mind was blocked. I just did not want to move. I was very hard-headed.

Robert! I better start seeing you working in that book or else. I'm only going to say this one more time. I've said this day and day again. This is going to be it. You know you're on probation, my teacher yelled across the room.

I knew I was on probation for three weeks to test me but I don't even last two weeks. I ignored her and then I heard her getting up, walking over to my desk with that final threat and her decision was made and I was out of there. I never completely gave up on one thing, baseball. I would play with my friends and neighbors and Robert all the time in the front yard where we had a perfect training ground. It was my very own baseball field with a backstop right outside my front door. Even though a lot of the times I 'd say that I would not go to practice or would not go to a game, I usually went. Adrian and his friends in the neighborhood would tell me to go, that it was a good thing for me and that I was stupid for wasting my time playing with them. They knew I had so much talent that I should have been out there playing the real game. I always felt like I was missing out on something when I was stuck in the house, mostly for some kind of punishment. I never failed to anger my mother who could take my head and pound it up against the wall after trying to get me to learn phonics from the hundreds of dollars she spent on that reading program. I would listen to tapes and repeat the words in books.

I got her so frustrated that I sometimes got my head cracked by my mother in the living room. Where a recliner was always sitting, tattered in maroon leather. The custom flower pattern fabric fitted not so snug, created by my mother to go over it. For me it was our playground, until my mother bought much more fancier furniture and moved everything downstairs. Our old couch had soft sponge, blue felt like fabric and a dark wood arm rails. She had my head and smacked it into the handcrafted pyramid armrest design. I only remember having the side of my head pushed down on the corner of this shape, as I would cling to the chair. My mother didn't play around. I always found myself wondering what the neighbors were doing when I heard other boys playing in the field or street. Or, my neighbors next door playing with my brothers. It was the same feeling when I was out there playing and my dad told me it was time to go to baseball--I didn't want to go. I thought I was missing something better if I didn't stay home. I always enjoyed it. It was my favorite sport and all my practice paid off now. As a thirteen year-old, I finally made it to the pony league and to that bigger field where the teenagers played.

All of the best kids were on my team. My coach was a very bald black man whose son was also on our team. I finally made it! Sitting on the bench was a great feeling we were for sure going to be in first place finally. I still had the same glove that fit perfectly. At thirteen years old I was still connected to that glove like an extension to my arm. I was still one of the shortest kids on the team, but definitely the most athletic and muscular even though I only weighed one hundred and five pounds. I loved pitching but I did not get a chance that year. I threw extremely fast but I didn't know how to throw curve balls even though I would switch up my finger positions. I just didn't know what I was doing. I even tried to throw what I thought would be a change up so my coach could see. He stood behind the backstop watching my ball fly fast and hard as I could and extremely accurate. I got a lot of practice in the field and in my backyard where my dad had hung a big black rubber tire from the old swing set. I would stand in the back of my yard between my fort and the shed, and sometimes right in front of my fourteen-foot circular trampoline, closer to the back of my house. I threw toward another tire up against the fence between the fig trees protecting my dad's garden. During jumping sessions on the trampoline, Jeff and I were always soaring as high as we could, trying to top my consecutive back-flips of fourteen. All night we'd jump, even sleeping out there on warm summer nights. We'd practice pitching at the tire even taking my baseball bat and practicing my swing hitting that tire-swing. I was strengthening the muscles in my forearm, extending my arms like a true baseball player perfecting my swing. I took my greatest wing envisioning a home run and contact with that baseball with every whack at that tire.

I was on that field trying out for pitching when I threw that changeup and got a startled response from my coach who thought my arm was getting tired. I was only trying something different and explained I was not tired at all. I did not make the pitching roster. I was playing shortstop and outfield, my favorite positions that I played exceptionally well. To me shortstop was the prize position. The best player always got shortstop, especially being from Maryland everyone knew that was Cal Ripken Jr.'s position.

My dad came to almost every game and we always played on Sundays in our league. My dad videotaped a lot of my games and I could see him standing there behind our dugout at the top of the metal stands while I was yelling for him to just videotape me not everything else. When I made a great play following the ball, he'd get me just as I was coming down from a catch, after the play was over. My athletic ability on the field was allowing me to excel in a physical environment where I could take control and feel free. I would tease around with the other players on my team. I wasn't always the most social. I was always the most astute standing firm and ready to play when I was called into action. I could take a joke and I could give a few out and I could surely give a few poundings on my teammates. My favorite part of the beginning of a game was sitting on that long aluminum bench in the dugout hearing the coach yell out the roster, giving us our batting and field positions. I mostly played the outfield and backup. Any play I could put my glove right behind or underneath one of my teammates and if they missed the pop fly, my glove was right there to catch it.

Life! It Must Be a Comedy

I pitched a lot in the Bronco league with my coach Mr. Blue, a man with a rough face, and little overweight, but with a gentle, sweet coaching. When I was pitching he'd try to get me to move over on the rectangular pitching base, different sides, to pitch to home plate with different approaches. I stood closer to the edge of the base to the side the batter was closer to, trying to get an advantage over the batter. I recognized a pattern too. The years that I pitched the more my batting average went down and I didn't have a home run swing. I could hit it hard and accurately faster than anyone on my team. The years that I was not pitching my batting average went up tremendously. I only saw my teammates in the summer and part of the fall-ball, playing or football for the Buccaneers. So I don't remember all of their names. There were the twins that had the same athletic ability and we never were on the same team except one year. I remember Randy because after a winning game in the Bronco league we went to the concession stand which sold its famous big league chew. I always got the shredded cherry-flavored that mimicked tobacco.

We always passed around white giant baseball gum drops with baseball words on them. Words like "strikeout" or "home run". While sitting together on the wooden benches, under the giant trees in front of the concessions stand, my mother brought a giant pizza. Sometimes she'd volunteer to work during my games. Once, a tiny chipmunk fell out of the tree. We were all kind of just stunned. Randy sat there kicking dirt in its face and I was disgusted seeing it choke, stop breathing, sand in its eyes. I was a huge animal lover. None of us did anything to stop him. This memory still haunts me. Randy was a tall, brute kid who played catcher. Jason was also on the team. Every time I hit a line drive over the shortstop's head into center field, he would always match my exact hit. I would do the same thing if I was batting behind him. It was a great kind of camaraderie where seeing your teammate doing good inspires you to do even better. Especially since we batted right after each other in the lineup. Playing shortstop I'd field grounders, keeping in close communication with the second baseman about who was going to cover second on double plays, according to whether or not the batter was a lefty or a righty, knowing that he would most likely pull the ball in one of our directions. My arm strength was getting much stronger now in my first year in the Pony league since I was lifting weights. I would grasp that baseball when I caught it with an accurate and strong throw, remembering the first baseman telling me.

Rob, man you don't have to throw it so hard you're not pitching, my teammate said.

That's just how I throw, I said back.

Life! It Must Be a Comedy

That group of boys was a real team I had an honor to be on. It was a great opportunity to see my progress through the years, my development of my talent in baseball. We ended the year in fifth place, though I felt we played much better than that. We had so much fun! One of the boys on my team, Michael, who was a year older than me, had a sister named Tammy who would sit in the stands. I had a huge crush on her. I would psyche myself up by yelling at Tammy, while I was up to bat, that I was going to get a hit for her. I was always a ladies' man and I think she had a crush on me too, but I never acted on it. The league I played in was closer to where my mother worked at North Arundel Hospital where she cleaned and sterilized medical equipment in central supply. So I didn't get to see a lot of my teammates outside of baseball. My schools were always so far away from home that it was the exact same way with my classmates. The more trouble I got into the further I had to travel to find a school that would accept me.

I finally came to a stop like an airplane circling the landing field, never leaving the area, hoping it doesn't run out of gas. Every school I went to added to the confusion in my mind, not giving me time to discover who I was. I was again looking for a way to understand my life and no one could nor would take the time to help. I was at another private Baptist school not far from the last place I'd walked out on. It was another work-at-your-own-pace school, but this time I figured out how the system worked, so I got good grades.

I continued my antics, never raising my flag except a couple of times, picking holes on the side dividing bar where my desk was. I tried to change my hair cut. It was rather short and growing out wildly, so in the morning I would stick it up in the front and spray it generously with hairspray. I would sit with my hands on my head picking the little pieces of dried hairspray out of my hair, hearing them hit the paper on my desk. I would ask help from the older high schoolers. We were all in the same room. It was more like a church with a couple hundred people size auditorium, we rarely used, with a parking lot that went all the way around the building except for the far other side was a one lane driveway to enter or exit school. During lunch I would play with friends in a constructed giant boat. All students would pass by, walking up the several stairs on a little hill, another twenty feet on the concrete walkway to the front of the school's church. It was set on a busy road that further down, intersecting a highway not far from Wal-Mart and that other school I walked away from.

I made friends with Paul, who was a very tall seventh grader with a long hair cut like a bowl. Near the end of the school year, Paul had an epileptic attack. I remember sitting in my chair and from the corner of my eye seeing him walk through the doorway and then roll back his eyes hit the floor, and collapse. In an open field next to the parking lot, we would play baseball over a huge concrete form about ten feet high. He was always being yelled at because he was off his medicine. Kitty was one of the prettiest girls there who attended there with her brunette but slightly red hair. Paul's mother was one of my two teachers for all of us high schoolers. There were two main rooms. The first about twenty five of us from seventh grade and up, and in a separate room of another twenty kids from fourth to fifth grade. When I was in trouble I would spend my time in an empty room where teachers would have one-on-one sessions with certain students doing separate activities. Surrounded by some school supplies and sitting at a very large desk, cramped up against the walls of the small room, I found myself bored and entertaining myself. Only one overweight teacher sat across from me occasionally teaching another young student, we had a conversation with each other and awkwardly, mostly with our eyes. She was always doing one-on-one sessions with younger students. I was really never told to do anything. I was pushed to the side so the teachers did not have to deal with me and I would not disrupt the class anymore. I would sneak my way through one of the doors in the corner of the room. It went into some sort of closet but also had another exit on the other side. I would sneak across the hallway that connected the older kid's room and also separated the hallway for the male and female bathrooms. Whatever I wanted to do I got away with and I would sneak away to the boys' room. I quickly jumped across the hallway directly into the bathroom directly across from this little closet. I didn't want the teacher in the room at the end of the hallway to see me.

During lunch I would sit in a circle in class with the older kids while I took dares. We talked about smoking cigarettes, marijuana and having sex. Kitty was definitely in my sights. I told her I would be good for her and she was definitely interested in the idea of how good I might be in bed. Some of the most daring upper-class high schoolers learned a lot with the other girls. One particular guy took a tall blonde girl into the girls' bathroom and had his way while she got him off. Everyone teamed together watching out for the teachers to come around because we knew their schedules and when they were not in the room. As a seventh grader I was sexually curious about my own body. Wishing to be with one of those older girls was always on my mind. I peeked over my shoulder watching Kitty and the other girls laugh with each other and goof around. It was a lot of fun hiding in bathrooms and being look out for the older guys. In almost every school I was in the dominant demographic, mostly white and a few white girls. The black girls were always jumping around, being vocal standing in the hallway making sure the guys and girls were having some fun. During one of my punishment sessions I was standing against the wall near the rear of the room with my face close to the light switch, told to keep my hands behind my back and not move. I thought I would be very funny if I turned the light switch off and on with my nose. The older high schoolers kept telling me to do it more. I tried anything to impress my peers, especially the girls. Everyone was laughing.

One time my father had to be called into the office and paddle me. At the barbershop I would tease my dad. I would sit on the little spongy gray leather platform he created to go over the arm rest. The chair had tattered brown leather upholstery. It would crank up with a silver cylinder handle and recline. Hanging from one of the sides was a thick black leather belt used only for decoration, but rarely to actually sharpen a razor for a shave. My dad joked around that someday he might have to bring that in and actually teach me a lesson. I should've never teased about that because that's what I had coming to me that day. My dad did not always like smacking sense into me. He was called in to do it himself once, but enrollment at some private schools parents had to agree to the policies. It was always three slaps and the third one was always the hardest. I was a little bit afraid, accepting it, I was able to hold in my laughter thinking how ridiculous it was. At the same time I was cornered, like a snake coiled ready to strike back, not sure what to do. It sure got me angry.

It was the very last day of school. I had made it through the rest of the school year. I ingeniously faked my grades by coming up with a numbering system of notches on the side of my book and looking on the self testing table for the answers for all of the tests for my pace books. I went back to my desk sat down and deciphering my code to pass everything. Like any inmate living in a prison, I survived by hiding all of my secrets and cheating. I surprised my parents by getting a good grade average of C+ and no one could understand why. The last day was party day so I wrote my gang member name in black permanent marker inside the wooden play ship. I signed it "Bugs" the name I gave myself because I like Bugs Bunny and I had teeth like a rabbit. Bugs Bunny was always a good role model for me. Paul and I walked to the back parking lot hiding behind a little bush separating the lanes. We were hitting off a cigarette and quickly scared out of our minds but getting a little buzz out of it. I brought my best friend Jeff's water pistol into school thinking it would be fun to play a prank on some of the kids shooting at them with it. I finished off a whole roll of film with the camera from home, hoping to capture some memories of friends. While walking back to class, passing the Coca-Cola machine outside the door, I heard that my teacher was looking for the water pistol, so I decided to hide it underneath the machine.

Life! It Must Be a Comedy

I was confronted so I walked over to where it was hidden and gave it to the teacher. I feared that Jeff would be so mad at me that I lost it but the teacher told me I would get it back at the end of the day. I was still upset. I paced around for a moment in front of the machine then I decided to walk to class to finish my day. Nobody was doing any work and everybody was just standing around when bluntly said how frustrated I was. In the doorway connecting a little hallway with a microwave and refrigerator I saw my teacher start to cross my path as I began to blurt it out. The entire room I think heard me. The start of something great in my life was about to crash into a dead-end.

God she is such a bitch! I blurted out.

I didn't have time to stop myself from saying it. Immediately she pointed at me and grabbed me by the arm telling me that I was in trouble and walked me to the principal's office where I would stay until my dad picked me up.

That's it Robert you're out of here, my teacher said.

It was those same famous words that I've gotten used to and even though I was going to miss my friends I just accepted it like every other time. I got a little bit of a kick out of it. At the same time I knew I would have to start all over again someplace new. I played it off as if I were cool. I was expelled from the school on the very last day of class. On the ride home in my dad's old baby blue station wagon, he was angry not saying much at all. I could just feel his frustration in his posture. When I made my parents angry, I could feel their energy like a radiating force, invisible, but plenty of signs. It didn't help that I ran out of school right before he got there, fearing he brought that belt again. He had to go down the street some way to see me hiding behind a tree to pick me up. I have the summer to look forward to. Finally I made parole and I was out--on bail. I put away all thoughts of school. Awaiting me was more snow boarding, hanging out with Jeff, riding my dirt bike, jumping on the trampoline, a little bit more exploration and looking forward to playing baseball for my second year in the Pony league. I had no sense of direction and no cares in the world or any conceptual understanding of education. My future and formidable teenage years were ever closer. When I turned into a teenager I felt I'd be able to do the things my brothers were doing when I was little, looking up to them. Somehow I was still treated like the little child, the baby of the siblings, fighting for respect at home, demanding it anyplace else I went. I could feel my

78

body becoming stronger and was looking forward to turning fourteen and all that I would be able to accomplish. I was also turning into a very handsome young man.

Chapter 7
Jesus Loves Me

Life was turning into a storm of pain. I was not in control.
Things weren't going my way. I started searching for ways to regain
control. I wrote in my journal about wishing I wasn't alive. I did not
want the path I was on, skipping from school to school, feeling like my
dreams were slowly fading, even though I had not even started working
on them. At the beginning of eighth-grade I spent the first month
bouncing around schools again, finally landing at Odenton Christian
School.

My mother tugged on my pants, getting me dressed while I slept,
pushing them up, while I slowly woke up, fighting her drive to make me
go to school. Those gray dress pants had a seam down the front, with a
black belt, a blue, long-sleeve button up dress shirt and dark blue tie.
Every school I'd gone to had almost the exact same wardrobe. I knew
exactly how to do my tie. It was second nature to me by now. Stuck in
my memory like a drill sergeant, forcing me to wear horrifying,
uncomfortable clothing, the only pair I had. It was the only clean pair
because my mother tried to get me to wash my own clothing, but I never
did. Other days, I pulled those pants over my legs, feeling the fabric
against my skin wishing she would have washed them at least once. The
first day of school was the only day they were clean. I didn't learn
responsibility like my brothers did, washing their clothes. I'd stand in
the shower for an hour, regretting my day before it started. I looked

forward to getting on my dirt bike or seeing my family and friends or being with my dog Fluffy.

It was the first day of school traveling almost an hour in my dad's blue station wagon every morning. I got the same butterflies listening to the lady on the radio. She reported the traffic with stale, uncomfortable, repetitive work voice. My dad was used to it, with his strong mind for hard work. I didn't have answers and I was always in situations where I had no control. I did not want to be told what to do, even staring at the road surface flashing by, wishing I could jump to escape. I arrived at school tense, but school did seem to be fun because I made it into one big joke and game.

We pulled into the parking lot close to a busy road near the Fort Meade military base. I could not see any military trucks but my dad was telling me it was close. I knew I was not going to boot camp though. My backpack was filled with every single book I needed. I had on my Forty-Niners jacket, still hanging baggy. My pants hung below my hips. I stepped out of the car, wearing my penny loafer shoes. It was a small parking lot and a small one floor school. There was a one-lane paved road going up a hill and around the building. There were several trailers with paved skinny walkways to wooden steps to each door. My skin crawled. My penny loafers, tightly fitted, gave me no traction if I chose to run away. I looked at my hair in the driver side after slamming it shut. I still had my part. The homemade bleached streaks were still looking good. My hair was cut in a bowl, long in front of my eyes and hanging past my ears. My dad and I hadn't said much on the ride there. Waiting for the ride back, my mother's maroon station wagon was just a trade-off. The same uncomfortable ride, except I had a working radio not my dad's old eight-track radio.

I walked up that hill while my dad handed me my lunch bag. I said something back, but it wasn't very reassuring. In his heart, I know he wanted me to excel. He was hoping something would click, that I would finally start to get it. I knew he had gone through so much trouble with Adrian and Carlo in school. I passed the front office that had two double glass doors and a sign to the left that said Office. A hallway straight forward led to the younger grade classes and the chapel. I clearly pinpointed the principal's office facing the doors and gave it kind of a grimace, with my head down, hunched over with my giant backpack walking up the hill, straight forward to my class. I arrived late.

Life! It Must Be a Comedy

I'll see you later son. Have a good day okay, my dad told me.
Here is your lunch. Be good, my dad repeated again.
Yeah-okay I'll see you later dad, I kindly replied.

The door was cold, rickety and flimsy. There was barely any room for the twenty kids sitting in tightly fit brown-top, curved, classic style desks. All the students were facing me and I could see the blackboard to my left and the tall teacher, Mr. Frankston staring me down with his big bushy black eyebrows. I walked to the right, down the four rows of chairs. I could see the lockers up against the wall. On the far side opposite of the door was a little table and a microwave, three possibly four windows surrounding the building. The trailer was very long and split in half for two classes to be taught in one trailer. I was standing there with my hardened face.

You are Robert, right? Well go find a seat, Mr. Frankston said.
Yeah, I replied.

What's up dude? You can come sit next to me back here, said a student named Steve standing up.

I acted like I didn't hear him, giving a little look, but totally established my dominance from the first day. He was standing up to share he was the cool guy in town, wanting me to submit to his gentle kindness. I sat down with my starter coat on, hunched my back with my butt on the edge of the forward part of the seat. I sized up everyone. A few really cute girls caught my attention but no one else that I had to worry about. Steve kept trying to nudge his head my way, but I never let him have any satisfaction that he could bribe me or think I was weak. To me, this was boot camp. I was in a very small crowd, where I always thrive and take control easily.

For the first few weeks, I gave just a little effort. Charles, a short black kid who wore glasses and was very gentle, sat next to me. He encouraged me to learn my spelling words and I did. I got a C on my first test. That was a good experience. This was the first time, in a while, that I actually applied myself again. The cramped space quickly stirred me up. I surprised myself, even though it was a very brief moment, I was able to focus a little bit. I tried flirting with one of the girls who had red hair parted down the middle and an amazing smile with braces. She had the kind of spirit I felt very attracted to. I had a crushes on three girls in my neighborhood, Megan, Stella and a new girl Sherrie. Sherrie and I would jump on the trampoline together for hours.

Life! It Must Be a Comedy

Sherrie was a petite girl, with flowing brunette hair. She always wore several bracelet rings around her wrist. Sherrie would only visit her uncle around my neighborhood occasionally, but when we were together she became my first blood rushing crush. Sherrie was a very flirtatious and provocative. She loved Alanis Morissette. As we'd jump to its beat she would tell me it was her "yes music". When I asked what that meant she said it was music that she could make love to. I was very sexually curious and she was my trigger.

Teachers changed classes not the kids. I had a history teacher and an English teacher. The history teacher caught my attention. I could see the brim of his glasses pattern, some sort of yellow and orange mixed with swirls of black. When he stood at the podium with his head bent it seemed he was staring right at me all the time. Little black circles appeared like the pupils of his eyes. I would sit through his entire class staring at him thinking he was staring at me. One of my most memorable demerits came when I was caught doodling on my notepad. I drew my history teacher with his glasses on and his hand down his pants playing with himself. My notebook had many more drawings of my newfound friend and classmate Curtis and I smoking cigarettes and me skating on ramps and half pipes and playing baseball with spiky hair on my head. I made myself appear to have large muscles, a cigarette in one hand and a baseball bat in the other hand and my shorts tattered, ripped on muscular legs. The teacher caught me, immediately giving me one demerit and then a second one as I walked to the adjacent trailer with him. I was giving him lip for the first demerit in front of the ninth-grade class while they laughed at me and my frustration.

Curtis was sitting next to me in class when the same teacher was getting mad at him for laughing and having his foot out in the hall between the chairs, making it look like the teacher would trip. Our teacher slammed his books down hard on Curtis' desk making Curtis erupt in tiny fits of accusations that the books came too close to his hands. We both just started laughing.

Come on you got to be kidding I'm getting a demerit for drawing? I said sarcastically in front of my eighth grade class.

Yes, and if you don't stop talking like that you're going to get another one, the teacher replied.

I looked over my shoulder and could see Curtis and a few other students laughing and Curtis shaking his head because I was so funny.

Life! It Must Be a Comedy

You can give me all the demerits you want I do not care. Do you think this one demerit scares me? I've got many more than that. I don't care if you give me three and I get a paddling, I said with even more attitude as I was walked to the front of the class.

Okay, if that's what you want. Here is your second and third demerit, the teacher said, happy to write that third demerit sending me to get a paddling.

I was used to being sent to the principal's office for that. I was clenching my fist ready to turn around and strike back that red hair sucker. The white plastic ping-pong paddle that was once connected to a rubbery string and a red rubber ball to play that silly little game was cracked. The swings got stronger with each hit. Three swings was the count, and he wasn't missing. My head was wedged against the cushioned seat and the back of the chair, my hands on the sides. When it was over I stood up, in his face, with my fist tighter than ever. Then he sat me down and prayed with me. While my eyes were open the whole time. I got up and walked out of the office, back up that hill to the class, starting to laugh to myself. I entered the class frustrated and mad but still laughing. There weren't too many paddlings and if anyone was getting it, it was either me or Curtis. The look on the students' faces was genuine, trying to read whether or not I was crying or if I was playing it off. They were expecting that so I knew I had to be strong. I sat down and high-fived Curtis over the hand.

Dude did you get paddled? Curtis asked.

Yeah, I did man, I said and we both started laughing hysterically about it.

My English teacher had a very strong Southern accent. I didn't pay much attention to what we had to do. I never read the books, just wrote my report word for word from the book jacket, such as the report we had to do for "The Call of the Wild." Even tracing through the paper the exact word and lettering with the book placed under the paper. I never got caught because I never gave my English teacher the book that she wanted to look at and I knew why because she knew I did not write that report. When my English teacher called my house I picked up the phone and blasted the volume on the television speaker and put the phone right up against the speaker until my mom would came downstairs, screaming at me. I sat acting like I didn't know what was going on. I did have some credible efforts I put forth, when reading most of that book but quitting before the end only looking at the drawings to find out what happened. I brought a big poster into class. It was almost an exact replica of the cover of the book that I drew.

The cute girl that I liked quickly saw me for who I was, someone that was just out to have fun and goof off. So, she lost interest in me. I had to nurse my right arm back to health after a dog bite by my neighbor Stephanie's old dog, Boner. The dog did not recognize me. He was more in guard dog mode, in different living conditions. He was a very large dog, a very rare breed with black and orange swirl short fur. I walked around grossing people out, exposing my stitches--eight of them over my right elbow and three of them under my elbow.

Curtis and I ended up becoming friends as he enrolled to the same school a few weeks after my first day. He looked dazed and confused--the same expression and feeling I did have. He had a striking resemblance to me in his attitude and personality. Curtis had a little hunch and was a very skinny boy with no real chest muscles like the ones I was building. Curtis had nearly the same haircut except not as long as mine and it was parted to the one side. I didn't say anything to him and we did not get acquainted for a couple of weeks. I was building a reputation as the tough guy standing in front of a little group of mine. Leo was a very tall kid with blond hair sporting a pullover starter jacket just like mine, with the New York Giants colors. Steve would also walk around with us. I would bring my hacky sack to kick it around. I'd do my roundhouse back kicks with my karate muscle memory coming in handy, showing off as the sack flew over and behind my head. I would do a spin kick into the middle almost perfectly every time. Another senior who had very similar physical features (though I felt bulkier from weightlifting) joined us in our circle.

It always seemed to be very cold and we'd play and joke around during lunch break, which was like prison free-time. We were surrounded by tall leafy trees and a patch of forest and breaking through some kind of construction. The road that went around the building between the trailers and building connected all the way to the back of school property where there was a playground, baseball backstop and the red-haired pastures house. Six steps led down to the gymnasium that I enjoyed.

Life! It Must Be a Comedy

The bigger part of the church had a carpet floor, basketball hoops and a basketball team. We'd use the bathroom in the gym or skip class. We'd ask for a pass and hang out there for a long time. There were three classrooms on each side of the gym and a stairway balcony where spectators would sit on a aluminum rising benches to watch the games. At the far end we would play baseball on a horribly managed dirt field with bumps and torrential rain dirt trails. There was a metal backstop. One school day I was so anxious to get on the field to play baseball with the rest of my classmates that I took off my shirt in the playground instead of running back into the bathroom to get changed. I took off my shirt, revealing my washboard chest and muscles to some younger students, feeling exposed, but tough.

I started racking up demerits. Sixty of them meant expulsion. Curtis at the time, started following us around. We talked to him more and stopped teasing him. From then on Curtis and I clicked. What I did he did. We were sent to the office, demerits in hand, getting paddled many times and came out laughing. Our teachers signed white note paper, like demerits were the prescription for our cures. We liked dirt bike riding and goofing off. Our attitudes fed off each other's energy. Curtis tried to keep his grades up so he could stay on the basketball team, but failed. The two of us would sit outside the principal's office on the floor with our backs up against the wall throwing little pieces of the erasers at each other. When someone came by we would stop. After school one day we were waiting for our parents to pick us up. We stood in front of other students getting in their faces, while Curtis and I asked all the students.

Do you have, ha' h -ppiness?

Do you have, ha' -ppiness? Do you have, haaa -piness? I would try to change up the pronunciation so it sounded more-funny.

Robert! I can see what you're doing, the supervising teacher said under her breath.

What! Come on, I'm just asking if everyone has happiness, I explained back.

That's it you two. Come with me, the teacher said, semi-laughing under her breath.

We were like Beavis and Butthead, my favorite characters on MTV. I wasn't able to watch MTV because my dad had cut the power cord to the back of our television because I was misbehaving. Our heads bopped and our posture resembled Beavis and Butthead. We walked along laughing the same way they would. When our mothers picked us up, they walked down the hallway behind us and we were laughing.

I realized having a friend exactly like me, no matter how much trouble I got into, it was worth getting in trouble. Hopefully, we could stay together for the rest of high school. My grades averaged F. A bad grade was one thing at least that I was great at staying consistent with. I attempted to change some of the letters on my report cards, but it did no good. One of my favorite things was to ride my dirt bike through the woods with my best friend Jeff. Curtis had a Yamaha one hundred too. There was a huge patch of woods near Curtis' townhouse and a long strip of power lines leading directly from a huge BG&E electric factory across the creek. We both quickly realized that we both lived right across the creek from each other, only a dirt bike ride away to one other's houses. Something had drawn us together against all odds. We were like twin brothers, so it was amazing to live so close.

School ended, we survived longer than any of us thought we would. Baseball season started up again. I was getting interested in playing with my team. I met a girl at school. She was Principal Gunnar's daughter Grace. She had an Asian background and she was a very petite girl. She was in the twelfth grade, and was a master at piano and the harp. Grace mesmerized me with her ability to play music. I went on a field trip competition for singing and she was in the competition for piano. I sang my lungs out pretty well in the class choir.

Life! It Must Be a Comedy

Listening to her play piano, I wanted to become her friend. I never
associated before with anyone so close to the school authorities. Grace
actually tried to help me. Leslie was a beautiful Hispanic girl, in my
grade, with long brown hair and a little bit of accent even though she
was a native of the United States. I was always trying to pinch Leslie's
butt in choir. She refused my invitations to go out. Steve managed to
get the attention of both Grace and Leslie but Grace more so as they
were kind of going out. Both these girls would smile at my
inappropriate humor.

I decided to skip the last three days of school because I knew I
failed anyway. Since baseball season had started, I was anxious to start
swinging new red Easton bat with a huge barrel that I'd bought at a used
sports shop. My new bat had not yet seen much action. Curtis and I
were together riding dirt bikes with Jeff through the woods. We went
snowboarding on my fourteenth birthday before the end of the year,
along with Jeff, Leo, Carlo and I. I convinced my mom to take me into
class on the last day of school even though I was practically suspended
so I just took off. My hair was looking really good, after being hounded
by the principal to get my haircut. He used to always check under my
hat during lunchtime. I stood out as the punk skater, wearing my black
wino jeans with pockets in the front and back past the knees. I never put
any liquor in those long pockets. I could feel my wallet, a gray and
white hand-me-down from my brother Adrian, at the very bottom of my
back right pocket right below the back of my knee. I had my skateboard
buckle belt hanging down the side, black with a silver tip ending. I was
wearing my low-cut air walks look-alike Payless shoes.

I walked around the campus proud of my lack of
accomplishments. Feeling comfortable with my strong tight muscles,
walking with that strut my mother always yelled at me for, barely able to
walk in those huge pants, so heavy in weight. I had my "No Fear" hat on
and my yellow Stussy T-shirt on with a longer slightly darker T-shirt
under that. It was my chance to walk around with the image I was
always projecting in my school uniform. I walked around to each
classroom saying goodbye to a few friends. I ran into Grace and Steve
in the ninth-grade trailer. We took a photograph together and I wrapped
my right arm around Grace's waste. Grace and I were the same height
but I was slightly taller. In my left hand I had the bill of my hat rolled
and in my right hand my fingers signaling the words I love you over her

hip. I did not want to leave and wanted to get an image of what would be my past left behind. My future was uncertain. I knew I would have to repeat the eighth-grade. I felt like running away.

I said a quick little goodbye to Grace and a few other friends giving her one last hug. I was hoping this would not be the last time I would see her. I did not know this would be the last time I would be standing next to her. My muscles were holding her tight and I was standing firm, leaning toward her feeling extremely comfortable. Jumping from school to school, I never had that feeling. I was a fourteen-year old boy, exposing my strength and muscles rather than my mind. My fragile mind was in disbelief, unable to cope with my problems, instead muscling through everything.

Life! It Must Be a Comedy

I felt a blooming cloud storming around me following me everywhere. Baseball season was well into its schedule. I requested transfer from my team of the previous year because I was not being given an opportunity to pitch. It was a panic decision. I knew I had a lot of good feelings with the team, but I wanted sole possession of the ball and I could only get that if I changed teams. I was excited on the first day of practice but immediately I knew I didn't make the right decision. I felt stuck on a team that did not have as much talent. My coach even said if I wanted to transfer back to my team I could. I looked across the field, while sitting on the bench looking over at my old teammates before our game started as my coach gave me the option. I decided to stay where I was. I made my decision. I knew I could help that team but it also felt good being looked up to by everyone, including the coach, as a star player. I was afraid to switch back. I didn't have the willpower to say I wanted to go back. I grew frustrated with my team. I was throwing hard strikes and curveballs. I watched line drives smacked back past me into the field while my players were lazy about picking up the ball, not running to catch it. Every father was yelling to his son about being lazy, especially the coach's son, followed by me yelling too- ---"*Get the ball*!" I wasn't the best pitcher, but I enjoyed throwing accurately and hard. I knew what I was doing, hoping to strike some people while being as fast as I could. I didn't understand all the mechanics of pitching, holding the ball, switching out my hand positions every once in awhile. I did not know if I was doing the right thing. My body position, my legs kick, and arm follow through was as natural as anyone could ever be.

I could hear my old team yelling from the dugout. I was torn up inside but I just stuck with what I knew and when they came up to bat I threw my hardest strikes. My focus on the mound was never unbalanced by any distraction. I could blank out everyone around me and put myself in a state of mind when I was training on my field at home. I was all by myself and I'm just playing catch with my dad or my friend, throwing strikes and no distraction could ever make me miss my mark. When they made their remarks I glanced over briefly and could hear what they were saying, but I still went into my wind up and threw as hard as I could.

We were going to have fun with you this year Robert, one of the boys of my old team yelled while holding on to the fence in the dugout.

Life! It Must Be a Comedy

We were going to let you pitch this year Robert, my old coach yelled.

I showed the most promise on my team. I was the star athlete shining like a bright star amongst every other player on my new team. Switching between shortstop and pitching I had line drives come to me and I naturally gravitated to them with perfect form, poise, stamina and footwork from base to base. I wore number thirteen on my jersey, and the previous year I was number three. We wore maroon jerseys with white straps around the sleeves, white baseball pants and matching hat. Harundale was written with cursive letters across the front of it. Every spectator, team player and coach saw my talent. I was the only person on my team to be sent to the All-Star game two weeks after the season about to end. Switching teams paid off. My talent was finally recognized, giving me honors. Combined with my amazing athletic ability my star qualities and moments did not go unrecognized playing shortstop. I stood there in my wide leg position, my knees bent and my hands poised, ready, leaning forward anticipating just like Cal Ripken Jr. played shortstop. My senses anticipated the swing of the bat and the first crack. I knew exactly where the ball was going to come from and what direction to move to get there. I never took my eyes off the ball.

I was setting up for a double-play with a man on first base. The first pitch was thrown hard. I started leaning to my left as the crack of the bat sent the ball careening straight down the middle of the infield, rising slightly. I ran as hard as I could toward second base, with my eye on the ball. It was perfect poetry, every foot step falling into place, my speed fast and keeping pace, my concentration honing in on the ball, me finding the bag. We were defender and offender in a race to catch the ball, racing to be called safe at a pinched meeting. I stepped on it with my left foot, running fast, planted, launching from the bag boosting high into the air then possible. My left gloved hand reached out looking like Michael Jordan flying through the air, my legs spread to full extension as the ball was trapped in my glove, high above the ground, higher than anyone could ever normally jump. I landed with that ball in my glove, quickly grabbed it with my other hand. I did a spin to my left to get my balance while still moving forward and grabbed the ball out of my glove. In the same motion, I stretched back my right arm in a coil of strength and released it toward first base for a double play. The inning ended on my two outs and all my teammates erupted in appreciation and the crown was clapping hands, in disbelief and amazement. I ran straight past Blue (the umpire) and he jokingly yelled out to my dugout benches shaking his head, wondering whether or not he thought what I did was a legal move. I knew he was only joking around, just struck in surprise that I actually pulled it off. I created a feat of agility no one had ever seen before. It was a phenomenal moment for me.

Hey, he's not allowed to do that is he? Blue said. Echoing words in repeated response from a different play I would make.

Life! It Must Be a Comedy

The same thing happened once when I was playing center field. I caught the ball in midfield and saw the batter rounding first base running toward second base, over shooting his anticipation with too much speed. I launched the ball as fast as I could directly toward first base barely missing the tag. It's a play that rarely ever works and you have to be strong and throw hard because centerfield is a very long distance, but I managed to get there in a split second. I waited for call by Blue. The player was safe.

Life! It Must Be a Comedy

I was looking forward to the All-Star game. I had the looming anticipation of failing eighth grade and wondering what would happen next because I did not want to repeat. We finished the season, but not in any standings for a trophy. My brand new Easton bat still did not get much play. I took it home with me and kept it in my closet, bringing it out a few times when playing in the field. Curtis and I were in a similar situation, with the middle of summer and returning to school on our minds. Now the beginning of June 1996, we would always run away together with our dirt bikes. I got in an argument with my mother threatening. I didn't care if I had to repeat eighth grade and that there was no way I would ever succeed in school. Her reply was more serious than ever before the threat that I would be put in military school next year. Afraid that day I would be taken for an interview to one of those schools, I panicked.

Sitting in my bedroom I waited for my mother to leave the house, called Curtis and told him to collect some supplies in a book bag for a couple of nights out and to bring the tent that we both found riding our dirt bikes through the power lines one day. We didn't know what purpose that tent would have, or if we would use it, but it seemed like it was placed there just for this moment, some sort of mystical power setting me up for something. I put my rollerblades in my backpack with some crackers and I hopped on my brand-new bike from the previous Christmas. All set with perfect transportation and backup rollerblades, I was on my mountain bike headed off into the woods to meet Curtis and run away. I knew he was freaking out and was only going through with it because I was absolutely serious. Curtis agreed only if I promised I was doing this permanently.

I jumped over a few fences of my neighbors', hidden behind the pool two houses over, waiting to see if my mother had left yet, and as soon as I saw the car go down the road I ran back to my yard for my bike. Twilight was approaching and I was frantically peddling down the street, a far distance from my house, into the little path made by our dirt bikes into the woods off of Nabbs Creek Road, passing all of the shoreline until the woods were deep enough, going around the creek. My adrenaline peddled through the dirt, through the mud and over the cut-down tree bridges we made over the stream, a foot deep and ten feet wide, at the bottom of the hill. I then raced across the path, up the other side, through the woods. As soon as I got to the top of the hill I got off the bike to push over the slippery mud and the deep trenches our dirt bike wheels made I began paddling fast around some puddles and down a little trail we always followed. In an instant Curtis came flying around the next turn popping out of nowhere from the dense thick woods. We were both frantic and our hearts were racing. We couldn't catch our breath and we could hardly speak to communicate what we were going to do next. I didn't exactly explain what was going on except for I didn't want to go to military school and decided to run away and just convinced him again to go with me and we were both one hundred percent on an adventure. We both thought it was going to be forever but we were just riding it out.

We stayed clear of all the roads, following the trails and the large opening in the power lines where a gravel path had torrential rain crevasses. We know down every hill several times trying to avoid another accident, when Curtis had once flipped over his wheels on the dirt bike on the same trenches. We could see the tall towering electric lines soaring a couple hundred feet in the air. We stopped at one of them climbed up about twenty feet and smoked a cigarette. We carefully climbed back down going into Curtis' neighborhood filled with townhouses a direct entrance right on the side of the power lines. We picked a trail, one of a couple that led from the power lines through the woods, but a different one than the trail that took us back to my house. This one stopped on the other side of a tall bank, directly across the creek in view of the Margo Marina that was at the bottom of a hill on my side of my neighborhood. It was a perfect site to see the road to see which cars were going by. Our campsite was located directly across from the marina. All the boats were docked at the neighborhood bar and restaurant. It stood out with a very tall and steep roof. It had giant windows lining the back, a couple of balconies and a street that went all the way around it to the piers and back up the hill to Nabs Creek Road.

Behind Curtis' house there was a peer and hiding in the tall grass was a small aluminum flat bottom fishing boat. We flipped it over and grabbed a couple of two by fours lying around and paddled over to a boat docked in his cove. We lifted up the pins securing this twenty foot speed boat, slid under its cover and looked around. We found a backup place for shelter and even discovered a brand new set of long-distance binoculars in a leather black carrying case. I decided to take them because they might come in handy. We were both trying to figure out our timetables and because Curtis took off with me he still had a chance to go back and get the tent for us to camp out. His parents didn't know he took off yet. Curtis went home to eat dinner and I staked out across the cove from his house. I was perfectly perched up on a hill at the water's edge. Between the trees directly behind me was his neighborhood docks with all the neighborhood boats safely secured away. With a perfect vantage site I got out my binoculars and waited for Curtis to signal me. I stood there quiet to myself, just thinking, panicking a little bit, eating my saltine crackers, keeping a close eye with my binoculars. I heard a loud scream and then saw Curtis racing down the road on his mountain bike with a giant piece of fabric plastic hanging over his shoulder, protruding from his back. I knew it was the tent. While the fabric was flapping behind him he was racing with his legs peddling fast. I knew that his parents would be worried. I waited for Curtis to meet me at our spot. Curtis was so anxious and panicked he started mumbling words of dismay that *we had to get out of there fast*. So I quickly laughed like we always did, got on our bikes and went to set up the tent for the night.

There was an old campsite littered with crushed beer cans, a bit frightening to both of us because we did not know if this was a local hang-out spot or if we would be alone. We didn't know what was going on in the woods. I remember hearing rumors, but we knew we were not old enough to really protect ourselves. With water in sight, we went off the path several feet, hoping if anyone came back there they would not see us. We cleared a patch of ground, moving all the leaves and sticks and set up our tent. We had an hour and a half of daylight left to work with. If it was going to rain we would need Curtis' windbreaker because the tent had an opening of clear fabric that would not block the rain. We had enough supplies of Oodles of Noodles, Pop Tarts, Saltine crackers, potato chips and even a fire-starting log lighter with a red handle. I started teasing Curtis that he could have picked some better food and that we did not have any pots to cook the noodles. We had plenty of water from both of our bottles on our mountain bikes.

We rode our bikes on the trail to sneak by his house and put them in our boat and paddled over to his neighborhood dock. We went from boat to boat, after getting up on the docks, searching for supplies. We found a couple of seat-cushion life preservers, with white straps, a couple of good double-sided paddles and a fishing knife. Curtis went down one of the connecting peers and I followed him. Curtis was laughing and happy that he found an amazing paddle that we could use. It was very dark we didn't have much light so we had to grab what we could see. The townhouses were in clear sight. We were hoping nobody would catch us, but Curtis was laughing with each step.

Rob! Hey man I found an awesome... Curtis said

I wasn't too far right in front of him when he took his next step. He didn't even get to finish his sentence when the pear in front of him went from very wide to extremely narrow. Curtis missed his step and went falling straight into the water. I heard a loud splash and Curtis flopping around trying to hold onto his paddle and yelling for me to reach for him. I couldn't help but start laughing. I was rolling in my gut while he yelled for me to come help and stop. I watched him do a doggy paddle and only the moonlight was lighting up his head movement with the dark black murky water making it seem like Curtis kind of disappeared.

Oh my god Curtis that was so damn funny! I saw you walking and then all of a sudden you fell in the water. That was so funny. All right, grab my hand, I said.

Curtis swam to the corner of the pier not far from where he fell pulling himself up. I was completely soaked with water standing there with the night wind blowing a little bit it was kind of chilly. I offered to give him one of my shirts I had two of them on, but he didn't want it.

I don't know what happened. I was showing you my paddle and then all of a sudden I fell in the water. Stop laughing at me man.... And then when I got out something electrocuted me from the pier. I started to panic, Curtis explained.

Are you all right? OK, well let's just get the hell out of here and get back to our camp. It looks like it might rain. Crap! I said.

We both giggled. Curtis was still soaking wet, but we got back in our boat and paddled back to our tent. We climbed up the steep incline covered with trees, wet leaves, sticks and branches using a rope that we found in one of the boats. We started a fire and left it burning, hoping nobody would see us as it started raining. Curtis fell asleep. I couldn't believe it. I could not sleep with that hard prickly ground and that plastic up against my face. I laid on my back with my hand behind my head for a little while, listening to the rain watching the fire dimming out. I could only see the faint flickering orange and yellow with the zipper closed. I swear I heard someone yelling my name. I was also wondering if someone was looking for me. The rain was stopping. I quickly made the decision to wake Curtis up. I wanted to get out of there because the place was creeping me out. I knew we had a safer place to sleep and this was our only chance to make our escape as the rain stopped. We put away the tent and grabbed our clothing that was still wet on the hanger we made above the fire. We took our bikes and everything back down the hill into the boat. In the pitch black I somehow managed to slip down carefully without getting hurt. I helped Curtis into the boat first and then I handed down the bikes. The operation was quick and smooth but even more dangerous than before and darker. We had to step over the paddles inside the boat. It was filling up quickly and there was barely enough room for me to get myself down the hill without falling in the water, or slipping on the muddy slope. I carefully got into the boat holding on to the tiny branches connected to the tree above us, and one hand on the rope, hoping they wouldn't snap.

The water was absolutely calm only the moonlight was shining our way and some of the light coming from the marina across the creek. We were both hoping a cop wouldn't be patrolling because we didn't really have any light except for one flashlight. If we wanted to signal him we couldn't, at the same time we didn't want to be caught. We gently paddled slowly picking up speed as the rain started coming down a little bit faster but not pouring yet. There was some water at our feet but we didn't have to bail out water too much. We paddled past the marina and the docks past Curtis' neighborhood right behind Curtis' house in his cove we stopped lifted up the pins from the watertight protection of that speedboat and slipped our slippery wet bodies in there for the night. We tied off our boat to the other boat and left everything else. We now had every commodity we needed clean, soft cushions, pillows and towels and blanket, two places to sleep and even a sink, working radio and a bathroom. We goofed around a little bit doing a little bit of wrestling, but quickly fell asleep. The next morning we woke up to the eerie motion of the bottom of our boat slapping against the wake and the sunshine peeking through the little hatch.

I made the decision to go back home and Curtis was furiously mad that I wasn't going to go through with the plan. So instead of going home we would use the paper towels we found to get rid of any evidence that we were there. We paddled over to Curtis' house and wrote a note as I told Curtis to write explaining we were going crapping. We fell victim to the comfort of Curtis' house, taking our time, getting a little lazy and eating some breakfast. We got too elaborate on the letter. We walked down to our boat getting ready to go paddling out into the water not knowing where we would hide.

Just as we were getting in the boat to push off we hear a voice. It was Curtis' mother. I guess the letter we wrote lead her exactly to us. She got home much faster than we thought she would.

What do you both think you're doing? So I guess you stole that boat and you were just going to paddle around? Curtis' mother said.

Dammit! I said under my breath.

Curtis' mother was furious and she dragged him home and offered to take me home.

Yeah...ahh... No thanks. I'll just ride. I said under my breath.

I sat in Curtis' basement thinking to myself. I gave Jeff a call. Nobody was picking up at his house so I tried several more times thinking I could ride my bike to his house and still stay away. I hopped on my bike to the street leading out of Curtis' neighborhood. I rode the medium strip on the highway. Speeding down on Fort Smallwood Road Adrian and a neighbor friend came up behind me in a long blue low rider old-style Chevy. Adrian tried to get me to go in. Immediately tears started running down my face and I yelled to get away. I paddled down Solley Road off of a shortcut. I pulled my bike up behind a warehouse staked out a little bit to see where that blue car was going. I stayed there for half an hour and made my way back down Solley Road. I was afraid as soon as I got to the power lines I was going to see cops and my mother's car and people looking for me. I stopped my bike when I got over a little hill and turned peeking over a little bit. Nobody was there. I continued home down the street fast as I could. My backpack still had everything I left home with. When I got to my house I did not go in. I stood there over my bike at the corner of my property. I knew I was in trouble so I waited for someone to come out. My mother came out to the front door. She pushed it open and stood above the steps on the front porch crossing her arms just looking at me. She knew if she was going to be any kind of threatening I would get back on my bike and just take off. We both stood there staring at each other for a couple of minutes feeling the situation out.

Life! It Must Be a Comedy

I'm not going to military school! I yelled.

I'm not talking about that. Just come in here, you're not in trouble, my mom said back.

I didn't do anything wrong, I explained.

I waited for her to clear the door and go back in the house. Then I followed and went right to my room. I waited out the next couple of days, just feeling like I was wandering around aimlessly. I knew that I was waiting for summer to be over, even though I had the All-Star game to look forward to. I decided to give my dog a bath. Washing him up outside gave me great joy. I was laughing at him while taking a picture outside. Standing in a white T-shirt of mine I pinned it around his stomach to fit tight. He never waited for me to dry him off. Even though he had a haircut, all that long goofy hair was everywhere and his shaking got me entirely wet. I rarely ever gave him a bath all by myself. It was a special moment connecting with him.

I wanted to take a picture of us together that day. I was sitting in the living room in front of my television downstairs with the camera. My back was up against the end of the couch and my left hand and elbow were resting over my knees, bent up slightly, my weight on my left foot. I had Fluffy down at my feet, petting him.

Hey Mah! Come here please! Take a picture for me! I said.

She came downstairs and kneeled down in front of me to take a picture and captured our moment together. The picture was priceless. I had my T-shirt off, wearing my smooth shiny fabric maroon George Fox shorts and no shoes or socks. I was proud of that picture. It showed me as a great strong man, good muscle development and me and my puppy. I had an overwhelming sense of preserving that moment inside me. I don't know what it was inside me, but I felt a great need to do this. I always want to remember this moment. I felt happy, peaceful and in control.

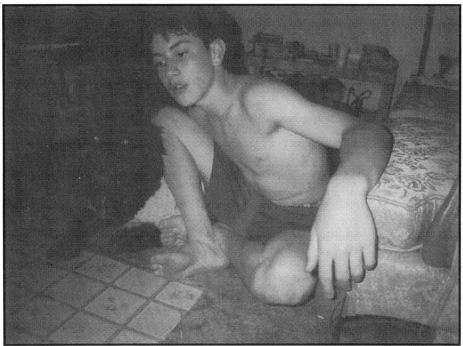

The All-Star game was coming closer, scheduled for the twenty-first of June. Even though I'd never been there before, and it was the furthest thing from my mind, I would think about it from time to time. I asked Carlo if he would take me to a friend's house for the day. It was two days before the game now. Curtis told me not to go to Jeff's house, instead to hang out with him for the day I decided to call Jeff back anyway. I got in Carla's brand-new single cab cherry red Ford pickup. He hadn't had his new car a month since we were at the dealership together all day long, trying to make the deal. I convinced Carlo to drive me, so I packed a bag even though my dad told me not to go, because he knew the game was in two days.

I got dropped off in the parking lot between all the houses at Jeff's Auto Body Shop's family property. I quickly said bye to Carlo, grabbed my bag and he drove away after waiting for me to get to the house safely. Jeff and I sat around the house most of the time. In the blistering heat, we swam in the pool, rode his dirt bike through the trails and played nerf guns attack in his house. That night we watched a movie with his little brother Buzz, his dad and his dad's girlfriend from China. Jeff's little dog was running around and Jeff's little new baby brother was in the next room sleeping. It was a double wide trailer, but still hardly enough room for all of us.

That night Jeff was teaching me how to create key chains by folding overlong skinny strands of plastic, some sort of technique he learned in school. By taking four strings you fold over the two and then cross connect the other two making a tight square pattern shape all the way up. It seemed like something interesting enough to do. We had Sega video game sessions in his bedroom. The game sat on top of a skinny, medium height, very flimsy wooden TV stand, on his little black television. The room was littered with toys. I couldn't walk around without stepping on something. Jeff and I shared the top bunk bed while Buzz slept below.

It was getting into the a.m. now and I stayed up another extra hour until almost three o'clock working on my weaving to make my little keychain barely two inches long. I stopped and burned off the edges connecting it to my keychain. The room was pitch black. I was sitting next to the far side window closest to the yard and swimming pool, at their little desk littered with toys and papers, with a little lamp over top, lighting up my hands. Jeff and Buzz were sound asleep, turning in an hour before me. I felt the forces of the world weighing down on me. Even though my little worries were nothing too substantial, I felt like I was in some kind of hunt, waiting to be caught by something or someone, some situation that would trap me. I never guessed it was the little things that would give me away.

I leaned toward God to say a prayer because I thought I needed it. I wanted to feel safe and I didn't want to feel like I had to worry all the time. I wasn't exactly sure what I was running from. I knew that I did not have anything telling me that my future was secure. With this heavy burden held inside my chest, weighing me down, keeping me up that night, I said a prayer to help me for the next day. I did not know what I would be walking into in the morning. I was not even thinking about the game. I knew that I needed this moment to reach out to a Higher Power to help me put things into perspective and could help me find control. It was an innocent cry for protection.

Dear God. I need to ask you tonight to help me. I feel like my life is spiraling out of control. I need you to protect me. God, please protect me tomorrow and give me a safe day and please look out for my family and take care of them. In Jesus name I pray. Amen.

Life! It Must Be a Comedy

I woke the next day with no worry and no thoughts of praying for anything. I had no care in the world. I felt free for the moment, rushing out the front door, across the little porch, out the screen door, jumping down a couple of steps. Jeff and I were ready to go swimming. I had my towel over my shoulder; I was in my bright orange swim suit with my shirt off. Jeff and I set up the Slip and Slide with the hose. We began running down the Slip and Slide next to the pool on our bellies, hitting the bump at the end and splashing into the little pool. In between Slip and Slide we would get back into the pool, walking up four or five steps onto the large wooden deck or even climb up the side fence railing an extra four feet above the pool to jump or dive in. The pool was a round shape only four feet deep. I grabbed a pair of goggles, flipped over on my back in the water and sunk my body all the way to the bottom of the pool lying there on my back just watching the surface ripple across, looking at the magnified sky, laying there and trying to hold my breath.

I decided to get out of the pool and do what I've done hundreds of times. Seeing Jeff at the other end of the pool up against the wall in the middle, I thought if I dove slightly to the right of him and went around him, I could swim behind and grab him. Standing on the edge of the slippery wet planks I went one step up and dove out. With feet free and hands straight, arms and body stretched out for my dive, I entered the water fast.

Something went wrong!

It all changed. I entered a new world. Everything that felt familiar to me had vanished. I was suspended. My head was ringing a loud crashing sound that echoed through my mind. My entire body was numb and paralyzed, though I felt like my arms were straight out at my sides and my legs straight behind me. I felt like a ghost form of myself. I could not move a single muscle except for shaking my head. I could not feel any part of my body except for my face. Suspended, floating for a few seconds, I knew immediately something was wrong and I was going to die. Holding my breath, motionless, at the mercy of anyone and anything, I hoped that somehow help would come. The current started pushing me. The water pressure from the filter close by was pushing me around the pool as I floated to the top face down. My life was over, floating there in a horrifying state of shock and uttermost disbelief and submission and panic. Furiously shaking my head left to right, time and time again, crying on the inside for help.

I floated for another minute or two slipping in and out of consciousness for what seemed like an eternity, witnessing my own demise. My head was lifted out of the water and I could hear everything around me amplified; the waves splashing, the wind blowing, kids yelling and sounds of car motors passing by. It was the sound of existence and consciousness of my life, and the only thing to me that felt familiar to being alive. Jeff pulled me out of the water for a brief second long enough for me to tell him to go get help. Not believing me, he let me go and I sank back underwater feeling that was my only hope, my only chance, and it's gone...

Jeff! You have to go get help you have to call 911. I cannot move, I said with whatever breath I had.

What? Jeff replied with a giggle.

Jeff did not believe me. He thought I was joking, understandably nobody knows in these situations if someone is telling the truth. Underwater again, floating, not moving a single muscle or knowing where my body is, completely disconnected from everything except for my face and my eyes. I was in a horrific new dimension of existence, pleading for help, screaming on the inside. Unknown minutes go by feeling like this was the rest of my life, as I start slipping in and out of consciousness again. I was only slightly able to keep awake. I felt myself being lifted out of the water one last time and I repeated myself. I was trapped in waves of consciousness, flooded and left for dead.

Rob! Come on man! I heard Jeff say under his breath with no extreme worry.

That was the last time I caught my breath. The waters moved slowly again and I was floating, waiting for the end. I held my breath as long as I could again for what seemed like the full extent of anyone's capacity to hold their breath. Fully aware of my last breath, my last bit of consciousness, I began to pray inside my heart and mind...

God save my soul. I accept Jesus Christ into my life as my Lord and Savior. My life is in your hands now. Please look after my family, I thought to myself saying the words in my mind.

I had to ask God to save my soul for the last time and I had to do it one more time, fearing the life I was living. The promise I had in me from repeating this as an eight-year-old boy with my mother was not good enough. I had to do it one more time. I did receive Him into my heart, but it was not good enough in my mind, so I had to do it again to make sure. I was so frightened and lost holding onto anything I knew from my childhood that might save me. It was this moment when I lost consciousness for good.

I entered the blackness of unconsciousness with no worries. For the moment, I thought I was going to die. I do not know how long I was under when I began to wake up being pulled straight up out of the water. The sun was shining down on me. I was being lifted from a grave, rising to sense my body was not moving. I could not feel anything and still could not move but the moment my face felt the air I began to wake up. I felt a warm bright sunshine in my eyes. My head was hanging down, pulled back, put on my back, and slightly turned on to my side. Someone screamed to roll me back onto my back. I felt the presence of three people. One was Jeff's grandmother standing over me frantically asking me if I was saved. I could hear the ambulance in the background shortly after being pulled out. I did not know where my body was and it felt like my knees were bent and my arms were straight out in front of me. I immediately began to ask where my body was and where my arms and legs were. People told me they were right there and I couldn't believe it. Where I was told my arms and legs were felt the opposite of where I thought they were. I could only feel some ghostly resemblance of numbness nothing at all connected to any sensation. The mind has its own phantom positions.

Rob! Are you saved? Jeff grandmother stood over me I could see her face asking me if my soul was saved.

Yes! I repeated.

The paramedics placed a board under my back and my head was strapped on to something, but I could not tell what it was. The paramedics quickly asked me who I wanted to ride in the ambulance with me and I quickly said I wanted Jeff.

Jeff was my brother and the closest to being like family. I was placed in the ambulance being carried down the steps and into the vehicle. Suddenly, I was in the ambulance with my head all the way toward the front side of a vehicle. I could see the paramedic calmly cutting off my clothing and starting some kind of clear tubes to connect to me. I did not know what happened to me, but somehow I felt like I knew. The ambulance was blasting the sirens and I asked if Jeff was there, while the vehicle rocked back and forth. I could move my head slightly, tilted back to look behind me into the passenger window in the wall dividing the vehicle. I could see Jeff's face looking back toward me. I relaxed my neck again after being told not to move.

Robert do you know what has happened to you? The paramedics said.

I think so, I said

Where is Jeff, is Jeff here? I repeated.

Yes he's in the front, please don't move, the paramedic said.

I felt trapped and stuck but completely submissive because I could not move. I knew I was in trouble. For the time being I was breathing fine all by myself. Getting to the hospital seemed like a moment in time that was fast-forwarded and then rewound and then fast-forwarded again. All of a sudden I was there, being pulled out, going down a cold unfamiliar hallway with lights on the ceiling passing steadily. I felt like I was being taken to a place of unknown nothingness as I started slipping into unconsciousness. My mind didn't have much time to think, just exist. I remember the images and the feeling of being completely disassociated and disconnected from the world and paralyzed.

I woke up in a room with my mother next to me, slipping in and out of consciousness, hearing the horrifying echoes of her voice and my father talking in the hallway, not knowing where I was. I was kept alive by tubes in my mouth, not being able to see anything except for the ceiling above me. It felt like a tunnel and I could not see anything. I could not feel or communicate. I felt like I was in nothingness again. I was lying in the hospital bed waiting for three days for a spinal fusion because the doctors had just came from a very long surgery and did not want to risk anything. It was the weekend, so we had to wait for them. I did not know what the results of that delay were going to be. At the moment I was at everyone's mercy. I was feeling the effects of severe sedation from drugs to shield me from the pain and I was having a hard time focusing to stay awake. I began struggling with the outer body experience because I did not know where I was. I had phantom movement and horrific dreams from the worst situation anyone could ever be in, with no control over anything I saw, heard or felt.

Life! It Must Be a Comedy

My friends began visiting me while I was semi-conscious, hearing their voices and my sister's voice echo in my memory, as I felt the despair she was feeling, even though I was not awake.

Oh Robert! I heard Hellen say.

As I fought and suffered in the white nothingness, I felt like I was climbing out. My spirit was fighting hard, as my phantom movement allowed me to feel like I was grasping onto something, climbing with my feet, even though my body was completely flat. I could hear voices talking to me and I felt like I was getting closer and closer to the white light with a white haze surrounding me, falling back and then climbing up again, feeling a huge amount of pressure forcing me down. I did not know what my hands were holding on to. It felt sticky and cold, like holding on to something only in my mind.

Some moments I broke through and I woke up slightly, enough to see what was going on. I felt my mother next to me, rubbing my face, as if she always was right there next to me. I immediately started to hold onto something that was in my heart ever since I was a child. I remember praying over and over again, like a beacon of hope, a symbol of remembrance, to tell me to keep my strength, that there's hope coming, no matter what. It will always be there. Like a broken record or the sound of the ice cream man bringing joy into my childhood, I repeated to myself endlessly this song from Sunday school. That reminds me that there's a Higher Power. It was so innocent. It will always be there for me. It echoes through my mind, horrifying me at the same time. I can only say it in my mind. Nothing can save me now except for one thing and I hope I get that. There's a Power I feel connected to me from the One Person that I reached out to the most in my thoughts, in my dreams and in my waking moments. All the promises and hope coming from One Person I never thought could let anyone down. In my little words, I pray to myself. It is a repeated, haunting empty opportunity for me to find some peace, even though it's not working, as I expected to be healed immediately. I repeated it to myself as I would fall into the darkness again.

Jesus loves me. This I know, for the Bible tells me so...
Jesus loves me. This I know, for the Bible tells me so...
Jesus loves me. This I know, for the Bible tells me so...

Chapter 8
I Dreamt I Was Missing

I was sleeping in the darkness, my body was disconnected from the world, from all sensation and any positive stimulus, resting, hoping to wake up to a better world. I came out of my sleep three days after my injury and I attempted to get up, muscle memory telling me it was going to happen. With complete belief that I was going to sit up in my bed, I moved my head and neck muscles squeezing my pelvis and leg muscles together. For a moment I had forgotten I was paralyzed, not able to move. Coming out of my haze in consciousness, my mind was thrown back violently, strapped down, remembering what had happened. I could not move. Only my head lifted slightly. I was not supposed to move while lying in bed with a brace stabilizing my broken neck, waiting for a spinal fusion. My life was being monitored and controlled by the staff of Johns Hopkins Medical Center.

Waiting patiently in the hallway, my parents were finally given the news. My brothers and sister were nearby. In my dreams and in my waking hours under sedation I thought I would hear my mother's voice talking in the hallway. The news was bad, but the doctor made my parents aware that there was some good news and gave them that first, because my dad asked for it. In my imagination I wondered how my parents were reacting.

Mr. and Mrs. Florio I have some good news and I have some bad news, the doctor said.

Alright well please let us hear the good news first, my dad said.

Life! It Must Be a Comedy

The good news is Robert did not sever his spinal cord, the doctor stated.

Okay well what's the bad news, my dad asked.

I'm sorry to say this, but your son will never walk again, the doctor replied.

A spinal cord injury is something my parents and I didn't know anything about. Before the surgery my mom fed me Jell-O. My lungs felt strong. I was breathing on my own. My mother comforted me, keeping her hands on my face because it was the only thing I could feel. The sedation was making me tired. I would fall asleep for hours. No one told me what was happening to me. It felt permanent. Everyone thought the news would have been too hard for me to handle. Under so much sedation, my family did not know how much I would understand. Part of me believes nobody wanted to tell me face-to-face. They were trying to explain it, but I did not want to hear. I fell in and out of sleep again.

I was laying in the darkness, comforted for now, not dreaming, only hearing voices in my sleep. I woke up in a very cold room, straps tight together on a hard board. I was being placed in a long tunnel only narrow enough for one person's body and no room for moving anything. I began to feel even more tortured, never any explanation and waking up to strange things and noises around me, sedated and hallucinating, hearing the clicking thumps of the MRI machine moving like a clock in a circle. Every time I heard a click it was like a hammer hitting a nail. I heard what sounded like a spinning fan, only I was in the middle of it. The vortex was getting faster and noisier, as if I was being sucked into an engine. Already in a catastrophically vulnerable state of mind, I did not know where I was and I'd never been in this situation before. The lack of sensation and movement was driving me crazy, hearing a voice talking to me through a microphone every few minutes so that I would not move. I remember thinking I can't move, how much more do you want me to stay still? I focused on what I could feel and move, and what was probably only a centimeter of movement, to me was a mile. I feared that the tests would have to keep going longer and longer. I always failed every test I took in life, and now with no abilities and only a flicker of a nerve left, my heart and mind would be the greatest thing tested. I saw my mother's face before I went in and her hand reaching out for me as I yelled out for her, with no breath and energy left.

Life! It Must Be a Comedy

Mom don't leave me!

Click, click, click, click, click, bang, bang, bang, bang, bang, whoosh,---- whoosh --- whoosh -- whoosh - whoosh! the MRI machine would sound as it picked up speed and stayed steady.

Robert! We need you to say absolutely still or where going to have to redo the test! the man in the speakers said abruptly.

I desperately wanted the noises to stop. I was conscious, but I could not run away. I dreaded every trip to the MRI machine. Even the limited vision I had in the hospital bed on wheels, seeing the ceiling walls go past me and looking at the bed's beveled railing while being transported, I started to get lost in the loops and curves on the side, as if it was constantly stretching like a long limousine. My mind I kept playing these scenes over and over again. I realized what I was doing once and tried to stop, but my brain kept going, stuck in a loop of redundancy with no comfort from familiar stimulus. My mind was playing tricks from not being able to turn my head or body. The longer I was in recovery the worse my visions became. I had tunnel vision. Things started to deform mind loops all the time until my body was placed in front of something new.

My surgeon, Dr. Sponseller, was talking to my parents. He approached my bed holding a doll with some sort of tube in his neck. The doctor had arranged something without sedation so that I could be spoken to. I was completely disoriented and not connected to any part of my body except for my eyes and my face. Nurses walked around my bed. At other times I questioned whether or not they were there. I was floating around my room. I did not know what direction was up or down. My mind and body still has not connected to the phantom state of existence I was experiencing because the spinal cord is not detached from the mind. I did not know where my body was or what was equilibrium. For a very long time I felt like I was standing straight up on my feet. On each hand, my fingers from the tip of my thumb to the tip of my index finger were palm side up. My fingertips felt glued together. I tried to pull my fingers apart. Like the pose of the meditating hand. My mind naturally put my fingers in that position in my phantom form. I was locked in a permanent ghostly form in pain not in meditation, even though I felt that form. I began to question why everybody was walking on the ceiling or on the wall behind me. I didn't realize that wall behind me was actually the floor. I could still see some light coming from a window to the far left of my bed. I was hearing the beeping sound of monitors and occasional footsteps and voices outside the hallway or next to me. Whenever I heard a voice I tried to identify it. The voices always sounded like my mother and I felt like I was screaming for her to come help; like she was right down the hallway talking to someone but no matter how much I tried she would never come.

I was told that the surgery would fuse the bones together in my neck at the third, fourth and fifth vertebrae. When the doctor showed me the doll with the red tube in his neck I remembered seeing a kid in a special education classes at George Fox Middle School who had a trachea tube. I was not very approachable about this, and instead of listening I told the doctor to go away because I knew what they meant. After the surgery I would not be able to breathe on my own. The surgery lasted seven hours. When I woke up I felt even more drugged than before. I was short of breath. I could not breathe on my own. I could feel something hard and cold in my neck but I was not in any pain except for the tears running from my eyes because of confusion and the control that I had lost. It was never explained to me, so I am not sure if the reason I lost the ability to breathe was because of the surgery or not. I was told not to drink or eat anything as I had a feeding tube going down my nose into my stomach and I was dependent on a ventilator giving me every breath. I explained that I felt short of breath and I could not breathe. I would pass out often because of anxiety attacks. Whenever any attempt was made to move me my blood pressure would bottom out. The room would turn completely blood red, my ears would start ringing, I would get short of breath, and then I would pass out. There wasn't much anyone could do for me except for the pressure relief foam moving bed that was given to me that floated on air. From the sound of the motor, it was positioning me from left to right, all the way up to a forty-five angle.

My entire body was on life support. I wasn't given any hope that I would ever recover any movement or be able to breathe my own. I had a tube running down my throat in to my mouth and I would always bite down on it making the alarm go off. I began to dream again. My waking days did not give me any control. Neither did my dreams. Many times I didn't know if I was dreaming or awake. I was stuck in hell for three weeks of recovery in Johns Hopkins Medical Center. I continued to see images of my friends and family in my dreams. My hand barely floated above the surface of water on the inside of this gigantic rolling wheel almost three stories high, as if my body was part of the rim and only my head was existing, barely surviving from drowning. Miss Grindy, an old friend of my parents, used to hang out with my parents and me all the time, her smiling face sometimes turning into a frown of serious concern. She had very short hair, kind of fluffy with salt-and-pepper. She was a slightly chubbier woman with very rosy cheeks. I saw my mother and father, my brother Carlo, Adrian and Hellen. All of these kept going back under the water, as if it was my job to keep this wheel spinning, running out of control, through the neighborhood, running over houses, crushing them, cars, telephone poles, heading straight down a long road toward a lake. I did not know why I was in this illusion and I didn't feel in control. Every twisted manifestation and imagery was unbearable, like a complete transformation of my mind to be someone I never knew I had to be or even could possibly imagine. I was just another head trying to stay above the water. These images were drowning. I was trying my hardest to keep them afloat, feeling it was my fault. I could not reach out to help them stay afloat and I was losing them forever.

When I woke up again someone brought me balloons. I was staring, watching them move very slowly. The shine of their circular shape reflected around the room from any light source, any glisten of material that would sparkle. I don't know what the two balloons had written on them. They just swung in front of me, teasing and torturing as they transformed in front of my eyes. I wished these images and thoughts would go away. I only wanted it to stop. Suddenly they transformed into something perverse. It looked like a man and a woman in each other intertwined sexually. I was entertained, but disgusted and very confused and screaming inside for the images to go away. Every time I woke up and saw these balloons I had to deal with the images again. I had completely lost the ability to talk, not being able to pass air through my vocal chords. When anyone was asking me questions I had to use a chart of letters and when they stopped their pencil over that letter I would either blink my eyes once or twice meaning selecting that letter or the other letter so I could finally clarify what I was trying to say. There wasn't a lot to say. Nothing would be the same and I only wanted to go home. It was only when I reached closer to the end of those three weeks when I was given my favorite food choices. Piña coladas were my biggest request. I was left alone a lot, to rest. I was always looking around for someone to help me--some family member, mostly my mother, to be there for comfort.

Little did I know my parents were spending every single day at the Ronald McDonald House next to Johns Hopkins. It was a center created by donations for family members of sick children in the hospital so that parents could actually be close but also feel the comforts of home. While I was recovering, living in an unfamiliar world, my entire family in their way had too. They were given breakfasts and beds when they needed to rest.

I continued to dream, the perversions feeling worse. I could hear doctors talking around me as my mind started to fixate on my genitals and my spinal cord, near my neck. I had one arm fist-clenched around my neck, hovering over my hospital bed, seeing myself lying there. I had my other fist wrapped around my genitals. I squeezed in my fist so tight they were bursting and like play dough, completely masticated. I could feel the bones around my spinal cord in my other hand crunching together. I permanently destroyed whatever was in my hands. I began to swing vertically over my body, holding on tight, and not letting go. My body was smashing my feet, legs and knees against the medical table on one side and then the hospital bed on the other side. I heard metal clanging together disastrously, while someone was screaming over and over again. My body slammed from one side to the other side faster and faster, until I became a human revolving instrument going faster and faster, spinning like some sort of mechanical beast. I could hear the whooshing as I continued bashing in one direction, through the floor, up through the wall, as my legs were being ripped to shreds, flying everywhere. I screamed inside for the horror to stop, but it would never stop it just kept going and going. In this disgusting hallucination, I was ready to pass away from my own disbelieving, panicking mind, completely debilitated, perverse, and not able to handle any more. I passed out, in the unconsciousness in the dream of a dream, sinking deeper in the darkest parts of my mind. I thought the real world was the dream. The only relief I found was to wake up again and again, confused if I was awake or dreaming in my own dream. The spinning got incredibly fast. I started hearing people screaming as the blood flew everywhere.

Life! It Must Be a Comedy

I was being taken for another MRI scan. I knew I was awake now and I yelled behind me for my brother Adrian. I heard his voice repeat that he was there, confirming that I actually was awake. My voice was very stretched, like a whisper. It was the first thing I had been able to say for nearly three weeks. The last thing I felt on my face as the large doors opened was warm air blowing down. I could see electrical wires and piping on the ceiling. I saw Adrian in the hallway and knew he would be walking behind me. Eager to know if he was still there, I shouted out for him.

Adrian are you there?

Yes man! I'm right here I'm not going anywhere! he shouted back.

On to the MRI scanning. I had the same words told to me, the same exact images of the bed rail on my stretcher, being transported down the halls. I only had one brief moment of laughter. It came when I woke up and saw a glass wall in front of me in the recovery room. In my mind I felt like it was a split foyer. I couldn't work it out, but it looked like a window into another dimension. I could see people walking around and I felt like I was hovering over them. It was the weirdest room I've ever been in, with geometry I'd never seen. "Achy Breaky Heart" by Billy Ray Cyrus popped into my head to the rotation of the ventilator doing its cycle. Every mechanical pump pushed out a forced breath that I whispered every few seconds, waiting for another breath and then sang another couple of words to the song. I had a big smile on my face and I don't remember why. I was laughing only because I felt released from what was haunting me. No matter how bad I wanted to get away from its possession, it would not leave. I had only one moment where what I was fixated on, was actually something good. My family was around, happy to see me smiling. I had a little peace of mind for a moment. The feeling didn't last long and I passed out again. I knew my family was around me, even though I couldn't see their faces. I could almost hear their voices and I felt their presence. As I was smiling, I heard someone point that out and somebody started giggling, but I could hear in their voices they were confused about why I was smiling. It was short lasted, but a very long awaited symbol of hope, seeing me smile.

I woke up again, more people around me than ever. Everyone was talking and they were motivated, ready to do something, but I didn't know it involved me. Three or four people were on each side of my bed.

118

More were supporting my head and neck, and others were standing in front of me talking. I started to whisper with every breath I had that I was panicking, asking what was going on, telling them to stop. One person explained to me that they were trying to sit me up. Immediately I felt my blood pressure drop. I had no idea what was happening, but I started to get light-headed like I was going to pass out. I heard my mother's voice yell out something while everyone kept attempting to get me to sit up. They turned me to sit on the edge of the bed while holding me up.

My body started to turn. As soon as I came off the pillow my neck started tightening up. I began to yell that I needed them to stop or I was going to pass out and that my neck was going to pop. I was filled with panic. I thought my neck was going to break again. I was furious these people would not leave me alone and would not listen. I thought I was going to die.

In one quick motion my neck popped, a tear rolled down my eye, and I passed out. I woke up sometime later, gazing from a perspective I thought was not real. I could see rooftops outside a tall rectangular window directly in front of me. I could not really see my legs, but they were in some sort of white stocking completely covered tight against my skin. I could feel the brace around my neck, but I still had a little room to move, though I did not try. Again, I was confused by what I was seeing. I could see a rooftop of brick buildings and I could see a statue of a human figure on top of one of these buildings. It was a feeling of removal, staring at a place I knew nothing about. I felt like I was in a city, but I had no idea where. I didn't see any other tall buildings. I began to call out for my mother again, but nobody came. I could see some kind of heating unit in front of me. I could feel the pressure and the weight of my body uncontrollably leaning to one side of a chair I was placed in. I could not tell what kind of chair. It seemed very snug to my body, but it was not designed for me. My brace was taking most of the weight and my neck was pinching it, rubbing against my chin. I cried out for anyone. Sitting there alone with no one around, I tried to plead, but I did not stay conscious long. I passed out, crying, feeling alone, trying to call for help, but nobody came.

I woke up again, more aware of my surroundings. Everything was not tunnel vision. I could see a friendly male nurse that was taking care of me across the room. He was on the other side of a glass wall that

I could see through. He told me that if I needed anything, as long as a nurse could see me, all I had to do was voice with my lips and he would come over. I could see someone lying on their back in the bed across from me in the adjacent room. I couldn't see much except that it seemed to be a child and her entire body was burned from head to toe. I began to panic, blinking my eyes, trying to click with my throat to get the nurse's attention.

He finally came over I asked what I was looking at because he could not tell what was worrying me. The nurse would ask me questions and I would blink my eyes, barely whispering to get my words out, if any at all. I would blink my eyes for yes or no. Blinking my eyes and motioning with my eyes toward her direction I finally got the explanation. The girl was in a terrible fire that burned eighty percent of her body. I felt sorry for her, knowing she must be in the same hell that I was going through. She was younger than me, probably eight or nine years old. The nurse explained to me that the little girl's entire family passed away in the fire and she was the only survivor. I didn't have any more questions to ask after that. I was filled with so much sorrow for her and even more for myself. I'd reached my tipping point. My body, mind and spirit couldn't take any more bad news. Every bit of fear or suffering a human being could experience had been thrown at me, coming in waves, and I was paralyzed, unable to swim away from them. Forced against my will, floating with the waves pounding over and over again, I was stuck on the shoreline, drowning, tumbling, unable to save myself as the horror crashed down on me.

I felt less drugs as my waking hours were prolonged. I would plead to the nurse in the room to get my parents. When people came to visit I could hear her turning them away because I was supposed to be resting. I grew angry and vengeful against this lady. In my heart and mind I was screaming out for them to come, pleading with her to let them see me, but she wouldn't. I wanted familiar faces. Lying on my back I was visited by teams of doctors standing at the foot of my bed. They hovered over me, studying my case as if I was some kind of dead cadaver left to science. I lay paralyzed, almost dead, but awake. Being studied by students I started to feel like I had become a freak of nature. I was Alice, tumbled down the rabbit hole always falling, never landing, passing images and experiences as if I was living in a new dimension, tortured all the time. One short doctor was in charge. He stood up on a stool at the foot of my head. Looking at his face I did not see any compassion. I was merely a test subject to him. Students offered me no comfort, no sign of human compassion or any hope that whatever happened to me would be explained. No one told me I would walk again. I would get an occasional pat on my feet or pat on the side of my toes to "*hang in there.*" I was always left hanging. The more often I was conscious, the more I was visited by the people in white coats.

I could barely see light coming from the window in my room. With no one around me, I felt the presence of someone there. I would call out with every breath. Often, I was not even aware if my mouth was moving or if I was just dreaming. I asked if someone was there. I had no emotional comfort.

Nurse? Are you there? Someone are you there? I would repeat.
Mom! Are you there? Someone! Are you there? I continued.

My mother kept a calendar on the wall near the foot of my bed. Every day I was in the hospital she would circle that day with a smiley face. I would stare at her meager attempts to draw the pleasant smiley faces for me. I found more comfort and compassion in those little faces than I felt from anyone. Each face was different and I would look to them every day as my friends. As I would stare at them day after day, some of them started to grimace and others started to look like they were snarling. Some had a good smile, but I focused mostly on the one marking the current day.

I was not allowed to drink water. When my mother was around she gave me ice chips and a chance to drink water from a straw. I was starving of food and thirst. Shortly after not drinking much at all, my stomach began to fill with gas and I let out short burps that would not stop. I started to smile and laugh a little bit as my father would tell me, just *let it out you will feel much better.* I wasn't feeling any better and quickly started to worry because the pressure coming up my chest made me short of breath. I waited for each mechanical breath timed on its own pace. My heart was racing but the machine never gave me any more oxygen to match my body's required level. The pain medication intoxicated me again and the whole time I felt as if my body was straight but completely vertical. It was like my head was sticking out of the pillow, and alternating through the bed and even as if my arms and legs were completely behind me and I was lying on my stomach. I constantly whispered if I tried to talk at all, *where is my body?* My father would stare at me and leave the room saying, *it's OK you are laying straight here*. I never knew where anyone was but imagined they were always in the hallway talking.

I was trapped again in the white nothingness. I could hear my mother's voice and familiar voices. I began to climb harder with all the force of my life I could feel. I had to get out of there. I was no longer human. I knew who I was and what life meant but this existence was beyond anything that no one could ever imagine it. I finally broke out of that place to open my eyes, but I couldn't concentrate to look at anything. I saw my mother over me.

Robert, Robert! Look at me baby! Why doesn't he look at me!? My mother was saying and looking around scared that I couldn't understand her.

I tried as hard as I could to look at her but I couldn't. I was stuck staring straight at the ceiling and I couldn't even blink my eyes. I woke up to the real world but it was a no better place. I turned my eyes to look at her and at the same moment I wasn't sure if I was in control, but I could see her. I looked at my mother and she smiled.

Waking again, I saw my mother standing over me. Still heavily sedated, I could hear other voices around me but I couldn't recognize their faces. I could hear Adrian's, Carlo's, my mother and father's voices. Lots of people in green clothing were all wearing masks over their faces. I could tell Adrian knew I couldn't recognize him. I heard the voices but I never knew when to believe the things I was seeing. I became delirious and panicked. Hearing their voices but not recognizing their faces only added even more confusion. I could hear his voice again explaining what I was seeing, telling me it was him. I glanced over at my calendar with confusion and delirium.

Robert it's me Adrian. I'm wearing a mask. Adrian explained.
What? Why? I said.
They won't let anyone in your room I think the patient next to you has something they don't want us all to get, Adrian explained.

I could not understand and immediately started slipping away, looking at my calendar. I feared it was all a dream.

No! It was all for nothing. I can't go through that again. What day is it? It was all for nothing. I don't want to go through all that again. What day is it? I said as I panicked.

Life! It Must Be a Comedy

I could see the confusion on Adrian's face. No one had any idea what I was talking about. I was hoping someone could explain it all to me.

Robert what are you talking about? Mom, what is he talking about? Does anyone understand! Adrian tried to ask.

Robert what are you talking about? It's okay baby. My mother said to me.

I could hear them all becoming confused as I panicked more, stressing myself out. Tears ran down my face, as I thought drowsiness, wishing I could stay awake, but I couldn't.

Finally, there was a new feeling in the atmosphere. For the first time in three weeks I could actually comprehend what was going on around me. The head of my bed was raised slightly for the first time. I looked at the calendar and three weeks were filled with smiley faces. I knew that it was time to go. I did not know where I was going, but I knew that I had to go to another hospital. The talk in the air was happier. The Make A Wish Foundation came to my room and they asked me what I wanted. I could have anything I wanted. I could only think of one thing. My mother got excited. She whispered out loud the name Cal Ripken Jr. He was my childhood hero, the baseball player I most wanted to be. We all knew I would never walk again. I'd never get a chance to play on a baseball field or be a major-league player. I was told my request would go through and sometime in the future I could look forward to meeting him. Cal Ripken was the best baseball player who ever lived, a hero to every child, someone that represented accomplishing the highest goals of life. I was trying to create my own hope and aspiration, knowing that I'd lost everything. I was a child trying to hold on to something, reaching out to Cal Ripken as a bright light in my darkest moment. I knew it would not come true right away, but just saying his name and being told that I would meet him filled me with excitement and gave me the biggest smile. My mother smiled too.

I requested somebody go home to get my red Easton baseball bat. I wanted to see it again. I had to know that it was real, that it wasn't just a memory. I could reach for goals, somehow. My bat was laid under my right hand as my fingers were outstretched. It was laid across my chest, up in my face. It was the first sign to me that everything I once did was still real. It was a harsh reminder that I would never return to those moments. It was an eerie feeling. I was happy with a large smile on my face. We took a Polaroid picture. The nurses requested these photos from patients they were attached to. They put them on a wall in the hallway when their patients were discharged. I had Carlo on my right and my mom and dad on my left, all leaning over me with big smiles on our faces, while I had my fingers spread out over the handle of my baseball bat. It was by no means a regular happy day. I'd never see myself smiling in any normal circumstance, but this was more than I ever thought possible, far beyond normal. I still could not feel my bat or anything below my face. I thought that if I had my bat laid under my hands something would happen, but I was struck by a heavy blow of reality, watching my mother grab my fingers, stretch them out and lay them over top of the bat, my fingers doing nothing and not holding on.

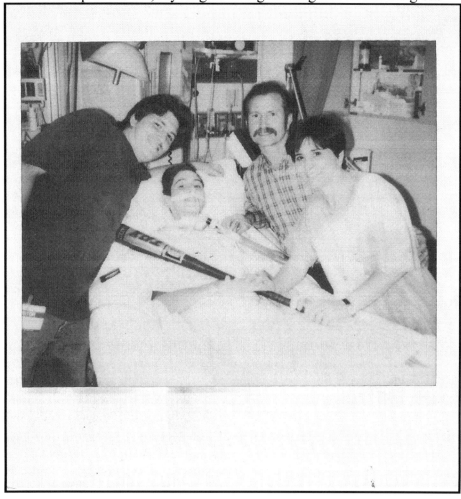

Life! It Must Be a Comedy

The nurses and doctors all prepared for my discharge. My temperature was rising, reaching one hundred and three degrees. My mother started to grow concerned, asking the doctor whether or not it was safe to transport me and if he should delay my discharge. If something had gone horribly wrong, the doctors might not have had my best interests at heart. I was no longer on sedating drugs, but nearly fully conscious, with tubes connected to my throat, while a breathing machine followed me everywhere I went. When I would be transferred from room to room, if the machine could not fit, I would panic as the nurses would take off the tube and hook up an ambo bag to manually squeeze breath into my lungs. I'd panic being pushed out of the room into the narrow hallway, arms reaching over me, monitors and beeps going off, the ventilator alarming everyone with loud beeps that it was disconnected. Gasping for air, my eyes would get large, panicking, hoping that the person squeezing the bag would do it faster, giving me more oxygen. Their hand would squeeze in a steady and slow pace, even though my heart rate was racing faster, requiring more oxygen than they were allowing me to have. I grew bitter against the hands in control of my life.

I was on a stretcher riding in the back of an ambulance with my mom and a nurse, being transported to the hospital where I would rehab. My head slightly lifted on the stretcher, every turn was an encounter with gravity. I couldn't keep my body from leaning one side to the other. Every bang was painful to my neck, even though I was wearing a brace. I clenched my eyes tight on every turn and bump. I heard the sound of the ventilator breathing in and out, blowing with its fans. The ambulance was warm inside and they gave me plenty of blankets too. It was an odd sort of comfort. I could just see out of the side windows. As trees whizzed by, I thought *I still don't know what has happened to me or what I am getting into.* I was awake, but it felt like I was still dreaming.

I arrived at Mount Washington Medical Center. The vehicle went around a curving road, up a slight hill and then stopped. There was an unfamiliar smell in the air. I had not had any food or water and suddenly desired some sort of normalcy. Expectations were building in my mind. Two therapists met me outside the ambulance. My mother and father were standing next to the stretcher, trying to comfort me a little bit from the sun, talking to the therapists and the doctor. They'd get me back to normal, as normal as I could be. I stayed quiet as we went up the concrete ramp around the front entrance of the hospital. Through sliding glass doors I could see I was in a lobby. Another set of double doors opened up and the hallway got colder. Another doctor introduced himself and shook my mother's hand, speaking to her consolingly. The ceiling tiles were going past me again. I could hear nurses talking. One of them came and said *hello* and introduced herself as Beth. I felt an immediate surge of comfort from her. Her voice and touch were very soft and gentle. I was relaxed by her manner, long dark hair, round face and a gentle smile. She continued talking as I entered a new hospital room. I could barely see the foot of my stretcher, coming closer, with the overwhelming sense that I was being put into another place that I would never come out of.

Don't worry I'm going to take care of you sweetheart. My name is Beth. You must be Robert--the Robert that I've heard so much about. Let's get you into your room and make you as comfortable as possible, OK? Beth asked.

I could see a room number above the door and things started to turn into slow motion for me. I passed through the door into a little room and then I passed through another door into my room. I could not see much, only the ceiling and the door exiting my room. The stretcher was laid next to the bed and everyone grabbed my sheets counting to three and slid me on to the bed. Once again the ventilator was disconnected, alarms blaring frantically, the most uncomfortable, unwanted sound I've ever heard, welcoming me to my new room, causing me to panic, gasping for more breaths with the bag again. I would plead with my eyes to the person in control of my air to give me more, faster.

I become congested with mucus in my lungs. My fever had not subsided and my mother was furious that I was transferred too soon. The nurses immediately went to work, calling a respiratory therapist to help get the congestion under control. He had a friendly face, an older man with a white beard, a jolly smile, and a deep voice. He tried to cheer me up calling me Roberto. He introduced himself as Birk. He wore all-orange medical clothing just like the nurses and a stethoscope around his neck. He explained that I had a lot of congestion and he was very worried he would get the mucus out. I was conscious, capable of making sense of things, being suctioned by a long clear plastic tube put down into my throat by a tube that was in my neck. He took off the ventilator again and with a gentle voice explained he would give me three or four puffs of air or as many as I needed and then drop some saline down my trachea, use the ambo bag, and pound on my chest with his hand to loosen it up in my lungs. Then he'd suction it out with the tube. I did not want to give the OK, I only wanted more breaths. With authority, Birk made the decision. I began to gag furiously as tears streamed from my eyes reflexively from all the gagging. The suctioning machine pulled white and yellow liquid out through the tube. Birk's concern grew. I did not know what that meant. It was going to be a very long rehab. I could not get my lungs under control and with a fever I was at risk for pneumonia. Nurses and respiratory therapists would come in every other hour, turning me on my side, pounding on my chest with vibrating machines, giving a nebulizer treatment. Then more suctioning and the ambo bag together.

The comfort that I longed for and was promised when I first came in that room now turned into one week, two weeks almost a month of suctioning and pounding. I started to slip into a constant state of refusal and depression. Shortly after my arrival I developed severe pneumonia and my right lung collapsed. I was starting to recover from that pneumonia with the most severe suctioning I've ever seen of brown liquid, extremely thick and crusty coming out of my lungs. The congestion was getting worse and worse and I was having a hard time staying awake from the lack of oxygen. My condition was so bad I had to go under surgical precision while I was unconscious. The doctor had to look in my lungs with a camera to get everything out. I was not in a good state of mind or physical condition for any rehabilitation. I had traded one place for another with less sedation, but the same hell to deal with. What awaited me now was five months of rehabilitation. I was slowly discovering this was the wrong place for me to be. My condition would be monitored and any hope of returning to functional feeling and movement would come from Dr. Sponseller's once a month Friday visits. My family and I hoped something would change. Lying in bed, I was faced with memories of the person I used to be and everything I used to be able to do. I spent my waking and sleeping hours remembering everything I lost and fighting for a way to make sense of everything, holding onto faith because it was the only thing I felt I had any control over.

Chapter 9
The Road Not Taken

I need You now God. Give me something that I need that makes me the best again. Help me find out who I'm supposed to be and give me something, a gift, or something in my power to control. I can't see or imagine anything being possible right now, but I believe what is waiting for me will make me the best and show the world everything again. I don't know what that is but please give it to me when I'm ready. Looking out the window to the left of my bed, whatever sky I can see mostly blocked by another wall. I look at a recent picture of my dog and me from before. I finish my prayer.

It is very quiet and the lights are low. I am awake. Everything is now in real time again. I remember everything I have lost and it continues to play like a motion picture. All that's happened to me up until this point has been a memory. I'm stuck in this dark cave, having my eyes taped wide open, subject to images, without any outside source telling me whether what I'm seeing is true or not. I know I am no longer the same person. I need to figure out a way to tell myself if what I am seeing is true. Images are fresh in my mind. What I just experienced was in the past, but now I am in the present, consciously starting to see through new eyes like never before in my life. This can't be my life. I'm still connected to my mind, the only thing I have left. I am beginning to see a world I never knew existed, but I have to get out of this cave somehow if I'm ever going to figure out the truth.

Life! It Must Be a Comedy

I am lying in bed in a horrible place where I'm supposed to start my recovery. Mount Washington Medical Center is now my home. I do not find comfort, though it has been nearly a month since my injury. When I close my eyes and concentrate, I pray for my future, for a gift of something that will guide me for the rest of my life. I have completed thinking through every single scenario of it that I have left behind. My bed is rotating to prevent my body from getting any pressure sores since I cannot move. My parents bought me a fourteen-inch black television which sits eight feet from my head, hardly giving enough room for anyone to walk to the other side. To the left of my bed I have a window that opens to the sky, but mostly I just see another brick wall.

There's a bathroom to the left of the foot of my bed. There's a little flat chair for my mom to lie down on. I have a separate room that is divided from a small area of storage with a glass wall. My appetite is horrible. I cannot stand the food they are giving me. I feel no connection to any of my senses. I can't move anything and I can't feel anything. Days are lonely and long. While my mother stays with me a lot, we do not talk much and I can not bear any pictures of my previous self or any home movies. I can see a large white banner on the wall in front of me that says "Get Well Soon," signed by everyone who cares about me and loves me. I don't really care much about what it says and I take every day like it was the first, moment after moment, day after day, starting to blend into one long, endless, dark tunnel. I have the television on and watch people skateboarding and snowboarding. I've never heard of this show before, but I watch Seinfeld all the time now. I'm not aware of what season it is because all my thoughts and memories force me into deep depression. The monitors are beeping, regulating my heart rate as I can hear the ventilator breathing in and out. I frequently panic whenever the nurse, my mother or the respiratory therapist is in the room trying to get them to speed up the breath rate. I have to plead for more air. When I panic, I see nothing but red. My ears ring and I cry, struggling to calm down.

I don't get very many visitors, mostly my mother, Carlo, sometimes Adrian. I'm not sure what's going on, but I think Adrian has really serious issues and is not dealing with my injury well. My next-door neighbors visit me and so does Robert. I can see the concern in Robert's face and his voice as he tries to be here for me. Occasionally some relatives visit or some friends, but it's not very often and I can go weeks without seeing anyone that I left behind except for my mother. I can't move anything. My arms will not move and I see the nurse and respiratory therapist several times daily to be suctioned. The therapist comes back still and pounds on my chest. Sometimes he uses vibrating instruments to get the mucous loose in my lungs to suck out. I call out for Beth whenever I wake up. I've seen her face almost every day for a month. I have a very hard time adjusting to new people controlling my body. The nurses have to put tubes in my penis to make me go to the bathroom and suppositories in my rectum to go number two. I don't know when all of this is going to ever stop and I have no idea how to find any peace in my mind to deal with this. I have been abducted from the real world, and every day I learn more about the changes in my body. I have lost a significant amount of weight now, dropping to seventy-five pounds from one hundred and five. My body is starting to shrink and my shoulders can no longer take the weight of pressure when I am turned side-to-side to clean the bowel movements. With every turn, I cry while my left shoulder gets worse and worse.

I have a new nurse today, a lady who I am not familiar with and someone I do not like. She is a black lady who walks up to me slowly, talks slowly and when she speaks sounds like she had some sort of brain injury. Her lips are so big they hang freely and she has very strange-looking beady eyes and a very strong protruding forehead. I fight with her all the time. My temperature is hard to regulate and she always insists on turning me again on my damn left shoulder to check my temperature, rectally. I wait for each breath of the ventilator to give me enough air to shout.

Robert you have a low-grade temperature. I could take the temperature in your mouth but the only way to get an accurate reading is rectally, the nurse would explain.

But-no-other-nurses-do it-rectally! I desperately explain.

Days pass and I am hardly visited by physical or occupational therapy. When they come I refuse to do any work or to move any muscles. They put a hand splint on my fingers and then my feet, made from a strange moldable plastic material melted by hot water. They wrap them around my hands and my feet to keep them in the right position. That's the last I see of them for a few days. My occupational therapist Jessica is actually very cute. When she sits me on the edge of the bed or puts me in a wheelchair I can see right down her blouse, as her breasts are exposed and peeking out from her low-cut shirt. My eyes light up when she walks in the room. She is my only inspiration. Her perfume and physical touch makes me dream about her all day. The only people who ever get close enough to me to feel any kind of comfort other than, to take my vitals, are two strange women I awkwardly release the smallest amount of sexual frustrations with. I am like a prison inmate cut off from my growing body and any stimulus, and self-expression of any sexual exploration, at the beginning peak of my adolescence into adulthood. I am a prisoner in my own body. I spotted Jessica the first day I got out of the ambulance and she was smiling at me. My physical therapist was there to meet me too, but she wasn't much to look at, except for her huge rack. Looking at Jessica's breasts gives me a great big smile, the only smile I have all day, but I still refuse to do any work. She has long curly blond hair, a nose that hooks down a little bit and she's an average height and weight, with a pretty smile. On the other hand, my physical therapist reminds me of an ogre. She has long black hair, huge buck teeth with an overbite, and a very long hooked nose. She stands very tall and does not smell good when she gets close to pick me up. My playful fourteen-year-old mind allows me to get some giggles when she throws her hair over one side of her neck, exposing the skin. She puts me to that side of her shoulders to pick me up. He-She also moves me over her chest, forward and pivoting to the chair right next to the bed. I don't like going anywhere so I just stay in my room. I think about her smile and her breasts all day, but no one ever realizes my psychological struggles and physical needs for sex or what inspires me. I grow bitter toward the stupidity of therapists and doctors, who never fostered, never inspired my true potential or motivated me. The cruel reality of life is revealing itself to me. I am exposed every day to a new element of the ethereal world.

When somebody comes into my room, I throw a fit, telling them to not look at me. My parents always try to cheer me up, but I still cry and scream profanities. I know I'll never get back what I once had and I can't deal with it. I am aware of everything going on around me. The only way to get some control is to demand it. I tell everyone what to do. I am overly obsessive about having my body cleaned, especially when I urinate or have a bowel accident. I ask if I am clean and tell people to clean me again. I can't stand not being able to feel my body. I don't know if I am still on the bed. My body doesn't feel the same. I have not adjusted to this numb world. I don't know where my legs are most of the day and my feet always feel like they're in pain, as if someone is cutting my feet off. I go through panic attacks and anxiety attacks. My body feels like it's curled up and I demand someone straighten my legs, arms and fingers. It's extremely frustrating to be told that everything is straight while I scream it's not.

Days are the same with the same experiences. My hair is getting longer, completely unrecognizable from the haircut I had before. The nurse combs it a little and parts it, but it's so long there is nothing that can be done to make it like before. I haven't taken a shower in almost a month. I can't even stand the bed baths, being rolled on my shoulders. Beth tells me the hospital has a stretcher to take baths on. She tries to get me excited about this. I panic about being off the ventilator and how she would have to pump my lungs full time.

I don't have anyone in my room today, not even my mother. I wake up alone not aware of what time it is. I can hear someone walking in the hallway since the nursing station in very close by my room. My TV is on. Something doesn't feel right. On a rare occasion my physical therapist visits me. She tries to get me to sit up in the bed for longer periods of time, stretching my neck from left to right up, and down, trying to build muscles. It's terrible on my blood pressure. I refuse to do this anymore. She tries to motivate, but quickly gives up. I refuse to lift my head. It feels good to take off the neck brace for the first time. I feel like I can hold my head up, but the scar on the back of my neck, is foreign to me. There is no point of trying, if I don't exist anymore. I can't move anything. It doesn't make sense to me to try to strengthen my neck. My life is as good as gone. I am left sitting in an upright position close to seventy degrees.

Come on Robert can you please lift your head up just once! The ogre therapist asks me.

Will you please say something? I only have an hour with you and I have to get to other patients, the therapist tried to explain.

OK. I'm going to leave you in this position for a while. You have to start working with me if I'm going to be able to help you, the therapist said.

The therapist leaves the room since I refused to work. As much as the therapist tried, I still feel abandoned. There is no one that can motivate me or remotely tries. I'm stuck in my room alone remembering all I lost. I'm not trying to move my head hanging my neck down. I sit quietly, not saying a single word, muttering internally out loud-

Why did this happen to me?

I'm never going to get it back.

I was told that my mother is on her way. Sitting there, almost straight up, with my head hanging down, I slam the back of my head as hard as I can against the bed several times. I stop, afraid I'll injure myself. I feel the air in my lungs, trying to sip with my lips, not sure if I'm breathing or the machine's doing it. I feel a little bit of my own inhalation. I drop my head for what seems like a half-hour, giving up, and ready to die. I begin to scream for almost an hour, crying for myself, for anyone to hear me.

Is anybody out there! Please, somebody! I don't want to live! Somebody please kill me! Please! Kill me! Beth!? I can't live like this!

I can hear some nurses talking to each other, saying things about me. Somebody is coming. An orderly lady pushing the trash bags past my room, walks in slowly. I have no idea who she is. I'm not happy to see her because I didn't expect would could do anything for me.

*Are you okay? s*he asks.

Hey, it's going to be all right. All right? she says again.

I want to die, I say, slowly rolling my eyes, leaning my head back and looking up.

The cleaning lady walks out of the room thinking she helped me. Another half hour goes by. My mother finally arrives. The only person I am ever happy to see is my mother. She sees how I was left sitting straight up. I always refuse breakfast, stacking the cereal boxes up in the window dividing the room. My mother's little bit of humor doesn't faze me at all when she points out the stack of rows of tiny cereal boxes is getting bigger. I recognize her step, a repetitive, consistent strut, fast with intent. She's always dressed in the best clothing, representing her Mary Kay persona as a confident lady. The days and weeks are turning into months. She wears more sweatpants, occasionally in some fake tight leather jacket or a regular old T-shirt. She still does smiley faces on the calendar for me. If she's not there to do it, my Dad does, or one of my brothers, or a nurse. My room always seems dark, though some light comes from the window.

I left behind things I thought could cheer me up. Today mom brought photos I requested. Pictures of Jeff and I jumping on the trampoline, twisting high in the air, ten feet above the trampoline, upside down, leaning over the edge, with our hair long, almost touching the ground. One picture I was waiting for the most was of me giving Fluffy a bath. Mom puts my photographs on the windowsill. There's one taken two weeks before my injury. I am sitting in front of my couch without my shirt on. My arm is resting over the couch and Fluffy is sitting at my feet looking at the camera. Turning my neck to the left gives me a very good stretch. Every day I see pictures of my puppy. I can see his big black furry pointed ears, the tips of them just flopped forward, one ear having a slit in the tip from a dog fight. A white doggie T-shirt fits closely over his chest and through his front legs. It cheers me up hoping one day they will bring Fluffy to visit.

His furry tail flopping, curling completely back to his butt and his big red tongue was slipping up over his nose to lick his lips. I can see his big brown eyes and his fur curling between his eyes and around his mustache. He gives me some peace. At the same time, he reminds me what I lost. I can't feel his furry cheeks between my fingers, can't wrestle with him. His temper used to get the best of him, sinking his teeth into my thumb, spinning around in circles and chasing me around the yard.

Life! It Must Be a Comedy

On July 29 we celebrate my father's forty-ninth birthday. Dad starts telling his jokes, making some wisecracks about the cute nurses and telling me he hopes they're not gay guy nurses taking care of me. He calls the black nurses "the colored nurses" by a force of habit, with no bad intent behind it. There's a gigantic chocolate cake, my favorite. My depression stops me from thinking about anything that is good. Whatever I put in my mouth has a metallic taste, similar to what I get when nurses change the metal trachea in my neck. I try to enjoy the moment with my father, but my secretions come back, the air leaking around the trachea, dripping with some blood from the incision. I start choking on it and begin to cry, wishing I did do not have this in my neck. It's hard to move my neck with the inflated balloon inside of the trachea tube inflated, stopping any air coming out my vocal chords, sometimes stopping me from talking. My father offers to help me go to the bathroom to go urinate. I don't want him to do it. My diaper is taken off, my penis exposed, urine starts shooting straight out by it self before he can get the catheter in. I tried to tell him not to do it, but my parents do more of the work for me now. My mother does the most; my father just sits by with his arms crossed in the corner, most of the time, staring at me, watching TV, trying to figure out how I can be helped, while I sit frustrated, not wanting to be stared at.

My father was excited to cheer me up today, bringing some home videos of me playing baseball at the field. As soon as I hear the kids yelling and the sound of the bat hitting the ball, I began to cry uncontrollably, demanding the video to be turned off and never turned back on again. I hear my father's voice in the movie yelling out to me. Alarms start going off and I become congested from crying. My secretions get worse, even though they are suctioned again, as the long skinny tube goes down my throat time and time again, irritating me, gagging me to the point that blood starts coming. Oddly, I get some comfort from the excessive gagging even though it's painful. It forces my lungs to work, to gasp for any air on my own. It feels like it's working, so I welcome the gagging, finding a weird sense of pleasure. I am being stabbed with every twist of the skinny suction catheter. The nurses and mom search my lungs, poking in and out, stopping the ambo bag and then continuing. It sucks all the air out of me to the point that I feel like passing out from anxiety.

Life! It Must Be a Comedy

Another week or so passes. At this point there is not much recovery, only hopes for keeping my spirits high. Dr. Sponseller visits on the last Friday of every month, monitoring my progress, giving me hope, telling me two months is the average time for seeing any function coming back from a spinal cord injury. With no progress to report, I am now on a wide variety of antidepressant drugs, but nothing is phasing me to help me feel better about myself. Nobody comes to give me a chance. I still feel abandoned. The pills aren't going to solve the problem. What happened to me is not curable. For the rest of my life, no medicine can ever make me feel better. If only someone would have given me a chance to reach out, but there is no one to save me and bring me to a better place. Though my family is there, I need more. I continue to refuse everything the hospital gives me and even therapists, who continue to fail to break my mold.

My mother requested that I get a chance to feel the warm weather on my face, so the nurses put me on a movable structure. For the first time I'm going down the hall and I'm seeing some paintings, back in the lobby that I first saw my first time coming here. Into the elevator, I went downstairs past a rehabilitation room that is very small. I noticed there isn't hardly any person with spinal cord injuries. I'm taken past the exercise room, connected to a recreation room almost as small as the therapy room. On the balcony I can see the trees and sun more here. I have not felt the sun in over two months come through my face and nose and eyes. I have not gotten out of the hospital gown that I am put in every day since my injury. Though I was lying on my back, my mother took a picture of my smiling face looking straight up, my head slightly elevated, with white blankets all over me and a pillow under my head, my hair kind of parted, overgrown, greasy from not being washed, with crust on my face. My mother is always trying to clean my face with her Mary Kay cleansers and moisturizers. I always hear her complaining that the nurses don't know how to take care of me. If not for mom, my toenails would be overgrown I would not get any arm and leg stretches. My face would start looking older. The sunlight is so bright in my eyes that my ears start to ring from anxiety as my blood pressure continues to drop. I feel the hot air around me and a sense of unfamiliar territory, not knowing where I am, feeling left alone with my mouth chapping from dehydration, fighting falling asleep. I start to reject anyone who is not my mother, fearing I'm not going to get the care I want.

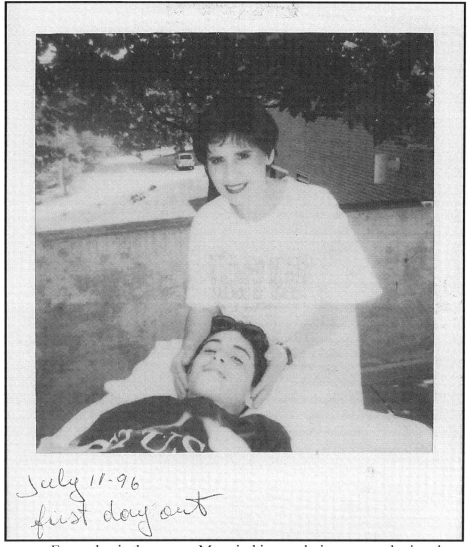

July 11-96
first day out

Every day is the same. My mind is wandering, remembering the past. I dream of love. The function I have now is nothing that can ever satisfy a woman or even myself. I remember the last girlfriend I had, the flirt she was, how attracted I felt to Diana. When I was around her she was like a goddess. My body wanted to take over and act on my feelings for her. The dark eye shadow around her eyes, her long brunette hair, and the bracelets around her wrists stimulated me. She was a year older, a delicate figure, someone I could pick up and carry. We felt like hindered spirits. This was my first glimpse into what love might be like.

My heart weighed down, attracted to her like a magnet, energized uncontrollably. My curiosity did not get me very far, jumping on the trampoline, smoking cigarettes, stealing a joint. We got away from the rain, going back to the tree fort in my backyard, the trying to feel her up. My hands were slipping up her leg toward her skirt as we sat facing each other on the weight bench inside the tree fort, surrounded by cobwebs on the ceiling and a dirty, bumpy floor. It was hardly romantic, but the excitement of hiding filled me with butterflies and anxiety as my sexual curiosity peaked.

My tongue was in her mouth, caressing her lips like a painter touches the brush to the canvas ever so lightly, studying every curve of her skin. My hands would go up her skirt and on her breast, or shirt, but time and time again my hands would be denied. Her kiss was teasing me, but now haunting me, not giving me what I wanted. I never had sex before. I only wish that I could go back to that day to feel that again. At least I would have that feeling of what it felt like to be inside her. I'd have that hope that one day a girl would give me what I was looking for without resistance. We were walking down the road. I was behind her with my arms wrapped around her belly, she and her friend, a blonde, both giggled and I whispered in Diana's ear. I was excited and I was rock hard. She giggled and whispered to her friend, telling her. Suddenly she stops, forcefully bends over and pushes her bottom into my pelvis trying to feel a poke. I embarrassingly pull away bending over slightly. I wish I would've pushed back into her. Maybe I would have known what it felt like. I would've been a little bit closer. Now I'm stuck forever only guessing. Love is one of thousands of things I left behind. I have prayer to comfort my mind, but it doesn't help.

Three months pass since my injury and I hardly see the people I love, especially the friends I grew up with. All of my friends have completely abandoned me. I do not understand why none of my friends visit. I want someone to understand me and be there with me, but I'm forced to find my own way. I finally took my first shower, lying on a stretcher, the ambo bag giving me my breath. Down the hallway I go, to this over sized closet with two huge heat lamps on the ceiling. It's a comfort even though I panic when the water gets around my neck and on my head, fearing that the nurses will slip and drop the ambo bag. To give me some comfort, a towel and chuck pads are wrapped under my head and around my trachea area, preventing water getting in my lungs.

Life! It Must Be a Comedy

The water reminds me of the swimming pool and I realize my phobia of water is permanent because of what happened to me. The memory of showering and standing tortures me. I derive no pleasure from it anymore. I find any sense of comfort and relaxation from the only played in my head that still has feelings as the hot water caresses me like a beautiful sensual massage. I close my eyes thinking of a beautiful naked woman wanting to love me, allowing me to love, her seeing me for who I am unconditionally and not making me feel like I have become something horrible. My thoughts get the best of me because they're the only thing I control. Love is always on my mind and so are all the memories of who I was and who I will become. My bed baths keep me clean except for the two or three days a week I can have hot showers. I look forward to them, but at the same time I'm frightened by so many little things I never feared before. Every activity now takes two or three people helping. The more I see that, the less I'm able to be calm. My mind fights accepting who I am, never wanting to live in a paralyzed body, never wanting to be the prisoner I have become. My prayers are starting to become pleas for parole. I tell God He has wrongly accused me. He has made a huge mistake in casting his own relentless cold heart of judgment. This must be a mistake. I must have been in the wrong place at the wrong time.

It's now the last Friday of the month and after three months Dr. Sponseller gives his final verdict that if nothing has come back by now it will not. Any function I have or do not have is going to be permanent. My mother continues to do her foot massage therapy on my toes, having read that certain places you stimulate nerves controls the growth of them in the spinal cord controlling function. I sit in bed with my head up slightly, enough to see the television, watching my mother play with my toes, putting lotion on my skin, cutting my nails, stretching my fingers all the time and annoyingly cleaning my face again.

My parents have changed. My mother has gained weight and my father has become more comedic, trying to cheer me up, to release the energy of the free child somewhere in me. I'm forced to see the world as I've never seen it before. My conversations are only with adults since none of my friends come around. There are no other patients here with spinal cord injuries. I worry if I'm in the right place, but I still don't care and I don't want to leave. My mother was getting closer to her Mary Kay directorship, with enough recruits to get her own pink Cadillac. All of that has changed. Now she is with me almost twenty-four hours a day, every day, only going home to sleep. After work she comes directly to the hospital. I wait all day hoping when I wake she will be there. I have perfect timing, feeling like I fast-forward time, sleeping until she arrives.

My dad is still working at the barbershop with my Uncle Sandro. Something is going on with Adrian I don't understand. Maybe it has to do with his friends but he seldom visit. I think he cannot bear the sight of me so debilitated, because there's no hope about who I used to be and how I used to function. I grew up with them. I would never want to see them in my situation. If I saw them the way I am now, how horrible it would be, how helpless I would feel. I'm sure they all wish I'd get better.

Carlo comes by and stays the night occasionally. We have grown a lot closer since my injury, even with all the teasing I had done toward him. I see the faults I had before my injury. I am truly sorry for treating him badly. We have great conversations even though I can't talk well with the machine. My lungs feel like they are working a little bit. I burst out in laughter or a quick request to scratch my nose or have some water. I love seeing Carlo's smile. He knows how to make me laugh. The little goofy things he does, a little joke or comment. Listening to Carlo talk I remember hiding behind the refrigerator in the kitchen while he was coming down the hallway and jumping out in front of him screaming at top my lungs, scaring him. Carlo always did this to me and my friends too. We talk about the past a little bit and I remind him how funny I always thought he was. He always suckered me and my friends in the kitchen, standing in front of the electric stove where the towels hang. Carlo would drop a towel and ask one of us to pick it up. I know it's coming every time, but I don't say anything because it's so funny. As soon as someone reaches for it, Carlo sticks his butt over their head and lets a huge fart rip.

My sister lives on the eastern shore, so I don't get many visits, but I see here more frequently since I was injured. She visited bringing her two beagles, Buzz and Girly. They remember me, wagging their tails and whining. Helen steps in to fix my pillow or offer me something to drink. I don't see grief and despair on her face. My brothers are quiet and nonreactive, emotionless almost, trying to fight being sad. I also enjoy Robert's visits. He seems to be genuinely interested, offering to stay the night or change the channel, reminding me he is always there for me and thinking of me. Robert is always interested in what I'm doing or if I'm trying to say something. Even though I'm older than him Robert I. always called him, "little Robert" and all of his sisters call me little Robert. He is always in my mind, the goofy kid with a slightly bigger head size, that short dirty blonde hair with those droopy eyes, his father's smile. Robert is like a little brother.

Dr. Sponseller hasn't left the hospital yet on his visit of, doom Fridays, with the verdict in. I am resting on my left side even though my shoulder is killing me from the lack of muscle that has disappeared over my shoulder bone. My feeling and pain sensation has increased to my shoulders. My mother is at the foot of my bed rubbing my feet, massaging my toes. The doctors dooming words play in my mind. Mom and I pray for God to let something good happen today since hope disappeared. The sounds of the hospital play a helpless tune. All of a sudden something happens. Something very little, but it feels like a miracle. I can't believe it. I don't know if it really happened or not, but it feels like it was my control. It's a wonderful feeling knowing that it's possible--something came back, just like that, in one second. Lying on my left side without even knowing I was trying, a feeling started shooting through a connection to my nerves. I tell my mother to look.

Mom I think I just lifted my right arm, I said with as much excitement as I could find with such little breath left.

What? Are you sure? Do it again! Mom said.

Look, see! It's moving. I'm doing that, I repeated.

Thank you God. Thank you so much, my mother and I prayed.

I flop my right elbow up and down on my ribs. It's something so little, but so wonderful. I can't help but cry and tears are rolling down my cheeks. My arm quickly fatigues. I did it seven or eight times. The nurses run quickly to find the doctor.

Is Dr. Sponseller still here? He has to see this! Mom says.

Without a doubt this means something has come back, so the doctor is wrong, Beth is so excited to say.

The doctor has left, but the nurses will tell him. Everyone is so excited. Mom calls everyone and my dad comes into the room. He comes to my side, hugs me and gives me a kiss. We are all crying. I am going to sleep very well tonight, knowing I have some hope. Even more might come back. I'm still wondering why it took so long. My diagnosis said this was the end date. If it didn't come back by now is that a bad sign if more might not.

Life! It Must Be a Comedy

In a few weeks the therapist gives me encouragement that my other arm might come back. They set me up in a manual wheelchair. I still don't leave my room much. Sometimes I go down to the gym to get on a flat standing table until my blood pressure bottoms out. I can't stand very long. My body is always being pushed around, either strapped down or twisted to keep straight. Nothing is under my control. The chair that they give me is very uncomfortable even though the brown leather goes all the way above my head. I always need pillows pushed against my right side to keep me from bending my back to one side. The pain on the right side of my neck can be horrible. The rolled towel under my ribs is always being adjusted. My hips are never straight. I'm getting picky as to how my clothes fit. I can't stand the diaper they keep me in. I can't control my bladder or my bowels. It's hard to have any kind of confidence. As soon as I get a smile from a pretty nurse or therapist I soil myself. I lean over them uncontrollably to transfer from my bed to the chair. I give up, feeling defeated.

I can see my mother getting more frustrated every day, fighting for me to get better care, not knowing what I need. What I need is not available for me at this hospital. My mother sees her child not getting the best care. She questions Dr. Sponseller, causing much anger. It seems all the odds are going to be against me for the rest of my life. I hope that's not true. I feel so abandoned and lonely in this hospital with no therapist giving me any help. They act like they do not know what to do for me. Even though I have no idea what I need, I know there is something that I'm not been given. My head is always itching like it's on fire. Nobody knows why. The doctor thinks it's the iodine that the nurses used to clean off the tip of my penis to help me go to the bathroom. My appetite is horrible and my weight is still dramatically low. I'm looking like a skeleton now. I wait for the electric wheelchair the therapist has ordered for me to drive with chin control. Meanwhile, I test out a sip and puff tube device that controls the wheelchair.

I try to go out to the hallway from inside my bedroom, sipping just a little bit and puffing the right amount of pressure, for forward speed, reverse, left and right. I want control so desperately. I'm eager to try anything to give my own power. The nurses push me out the door and into the hallway where I am clear to test drive. I hear the therapist telling me one puff for speed and another for slow down, or a suck on the little clear hose to stop. I give it a puff and I start moving forward.

My mother starts cheering. It's the weirdest feeling, like I'm connected, as if I'm part of it and it's part of me. I hate everything that my life forces me to adapt to, but I have to try. I don't know where I'm going, but I know I'm moving forward.

The ventilator is strapped to the back of the chair, giving me breath from a long organ-like, clear hose attached to my trachea. The only place I would ever feel comfortable doing this would be in this hospital, never outside. A second puff and I'm taking off too fast and then a sip but I don't slow down. I'm heading straight ahead at full speed for the wall near the big window. I like to sit there at the end of the hall, just past the front of the nurses' station. With whatever breath, I imagine myself yelling, but it's not loud enough. I can hear myself gasping, trying to suck that air to trigger another breath to yell. Everyone is screaming. I'm too fast for anyone to catch me heading straight for a bunch of wheelchairs. I feel excitement, immediately followed by terror. It is the first time I've tried anything under my control and I've failed miserably putting my life in danger. Yet, I still have absolutely no control. I've been taken by the mechanics of another machine. I close my eyes hoping I don't hit anything. I crash hard and I can hear the metal clinking harshly. When I open my eyes I felt lucky to be alive. It was a harmless accident, but everything in my life that was simple now seems like a huge accomplishment or a horrendous failure.

I keep trying to use my right arm as much as possible, but it only seems to move when I am on my side. With each day that passes the hope of anything coming back quickly fades. Every day I try moving more, the possibility vanishes. I attempt driving my wheelchair again. This time using my chin. As soon as it is strapped on I make myself comfortable and accurately steer out of my bedroom, pushing with my chin on a little black knob. This comes naturally. I feel relief for the first time ever. I am actually in control of where I go. My mother is filled with joy, as is the therapist. Both have bright smiles, giving the thumbs-up, telling me I can go anywhere I want. I motor out of my bedroom, and look around for a moment. Where I want to go is far as possible from this place.

Often I am left sitting in the chair with the nurses watching me. Some days I flirt, especially with the cutest nurse I had. I didn't get to choose who the head nurse assigned to me, but I got really frustrated when Beth became head nurse. She was no longer taking care of me very often. When I get congested and the ventilator beeps furiously, detecting a pressure, people know something is wrong. I feel like my life is strangled with alarms, going off everywhere. They try to save me, but really they're not helping me, even though they're keeping me alive. The alarm is torture to my ears. All night and day I hear the monitors and ventilators of babies and children in this hospital. I don't trust any of these people with my life. I don't feel comfortable with anyone except for Beth, and the really cute tall brunette named Sharon. Just mentioning Sharon's name brings flashes of joy. She's the girl that I keep dreaming about, wishing I had every night to make love to her. Some day I am going to have a woman just like that. I don't believe myself, even though that is what I want the most. I can't see past the impossibilities that are flooding my mind. I only know what I want in life, what I feel, and how life tells me that I can't have anything--unless I fight.

Now that I have some control wheeling around the circle hallway past all of the other rooms, I feel like I'm in some kind of otherworldly realm of existence. I wonder what else is around. With whatever sunshine is left this August, I am venturing outside a little bit, smelling the air. My respiratory therapist Bill accompanies me with a nurse, and we begin having really deep conversation about life. I like philosophizing with Bill about the trees, how life brings everything we need. How beautiful everything looks because it's the first time I've been outside. Feeling the sun on my face is amazing. I use the mechanical switches with my chin to tilt back, going down the slight incline around to the side of the hospital where there are some tennis courts. I can also see the highway, a parking lot and the trail near the back. Unfortunately because of the steps leading to the parking lot, I can go no further. I like to hang out in the curved area surrounded by little trees in a concrete path of ramps leading to another entrance and a few picnic tables. The rehab gym is right above that entrance, so I decide to go up there into the little cafeteria. Immediately I get uncomfortable from the looks I get from other people. I only talk to the people who are forced to be in my life and I refuse to talk to any therapist. No antidepressant medicine will work.

In the rehab department where the movies are located my nurse told me there are more videogames. I began feeling anxious and curious and more talkative and alert. It was a very brief moment, comparable to getting control back or being able to move my elbow a little bit. I love movies. I get lost in them now. There is one more thing that I wish I can do. My favorite video game is Earthworm Jim. My brothers, friends and I would play all day. I love the way Jim wears his big muscle space suit. Because he is a worm, he grabs his own head and whiplashes himself to a hook screaming "ouch!" I can hear that whipping sound repeatedly again. I hear the sounds of the videogames. I have only my head to move and feel. I'm in a straitjacket that I can't control. I am somehow whipping my own head around, as my world is rendered and programmed to whiplash, like Earthworm Jim. My life is my video game. Jim and his world are unique and hilarious. It's this memorable soundtrack and the uniqueness of the character that I am captivated with. I like when Jim is in some sort of bubble and I have to make my way up and down through a cave before I run out of oxygen, trying not to crash into the thorny under water cave formations. I love that sense of escape and I miss it dearly. Jim and I are both fighting for our lives underwater, trying not to crash. I have become Jim. I need to get to the end of the level in my game of life, just like that part of the videogame that is the hardest challenge. I try, but hardly make it past Jim's challenge, past that underwater world. I never did find out what happened much more past that level, but if I survive my game, maybe I will. I never made it to the end of the game, but I hope at the end of my game there is a princess that I get to rescue or maybe I'll get rescued.

I can't stand this controller in my chin and my back is curved, because this chair is not fitted for my body. My neck is pulling to one side. On top of the pain and anguish I am being told it was time to go back to my room to do some pressure relief. My chair tilts back to get the weight off of my butt, and the nurse shift was changing. I had to be in my room so the nurse knew where I was. It is starting to get dark.

I see children walking around, a few in wheelchairs, playing video games. A few look my way. I can't wait to see what videogames they have. Can I play them? Nobody is helping me. They can see my curiosity and my alertness. My drive and focus is motivated with a purpose, but vanish again like it never existed. I'm angry because they're telling me there's no way for me to play. I don't want to accept it. Submission is now my new role, accepting defeat like I never would before. I would just take challenges and run with them and do whatever I wanted even if I was told not to. I feel like a zombie stuck in the world of purgatory. Nobody stepped up to help me set the games.

Life! It Must Be a Comedy

Surrendering leaves a bad impression adding to and reinforcing my bad predicament. I never want to return to that area. I could see the screen where the games were located. I can't see the controllers but I can see wires. I want to see more but there's just no way to do it. I just don't understand why they don't help. I know what I want to do, I just can't express it. Leaving that area that place fades away into the darkness behind me. The flashes on the screens echo my past; remind me of my potential, all vanishing. There are strange people in control of my life now.

The next morning, I finally did get to see my dog. He ran away from home clear out to Solley Road, more than a mile away, trying to find me. I'm sitting outside in the picnic table area, with Jeff, Adrian, and Carlo, Beth my Mom, Dad and Fluffy. I love his tail wagging and that furry, cuddling face smiling up at me. As soon as I say his name he runs toward me. I have to get his picture. Everyone is standing near me. Jeff and Adrian are on one side, Fluffy, Carlo, and Beth on the other. We get Fluffy's face up close enough to my face so I can feel him again. I fought coming out here. It's the first time everyone sees me in my condition outside my room.

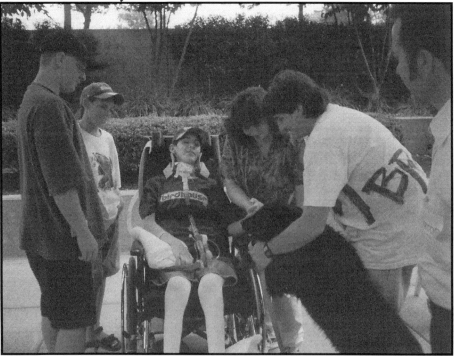

Life! It Must Be a Comedy

I still feel really vulnerable, embarrassed that I have no muscles anymore and my legs are covered with white thin stockings from my toes to my upper thigh. I'm wearing a hospital gown. I can see the looks on their faces. It's not a happy reunion. It feels like someone died and I'm the person lying in a casket on wheels. Even worse, I am sitting in that uncomfortable brown leather chair. It's all worth it to see my dog. I whisper his name with whatever breath I can muster. My hair is out of control, my entire body and life is out of control. I sit here, a spectacle because my loved ones want to see me and I want to see them. There's no replacement for what I lost. I completely detached from my body. I feel vengeful and resentful that everyone else has what I no longer have, walking around as if it's no big deal. Before I break down completely, I hope someone takes me back inside. I try not to make a scene while mom and dad and my brothers encourage me to stay with them. Nobody says much, they just look at each other trying to smile. I love seeing Fluffy. After taking him for a walk around the path, out to the front parking lot and back again, I have to say goodbye again. I break down crying. They're witnessing a family member tortured and suffering, but nobody can do anything to help me. They just have to watch. During this panic attack, I finally say goodbye and go back to my bedroom to sleep and dream and pray, holding on to what I have left in this prison.

Jeff is visiting me but it doesn't feel like a very friendly visit. There's something about his attitude and something about his quietness. He stands with his father and grandmother. They don't visit me often and there is a very uncomfortable feeling about their attitudes. When they leave, I feel like I'm losing my close friend who was like a brother. I want to remind him that we will always be friends forever, no matter what, like we always used to tell each other. While he's walking away I say that once. I had to get a reaction. I just want someone to be there for me. Even though I don't think he will, I just want him to know I need that. It could make a difference.

Friends forever Jeff, I shout.

I see his reaction as he is walking away. Jeff turns, pauses for a few seconds, stuttering a little bit, catching his breath. He emotionally mutters under his breath, finishing with a little more exclamation.

Yeah, friends forever Rob. That's right, Jeff said.

Friends forever Jeff. I love you man, I repeated.

147

Life! It Must Be a Comedy

It is the beginning of a lawsuit between my family and Jeff's family. There is not much that I know, only that my lawyers are trying to sue the pool company for fourteen million dollars. I can't understand why his family feels so uncomfortable. It would allow me to live comfortably. My parents, especially my dad, keep telling me believing God will give us the money when the lawsuit is over. I have never seen that much money, but in a way it would be a miracle, as if the money would be some kind of Band-Aid, healing everything. Some days the money is the only thing I believe in. Everyday I learned how much my medical expenses will be, and if I was to fully recover I would need a lot of money maybe to even pay for a cure someday. My eyes get bright and I grin a little bit when I hear my dad talking about the promise of the money coming in, that the lawyers are taking care of everything and soon I'll have all I need including nurses.

Jeff's grandmother visits me about as much as any other person. This day she brought her pastor, doing some sort of anointing with a cloth over my forehead while everyone stands over me praying. How do I explain the feeling of complete strangers hovering over my body praying in ways I'm not comfortable with? Like a Baptist tradition, there are unfamiliar words of the Presbyterian Church. They are Scripture prayers. The holy scary ritual is being performed over my body as if I were alive-but-dead. They stand around me talking to me, but not really talking to me, waiting for someone to start the ritual. Maybe I am praying the wrong prayers. Why is God sending me these people and why didn't it work? They were praying for a miracle that wasn't coming. They leave me with a sense of uncomfortable welcome, just like the unfamiliar rejection I have with the nurses I don't know and the doctors giving me pills without talking to me.

I'm so confused. All I know is my prayers, the faith and hope because nobody is helping me but myself. Everyone comes to see me, but they leave shortly thinking they've given me some comfort. They're only trying to comfort themselves. I do get joy from seeing the people I care about, but I don't feel any connection to them. I'm so lost and disconnected from my nervous system that I've lost all impulses for connecting to anyone. Now I'm trying to find a new way to reach out, with my brain. It's like I'm developing into someone I don't know.

My left arm is starting to wobble just like the right arm. Also now I feel my breath now is actually my own. It's very small, but

148

coming back. Every time I need suctioning and the skinny tube goes down my lungs through the trachea, sucking out the liquid, I feel a sense of pleasure. My lungs are being so agitated that it forces me to grasp for air with whatever ability my spinal cord nerves send. After the lungs are sucked out and the air is taken with it I tell my respiratory therapist that it feels like I'm trying to breathe and that something is coming in. I'm now ready to see if I'm actually breathing on my own. I think it's coming back. I show off for visitors that I can move my body over two inches. Really I'm just wiggling my neck and head while shrugging my shoulders pressing down on the back of the bed and lifting my elbows just slightly maybe one inch or two. When I wiggle, it feels like I'm moving a foot.

My holding cell has now become my cocoon, a place for me to rest. My mind never does. It's tortured by the memories and flashbacks. They are all I have, filled with everything that once was perfect. I have not accepted anything. I know that this is where I will be and there is absolutely nothing I can do about it, screaming inside, still wishing to die, but developing a different mindset, something I don't understand, but the only thing I have control over. My perspective has changed. I lie in bed, watching Mitch my respiratory therapist throw a rolled up piece of paper into the trash can behind the foot of my bed. I know he missed even though I couldn't see the trash can. Mitch was astounded that I was able to tell that by the trajectory path, hearing the paper hit the rim and then the floor.

Did you see that? Robert knew, before the paper even hit the trash can that I was going to miss. How did you even see that? You can't see the trash can from there. That's amazing! Mitch was astounded shaking his jolly gray beard.

The other shorter therapist, the same age as Mitch, also with a white beard, but softer voice, was hanging out with Mitch and me watching the baseball game. Bill came from the bathroom shaking his head, agreeing with Mitch.

You're an amazing kid Robert. Don't worry; Mitch is not that good of a shot. I could have called that he was going to miss too, Bill says, joking.

I feel very comfortable with these older guys, but when my friends visit me I have nothing to say. It's like we don't know how to talk to each other and were not in the same state of mind. Maybe it's just that at my age it's hard to understand anything. Somehow I'm lying in bed figuring out the world. In one revealing instead, now I can see something that arouses my conscience. It's as if I am aware that I am dreaming when I'm asleep, but in this dream I am learning how to do anything I want. I don't get anything from the other kids I know. I want to talk about baseball but there is something more interesting. My mind is completely open. There is an energy telling me that there is something else to discover. Even though I do not know what I'm talking about, I feel it. I have no one to tell me if what I am thinking is right. Somehow I feel like there has been a cover over my eyes, but I'm the only one able to see through it on this torturous trail that I'm being dragged down. My feet are tied as I'm on my back being dragged down a bumpy, rock and dirt road. I dig my fingernails deep to resist, screaming for mercy. Messages crash through me, thrashing me around, as signs flash by in chaos as I am towed. I cannot stabilize myself long enough to read them. I can feel a galloping horse steaming fast dragging me behind, as an empty saddle fitted for a hero pounds harder and harder. Every important message I hear and see posted in my wake is scrambled by my inability to find a way to take control.

I feel like I have a gift. Many people have been in this position. I'm aware that it's probably been millions. It's the people who think they live perfect lives that always think it can never happen to them, so they just have no clue, always thinking the world is perfect. I was one of those people. I close my eyes and imagine the future. What will happen to me? I close my eyes as tight as I can. What can I picture in my mind? If I can summon some kind of future image of where I will be, maybe that will give me some comfort. I know we must have some kind of control. Maybe those who suffer have minds prepared to see the future. The sun is about to go down and I'm lying on my side facing the window looking at Fluffy's photo. I close my eyes tight, trying to see something. It feels like a burst of dark energy pushing toward my eyes, ripping a circular jagged tear through the darkness, with spots flickering and shooting toward my face. I see a darkroom. I can see some kind of flat white board in a small rectangular elongated room. All shapes appear as dark shadowy figures with flashes of images of what they might be doing in concentrated tiny spots of focus close-up. Sitting close by a door are a few people painting or drawing on these boards. I'm too afraid to see more so I wake up. I don't want to frighten myself. I don't believe I will become anyone. I don't believe I exist anymore. I'm not asleep. I know what I'm doing but my mind is somewhere else. God please someday show me what my life is supposed to mean and why this happened, because it feels like this should never happen to anyone. I feel singled out. The whole world is swallowing me and I am stuck in this prison, forced to live like this.

I'm going to visit my home to see how it was renovated to open up a room for me to finally come home soon. Beth and Mitch are going with me. I'm so anxious that I'm having anxiety attacks, feeling lightheaded and short of breath. What reaction will the other kids have? I know they're going to be playing in the baseball field. They have no idea what I've been through and who I have become and how much change my life has taken on. I know they will see me differently. Not like the tough kid or the bully, making sure no one messes with me. I'm a completely different person and I can't face them, but somehow I want to see again. I've been envisioning everything in my memory. If it's still there maybe it will make me feel good. I feel I am sitting on a throne in this cumbersome retarded chair. I can't race past favorite spots or over familiar bombs with my skateboard. Now I must tilt back so the pressure of turning on a slant and stopping and taking off doesn't hurt my neck or make the ventilator beep. It follows me everywhere like a huge beacon for everyone to point at and stare. I spent so many years fearing, never wanting to become the neighborhood freak and always being the tough kid. Now, I've become that freak.

Turning on to my street, Pine Road, I can see the baseball field and the kids out there staring at the van. They stop what they're doing and walk over toward my house, gravitating toward me. Not like they used to, looking up to me as the coolest, but now with sympathy and in a weird way. I don't want it anymore. I don't want them looking at me because I'm afraid I am rejected. Rob is no longer.

My driveway is not paved yet. It is still full of rocks, but there is a concrete path four feet wide starting where the driveway ends. I take the first turn and see my swimming pool and those three purple hydrangea bushes on my right under the window where my brother's room was. Everything seems the same except for the path. Before, it was nothing but an over-walked dirt path. Now it has become the road I have to follow, the only one I have. I fear going on the grass. My body is changing. I notice tremors. Everything is holding me back. My body and mind are completely different. There is a cute little black lab tied to the aluminum poles under the swimming pool deck next to Fluffy's doghouse that Carlo built a while ago. Adrian brought home a puppy, but I heard he doesn't take care of it. My parents are so frustrated and it poops all over the downstairs bathroom. Fluffy is so excited to see me. He's right by my side, yelping at the gate, waiting for me to come, bouncing in front of me, leading the way into the house and down the new ramp, welcoming me. All my relatives who have any kind of trade are still working on the fixes for my new room. Going through my living room basement, the old brown carpet is removed, replaced by what looks like hospital-type blue carpet.

It feels like a dream returning to my house as a completely different person. I can't help crying, feeling like the torture will not end, giving in to every sad thought and every bad dream. It is refreshing looking at the back yard and the neighborhood. Robert walked up, to fence interested in helping me.

Hi Robert, I said.

Hi Robert, Little Robert said.

We all really missed you and wish you to get better, Little Robert said.

Thank you Robert, I said.

It's really odd. Without my body I don't know how to communicate. I know what they're feeling, seeing someone they care about. Robert looks at me with genuine concern. Other kids walk up to the fence. Jimmy was in the field and walks up to say hello and wishes me well. I feel some resentment. He never came to see me before. I expected he would be out in the field like usual, a normal day for him, completely shattered for me.

I go inside the house, down the hallway toward my brother's old room, followed by a nurse and a respiratory therapist. Tubes are hooked up to me while I drive with my chin. I don't feel happy. I just kind of digest what I see. Feelings force themselves on me. I have no way to get rid of them. The house smells different and I look and feel different. With my fingers spread straight out on the hard sort of spongy flat armrests and my legs bony, wearing a long sleeve shirt and sweat pants, I miss my old clothes. The bathroom is a lot larger now, with little white and blue tiles on the floor and white tiles on the walls. The large step to the bathroom has been blasted away. Carlo walks me through all the renovations. The wall dividing Adrian's room from the living room is completely gone. There's a large opening where my bed will go. I don't see Adrian anywhere. I don't think he wants to see me. It's still too hard for him.

Touring my house, being taken upstairs to sit in the old La-Z-Boy again while my family eats at the dining table, I start sinking into finding some control in my own house. My back is uncomfortable and all the pressure is on my neck no matter where I sit. I have an anxiety attack. My cousin Timmy looks back from eating pasta. My mother leans over me, telling me to stop making a scene. I burst out in frustration.

I don't care about this fucking life, God damnit! I yell.

They quickly finish eating the meal my mother prepared and then one by one some of them tap me on the shoulder not saying any words. They just go back downstairs to finish up the renovations. Fluffy never comes upstairs. He walks up to the middle level of the front door on his own. This time is different. He walks gingerly, hugging the steps, quietly up the steps to come see me, but doesn't want to stay, in nervous panic, thinking he's not supposed to be there. I pet him a little bit, encouraging him by calling his name *Fluffy*. He goes right back downstairs in spite of me calling him to stay.

My dad carries me up and down the steps as though I am a limber puppet. While not being able to feel my body I have no control of my arms. I am being introduced to something I used to do, but in an entirely different way. Wheeling around the front yard, all the kids come around me, curious with their eyes and quiet while I try to show that I'm getting better. Mitch takes the ventilator off my trachea and plugs it with a speaking valve. It's a big white cap with a crisscross on the other end and every time I take a breath in it lets air in but not out and sometimes even sounds like a little foghorn. I'm praying that it doesn't make that noise while I am trying to last maybe fifteen minutes off the ventilator. I quickly become lightheaded, so Mitch always asks me over my shoulders every minute how I'm doing. Watching the other kids play, standing around me while I'm accompanied by two people wearing blue hospital scrubs, I feel like the ugly duckling or Rudolph the red-nosed reindeer, fighting peer pressure and sensing ignorant stares and obvious rumors from the kids. They are playing baseball. I just wheel around them, barely able to talk, not really saying much, waiting and hoping they will go away instead of standing in front of me. I can sense the macho fourteen-year-old testosterone from one of the other kids. Jimmy, another friend in the neighborhood, just says hello. The kids call me by my nickname, Rob. It's nice to get the respect that I still carry, but I am ready to crawl away and hide because I'll never again do what they can.

Taking a quick stroll around the neighborhood, I become a lot more talkative with Mitch, trying to explain to him where I used to skateboard and rollerblade, how I was speeding down some of the slightly faster hills. It's a relief for me, walking around the edge of the neighborhood, down toward the local beach where I can always see the water between the houses that are along the waterfront. I know it's time to go back to the hospital, hearing the nurse and therapist remind me of the time switch of their shifts, irritating the hell out of me. Even though I chose to pursue my neighborhood, I hope none of my neighbors actually come outside to say hello. I don't want them to see me, but I wonder why they don't come out.

Back at the hospital, my mother is more curious about other treatments and finds out about Du Pont Medical Center in Delaware for kids under eighteen with spinal cord injuries. It's the best place to be. She thinks I should go there. I refuse to leave because I am in such great depression. It is my choice. Her frustration and anger were expressed to the doctor about why he chose to put me in a brain injury hospital with no other patients with spinal cord injuries, not knowing what to do for me! I don't want the therapy anyway. I'm not in any mood to make decisions. Given an opportunity to leave I plead to stay. I have a feeling this is going to be a very big mistake. It's not my fault I was put here. I have so much anger toward everyone, on top of my depression, and now ambition to try to move my muscles for recovery. I don't really know. The longer I wait the less chance I'll have of ever recovering.

The new wheelchair the therapist has ordered for me has arrived. While I sit up in it for a few hours a day, I don't want to go anywhere except by the big square window at the end of the hallway to wait for my mother's visit. It's a dark hallway with some fluorescent light on the ceiling. I stare at the red carpet and stare out the window at the trees and parking lot. I feel abandoned. I know it's not anyone's fault. It was an accident, but God has abandoned me. Even though I know my parents can't be here every day, I look for them. I suck in these feelings of giving up, remembering the past, and somehow praying for some hope. Staring out that window I can see my past and can't imagine the future as

Life! It Must Be a Comedy

I am now. I'll be going home soon. It's been five months since my injury. October has passed. It's getting cold as the leaves die and November approaches. I am disconnected from time and space without any embrace, looking forward to getting things under control. In my own house, telling the nurse what to do. I'm so tired of them walking into my life, dictating what I can and cannot do. I fear returning home, even though I am entirely sick of seeing those cereal boxes building up on that window sill and staring at those four walls every day and night. Though I'm excited, I'm still a slave to what I am doing and what I'm not doing. It's just the next step in my life. I look to my parents for everything. The get well banner is being rolled up and my family tells me that Fluffy is looking forward to my home coming. I can't wait to see my bird Speedy again too. I hope he is still alive.

The doors open for me by an electronic device. I hope I've been given everything from the hospital that I need for rehab for building the rest of my life. My congestion returns, threatening to give me pneumonia, as I uncontrollably breathe in fluid. I have been in a five-month awakening, sent off to a training camp for my mind, completely separated from society and from everything I ever knew. I feel like I sit beside myself, detached from reality. I do not know who I am anymore. Before my existence was always defined by the physical things I'd been able to express and feel. Now all I ever do is think all of those times and how losing everything has meant so much to me. I don't know how I'll ever cope with life now. I'm home, but can this ever really feel like home again?

Chapter 10
A Lonely Road

Lying in bed my first night home from the hospital, my nurse Sharon, is staying the night with me. She is the only distraction I have. I fantasize about being with her someday. I feel so stressed out and erotic. The presence of a beautiful woman, her tall skinny legs, waiting on me, relieves my mind. I want a woman like her in my life every day. I visualize and dream what it's going to be like being home again, living the way I am. My eyes are wide open, hearing every sound and looking at every shadow. I don't know if I will ever adjust to this life. I have become a vegetable. I have my own room apartment but I don't feel any privacy as anyone can come in at any time because of the open hallway. At night I hear the washing machine bumping and circling. I have no energy. I haven't slept in more than twenty-four hours. I am so jumpy and sleep-deprived that my entire body is twitching and aching from anxiety attacks. I close my eyes, find myself screaming. I feel like I am crawling out of my skin.

I am still on the ventilator hooked up to my trachea. I hear the machine breathe in and out. I still have no control. If I think hard enough, maybe I can find some peace, but there's no hope. I am so disillusioned in this cave I am in. It is just another cell for me. I am still a prisoner in my body. My eyes feel stitched open with sustained images. I am not sure what the world is like any more. I am brainwashed by disbelief and despair. I am chained down, dragging my burdens, clinking for all to hear. Every day I suffer my punishment.

Life! It Must Be a Comedy

The past, present and future remind me I am inevitably screwed. Everything I worked so hard to become has been taken away. I sleep in the room my grandparents lived in, waiting for their lives to end. I never really talked to them then or knew anything about their feelings. Now it's my turn. Everyone has forgotten about me too. I make it through my first night, without rest or sleep and hurt all over.

I don't get out of bed and just lie there staring at the lawn and my TV which I brought home with me. Looking out the window to my left, I see the sky and trees. I can hear children playing in the baseball field outside my house. This is what I was thinking about all night. Kids would look at me differently. I can't just can't get up and run out the front door to my own playing field that I had complete control. My territory is taken away. I bet they all laugh at me and tell each other that I got what was coming to me. I'm sorry for the way I treated some people, but at the same time I'm not because they treated my brothers disrespectfully. In my mind, I can see them pointing at my house. I hear the baseball clinking on the aluminum bat being swung by hands and arms and legs that run, mocking me, telling me to stay in the house and not come out to be laughed at.

I have even more losses. I occasionally get up in my wheelchair and drive around with my chin. It is too cold to go outside, so I wheel up and down the hallway, spinning in circles and figure eights for an hour, hearing the kids playing. I hear the ball, the bat, the backstop fence ricocheting off the chain-link fence. I hear laughter. I even think I hear my name being called, when I would grab my baseball bat and glove, run down the steps straight out the door into the game. I'm happy to be with Fluffy again. Everywhere I go in the house he hears any clicks of my wheelchair and gets up and follows me around. He has become my little companion. He sits up against me. His long fur has grown out. He always used to be pressed against my leg or resting on top of me. I can barely move, but I am gaining some strength. While my right hand stays pretty much in my lap, I can lift my left arm just enough off the arm rest and then flop it on top of Fluffy's head. I pick it up slightly and then let it fall off the arm rest to go down his ears and caress his soft fur. I still don't feel much of anything from my neck down. Some feeling and movement have slowly come back. I can feel my shoulders more, but with the loss of muscle and the pain from rolling on my shoulders, I am nothing but bones. I try to hide my appearance with baggy sweaters, hoodies and baggy sweat pants, sometimes parachute pants or khakis. I hate my body. I cannot look in a mirror or flex my muscles that I miss so much. My back is always twisted, putting pressure on my neck and making my stomach stick out. In my wheelchair, I try to fit little stuffed animals in the sides to keep me straighter. One of my favorites is Chewbacca. He is slender but shaggy and his head, shoulders and legs rotate. I have furry brown bears, from the hospital that I keep next to my face every night. I have a fatter bear a yellow classic Pooh. The ventilator follows me everywhere I go, connected to the back of my chair. I have the large wheels I requested on this chair made specially for me. The insurance finally approved it.

It's the little things in life that I use to make myself feel comfortable. I struggle every day feeling like there is no progress. I'm waiting for some sign, praying all the time and hoping that this lawsuit gives me the fourteen million dollars that I need to live. I fantasize all day. I listen to music, sometimes inspirational Christian music, a lot of country (Garth Brooks) and rock and roll. If I get one million, I can live my life comfortably and have any nurse I want. My desire and obsession over women increases. This is the peak of my adolescence and even though I fight every single nurse that comes, cursing up a storm about having to live in this cursed body. I still fantasize how I would use my body with a woman, pleasing her and getting everything I've ever wanted back through that action. I attach myself to things that give me pleasure using imagery in my mind. Most of it is about beautiful tall nurses that will be coming into my life. I keep getting the ones who are ugly, horrendously rude, insensitive, ignorant slow and lacking any common sense. It doesn't make me feel like I can trust these people. So I lash out.

I keep Adrian's little black lab female dog so my mom and dad won't take her to the pound. I've heard her barking chained up all day as my parents take care of their responsibilities. Adrian still rarely comes to visit me out of some kind of strange guilt. Jasmine is so a sweet, I keep her. She becomes another companion by my side. Both dogs come out from under my bed where they sleep and follow me everywhere through the house and even into the backyard. When I move from my bedroom to the living room, they are right there. I find some little pleasure as dad tells his jokes while Fluffy and Jasmine nip at each other. Fluffy's not neutered but Jasmine, a very young female, is spayed.

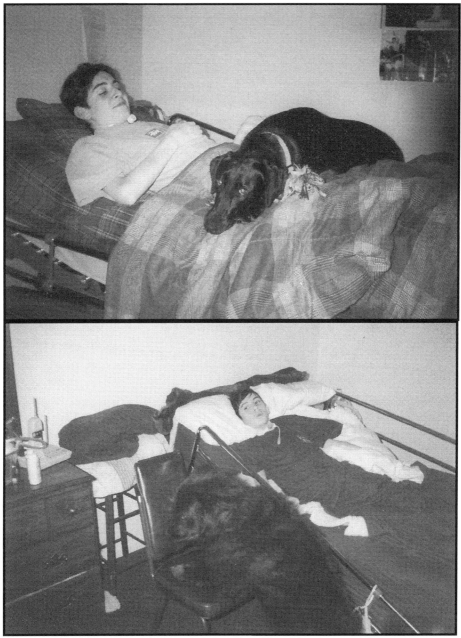

Fluffy's ears perk up straight, I realize I have more in common with my dog than I thought, sniffing and licking her, but Jasmine quickly turns around as he pushes her, snapping his face, so Fluffy turns away whimpering. Poor dog he can't get any, just like me.

Life! It Must Be a Comedy

My parents have become my best friends. I never thought they would be. I ignored both of them while I growing up, getting in trouble and thinking I had no worries at all. Now I have all the worries in the world. I rely on their knowledge, heart and sacrifice to keep me going. Every day I need their friendship, trust and love. Not my nurses, who don't do much for me. They act distant. I can't get close to anyone. I don't know these helpers, so it's not natural for me to feel like I need them to do everything, even though I do. I have a lot of barriers in my mind. I don't like getting near people I don't know. I ask my parents to help even when the nurses are sitting right there.

Every day is a nervous breakdown. Occasionally when my father gets home from working at the barber shop (around eight p.m.) he tells a few jokes he heard there. Or he tells me about the book he wants to write, a new TV show he wants to start, or about his experiences as a barber. But today is more stressful than ever. In my anxious need to control everything and trusting no one, I finally descend to a lower level than ever before. This fat lady nurse is getting on my nerves. I scream at the top of my lungs for her to leave me alone and to get away from me. My mother and father are both at work. I really hope my mother comes home soon. This nurse will be in trouble. She has no choice but to listen to me and do what I say. She is ignoring me now. I refuse to take my medicine. She tries to pull my shirt down my back. I tell her to get away, forcefully! I feel complete disrespect. I don't like her telling me how to live my life. I can do it myself, put on my pants and shirt and my hat. I wouldn't do it like that. I wouldn't do my hair like that. Even the time it takes them to do something, to get me in my chair, to change the channel, to get me something to eat, all feel completely institutionalized. I'm not allowed one second of my own. I'm at the complete mercy of strangers, taking their own sweet time to do things for me when I'm just used to just getting up and doing it. I don't know how some people become caretakers. It's like these people don't think how they would feel if they were in the same position. How would they want to be treated?

I shout out three or four orders at the same time. It's impossible for her to do it all at once. In my frustration I tell her to leave me alone and if she gets close to me I will bite and I will spit.

My mother comes home and hears me crying as the nurse closes the door and goes out in the other room, leaving me alone. She tells my

160

mother to let me be by myself, that I need to be alone. I'm screaming for mom. I just want to feel her hands on my face giving me the comfort of human touch. I can't do it with my own hands. I just need that. As the days have passed I grow more and more moody and depressed. I want my own hands to comfort me, needing that touch of love. The nurse had put a hospital mask over my face so I couldn't spit or bite.

Mom please I need you! I shout.

Don't listen to him right now he needs to be alone, the nurse says my mother.

Are you sure? What has he been doing? But he needs me, my mom says.

Just trust me ma'am, he needs to learn not to depend on you all the time. He needs to just be alone, the nurse tries to explain, convincing my mother in some weird way.

Mom please! I need you! Don't listen to that stupid bitch. She is tricking you. It's not true. She has a mask over my face! Please come in. I just need to feel you. God damn it! Fuck this life. I swear to God I'm going to kill that bitch. Mom please, I just need to feel you! I need comfort. Please I'm going out of my mind! I plead crying, as my anxiety attack lowers my blood pressure and I start seeing stars in the room. Everything starts turning red as my ears are ringing and I'm light-headed.

My mother finally comes through the door and I can see the nurse right behind her with her evil eyes. The nurse had some kind of animosity, as if she didn't get away with torturing me enough, tricking my mother. I'm not okay. It's like people like her get off on torturing poor little defenseless kids. Immediately Mom put both hands on my cheeks, covering my ears. It's my favorite place of comfort, keeping me warm. In my panic attack and crying and cursing, I tell the nurse she is fired and to go home.

I am stressing my parents, making them feel so burdened. I sense it in their tired behavior. They don't go out anymore and only cater to me. I have great support in them. My mother fights for me to get some good rehab besides the occupational therapist who comes out twice weekly from the state. I require more. The therapist comes to our house and is very nice and attractive. I look forward to seeing her. She has long, curly brown hair. She cuts blue styrofoam boards to go around my belly. I sit up in bed and push my hands and arms with force, sliding my biceps and triceps. She encourages me to develop my bicep because my left arm has more function coming back. I can raise my hand and keep my left arm up. She makes me a large white plastic board for my refrigerator. She writes my daily exercise schedule on it. My parents take initiative morning and night to keep my arms and legs stretched so my body does not completely stiffen up, becoming completely useless. I also spend my days staring out the window in my room, yelling to the top of my lungs for someone to kill me.

My friend Jeff still doesn't visit me because of the lawsuit between our families. My next door neighbor Robert comes over more often than anyone just so I can watch him play video games. Soon I will be traveling because my mother requested Governor Glendening of Maryland for three weeks at Hersey Pennsylvania Medical Center for spinal cord rehab. It was approved. My mother never gives up. She's always on the phone with the insurance company, medical supply company, demanding that I get everything I need. I don't get things like an elevator, renovations, or even any help for my parents, paying for their time when the nurses aren't there. I give Fluffy one more pat on the head. I'm at the foot of the steps in my basement. I look up toward the open front door, hearing the kids playing. In a few days I'll be off to Pennsylvania, about two hours away. I'll have the most intense rehab ever. I'm excited this time, wanting it. Something has changed, even before going. My occupational therapist Rob, who's very funny with a friendly attitude, sizes up my attitude about change when I'm at the hospital for my evaluation. They are not just evaluating what I am physically capable of. He reviews my chart with the doctor, looking at my history. They see how I just gave up and never feel to do therapy and how depressed and defiant I was. When my attitude changes, I felt like people believe in me and the therapists around me in the hospital actually help. The people at Mount Washington rehab had no clue how to help me and I felt doomed, so I gave up.

It would be a very tough three weeks. They told me that if I really wanted to do this it would be up to me to get the maximum benefit from that limited amount of time. I was also excited that Hersey Park is only about five minutes down the road. These people were actually going to get me to go places, to get my mind moving forward. I'm happy that someone is trying. I feel like this is my chance to show who I am, to discover who I am. Ross told me I had very bad scoliosis for being only fourteen years old. I thought of my mother complaining at Mount

Washington when they sat me in a regular hospital chair with no support for my spine to stay straight. Ross realized the terrible quality of care I was given at Mount Washington. It didn't give me much of a good start. I have a lot of work to do to reverse it, if it wasn't too late already. Every time somebody does a sensory and motor function test on my body to see what function I have the doctors and therapists are a little excited. Movement in my wrist and triceps muscles (which don't fire by themselves) needs to be worked on to make it more functional. The spinal cord to the brain is showing signs of hope, but it's usually a huge letdown, because it never comes back. I dread any further times this may happen. Doctors and therapists evaluate me have such cold demeanors, as if they didn't care how much it means to me. Any little *yes* makes me feel so much hope and at the same time frightened about crushing everything I ever wanted again. They say I should keep fighting, but we all know the spinal cord doesn't have any connection and it's probably not going to bring anything back that will help me. I sit on the edge of the therapy bed in the clinic.

Do you see that? Ross points at my back.

What? I ask.

Oh, yes I do, another therapist confirms.

You think this can be fixed? Ross says.

So, what do you think Dr., should we bring him into the program? Ross says.

I don't know, do you think he wants to be here? Dr. Dettorre says back to Ross.

What do you think Robert? You want to be here? Ross asks me.

I really do. I can do this if it's going to be good for me, I say.

Are you going to do the work I give you? Ross says.

Yes I will, I reply.

What do you guys think? Do you think he really wants to be here? Ross tries to get a response from my mother and the other therapist. I look around the room with concern in my eyes. I look straight at him. After a long haul Ross finally says something.

I believe you, Ross says.

It's been a couple of months. I come home from Mount Washington and I'm off to Hersey Pennsylvania. My mother and my father both accompany me. We head off straight to the rehab. We're driving in my brand-new van. I just got it from doing a fundraiser with

Life! It Must Be a Comedy

family and friends. It's a new large red and silver custom paint Ford van with an accessible lift and everything. I call her Big Red. It's freezing outside. I don't go anywhere without the scarf my friend Anna from Odenton Christian Academy gave me when visiting me at the hospital. Anything that keeps my neck, face and ears warm makes me feel like my entire body is warm. I brought my Bible, a little Ziploc bag with Old Bay seasoning in it to remind me of Maryland blue-steamed crabs, and Chewbacca and Pooh bear. There are four people in my room of the rehab department. They put me on the children's side where trains and teddy bears decorate the wallpaper.

I see little kids on ventilators and babies. I'm on a ventilator too. I only need to be on mine at night while I sleep. I can go almost all day breathing on my own now. Dr. Dettorre is my pulmonary specialist. I call him Dr. Doctor because his last name means doctor in Italian. He's a very tall guy with very short blond hair around the sides, bald on top, very quiet and gently friendly. I never felt comfortable around any other doctor before, until meeting Dr. Dettorre. Everyone has a certain way of talking in Pennsylvania, exaggerating the last letter of every last word in a sentence, picking up the pitch of their voice. It's kind of funny. Everyone is so nice. I feel very comforted and wanted. Maybe it's because I've traveled so far that everyone is being so over-accommodating, but whatever it is I feel like I can start discovering who I am. I know it is going to be a hard road, but I'm ready. I can't believe I'm actually encouraging myself. I'm anxious to do something. When I'm evaluated, they continue to talk amongst themselves about my potential, while I try to guess what they're talking about, making me feel again like they are evaluating more than my body. They stare at me with smiles on their faces to assess my resolve, to see if I really want therapy and if I will actually follow through. This new situation completely transforms my life. It's an environment that's good for my future. The only comparisons I can make is sitting in front of the principal to be accepted into another schools. Except, I really want to be here.

The therapist has me on a ridiculous schedule. I have to be up every morning at 8 a.m. The nurses usually wait for me to call them to get me up. I wheel myself with my chin down a couple of hallways to the therapy room. I'm actually making progress, trying to use my biceps as much as possible. My muscles and my mind are pushed to their limits in every sense. The pain rips one little part of my muscle tearing

164

sharply, giving me a chance to catch my breath. Anxiety makes me light-headed on the mat. They even try to sit me straight up on my arms for the first time with someone behind me. Occasionally someone will visit when I'm in therapy. When the therapy dogs visit I try to sneak as much time with them as possible. A much older quadriplegic guy with less function drives his wheelchair with his chin too. He shows how much Ross has helped him, giving me encouragement, but I'm not open to talking yet. Occasionally a psychologist will give me long tests to evaluate my mind. Sometimes they make me go down a long hallway into cold rooms, to look over pictures in a timed session. I explain to them how much I hate their cold, professional, and superficial attitudes. I wish they'd care and show it by being friendly instead of explaining what I already know about how bad off I really am.

My favorite nurse is Kait, a very tall slender redhead with a great smile and a goofy personality. She does not wear much makeup. I started this new thing with her just to pass the time when I'm not doing therapy called hall surfing. I'll convince her to grab onto the back of the handles of my chair, put her feet on the back of my chair, while sitting on an office chair with wheels. I pull her around the hallways, whipping her around the corners, trying not to crash in the food carts and medical carts. She has a blast with a huge smile on her face. The nurse's lineup for turns. A little part of my ability to get into trouble, being fun, perks me up just a little bit. I like to put a smile on Dr. Dettorre's face or my therapist Ross's or even my psycho analyzers. I smile and in my own way tell him to shove it up his butt, to leave me alone and stop trying to find ways to force me to feel depressed. I know the nurses can get in a lot of trouble. Dr. Dettorre tells me to *be quiet about it* as the chief doctor stands next to him. Quietly he encourages me to keep doing what I love, as I go flying around the corner with the nurse hanging on crashing into him, nearly knocking over all the food trays. It's like I am goofing off in the hallways at school and getting caught by the principal, but in a weird way getting away with it.

Shit, sorry! I yell. I stop to look at him and take off.

The other thing I do to pass the time is play the pinball machine inside the lunchroom. It has large buttons. It's on the same floor as my room and therapy, not far down the hall. With a mouthstick about a foot long I can use the left and right flippers and the two middle buttons with my left and right hands. I love trying to beat the scores. This is the first time I see my affinity for games. I am addicted to this distraction. I spend hours at it every day. The nurses check on me. Their shift changes at eight p.m. and finally I go to bed. At night I sat by my window and read some random chapters of my Bible. I have no idea what job I can do. I just want to give myself some peace of mind and direction. I've got a lot to figure out. I open to a chapter that is talking about lying in bed with a woman. I find ironic, because I think about meeting a special woman every day. I can't peace any of it together. I hope someday I will be with a woman I have always wanted.

Three weeks have almost passed. I anticipate my parents coming to visit to seeing me drive my wheelchair with my left hand. I didn't think it was possible even though my left arm had some movement. The therapist at Mount Washington would never give me the opportunity and told me I would never be able to use my hand to drive my chair. Fearfully, I believed them and it became my own insecurity. I also feed myself with a mechanical machine. It's tall and leans over me and is made of green painted aluminum bars, levers and pulleys. I put my arms out straight in front of me like a puppet with forks and spoons in hand. I try to use all the muscles I can to feed myself. I would've never imagined any of this as possible, but they threw it all at me here and taught me so much in just three weeks. Compared to the therapy I was supposed to get during the first five months, which were crucial moments for regaining anything, this place is faster and better. They truly care about my well-being. I want to stay longer.

Adrian, Carlo, mom and dad visit. Even though the weather is cold, we all go outside to the little flower path in the back of the hospital between the walkway that leads to the large five-story parking lot. There isn't much of a view, just a big grassy hill almost as high as the parking lot, surrounded by woods. In the far distance there's a highway. I try to show off for them as much as possible, driving with my left arm. I can only go short distances without fatiguing the muscle and stopping. It's really good to see Carlo, Adrian and my whole family with big smiles on their faces. They all give me hugs. There still is something missing. I see, not exactly disappointment, but grief still in their expressions. It's a big step for Adrian to drive all this way in his new, used maroon Camaro, showing it off to me. Walking with everyone, talking, looking past the swing sets in between the flower gardens and lovely little trails, I branched off a little bit with Adrian. He has been so distant, almost not around when I was home for the two months before I came here. I felt like I wanted to help that somehow. I'm starting to see a more genuine side of me I never knew was possible. I don't have all the answers. I just wish people would wake up and see things they have and not take them for granted. It bothers me when Adrian talks about his girlfriend because I miss that feeling of being with someone. We talk about secret things and I listen to his stories as if they were my own. We walk for a long time, sitting for a half hour a good distance away from everyone, just talking. My feelings are still bottled up inside me about not wanting to be in a wheelchair. I know everybody knows that, so I try not to bring it up. Looking at my face they can tell they would trade positions. They feel helpless.

I finally get to see Hershey Park, at least a little bit of it. Ross's wife, the recreational therapist, takes me and a nurse to the local tiny zoo right next to Hershey Park, where I can see the roller coasters and hear all the excitement. Afraid to actually go in, we stop by the little zoo. We walk through, seeing a few animals. A female lion eyes me up like I am her next helpless victim sitting in a wheelchair. Somehow this animal knows if it got out, I would be the weakest link. Seeing an occasional albino squirrel, thinking it is the most amazing thing, though not actually part of the zoo. The hills strain my muscles. I can't push up too much on an incline. I definitely have more courage to go out more places. I see myself doing more things. Though I'm in pain, the therapist suggests I ride a horse!

A few days later, I'm now face to face with a huge horse. I get on the horse. A brace completely surrounds my chest, correcting my scoliosis from my stomach all the way up under my armpits. The process of making this brace is similar to figuring out how I'm going to get on this horse. My body has been propped and pulled, twisted and stretched onto a tiny little beam. I feel tortured, scared and exposed, almost violated by this process, almost completely naked in a tiny fitting room. I'm only wearing underwear. They pick me up out of my chair with my spine resting on a two inch wide beam. I'm abducted, perversely suspended, freezing four feet above a hard linoleum floor. There's absolutely nothing on my left or right. Two big guys hold onto my body for about fifteen minutes while they take measurements for my brace.

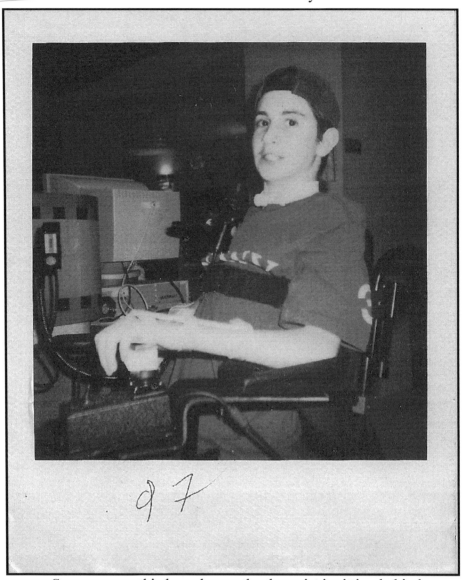

Secure, up on this large horse, the therapist is sitting behind me holding my weight. Another person holds the reins while we walk slowly inside a large barn and then go outside. It's an amazing experience being on top of this animal, taking me out of my wheelchair and making me feel like I can finally see and experience a completely different perspective. Instantly, I feel relieved and rejuvenated, while still very skeptical, being on this gigantic animal. It's not running out of control. The movement of its strength and the curvature of its body side-to-side, the sound of its feet and the horsetail wags and horse trots make me I feel a tiny bit free. I almost don't want to stop, but looking down between my legs they are hanging from the gravity. My feet are swinging. I start to get self-conscious, fearing that my genitals are being crushed and my underwear is giving me a huge wedgy. Those who take care of me know that I want my clothes straight and I don't like feeling contorted and crippled. At least the clothing I wear should make me look decent. They always get a big laugh out of me being so picky, but in my mind they would be doing the same thing. I can't wait to get this silly helmet off my head. It's really starting to have an effect on my neck. The ride stops even though I don't want it to. I am completely surrounded by positive strong-hearted energy. It's hard to say goodbye to the two tiny billy goats that ride on top of the horse with me. I've had an incredible experience that inspires me. I know that every exposure or reward gives me a connection to life. It means the world to me. I'm growing into a very passionate, deep-minded person, but still fear my own insecurities.

Three weeks have flown by. It's time to return home and see what I've accomplished. I did not expect to have my own custom-made joystick, U-shaped out of a dark metal, custom welded, driving with my arm. I have enough strength to pet Fluffy longer. I make my rounds, saying goodbye to all the people I have connected with. It feels like I've been here a long time. Some of my best friends are off shift so I don't get to say goodbye to many of them. I leave a message for them, Ross and Dr. Dettorre who wants me to join him every year at the ventilator camp in central Pennsylvania for all of his kids. He and his staff of great people will be there for us to enjoy ourselves. I agreed to go, but I have to think about it. Maybe I will go. I would be the oldest kid there and I'm still not comfortable being around other people with my same condition.

Once home, I go through over thirty nurses. They do some kind of trickery to me and I do something right back to them. From the first moment I meet a nurse I can tell from her attitude if we will get along. I'm visited every day by a new woman. They are fat, black, old, some from Africa, with the nastiest attitudes treating me like a job not a human being. The hardest thing about returning to my life again is having weird people I would never talk to being my hands and feet. I want to take care of myself a certain way, and they won't let me. I don't want to talk to someone I have nothing in common with, clashing with my personality, their religion or the things they were taught in nursing school, or there village, telling me philosophies they live their lives by. All the nurses at that agency spread rumors about me and my case. I have spit on them, cursed at them, tried to fight and even talked behind their backs to mom or dad just for spite. I prepare again for this new journey that I don't want to be on. My mother is convinced by Dr. Kennedy Krieger Institute in Baltimore that their Step Program would be the best place for me to go instead of public school. It will allow me to break out of my shell. I have to go to school, but I don't want to do anything.

I fight every morning because I don't want to get on that bus. I have become the special needs kids I always felt uncomfortable around. I hung out with my friends being the coolest one, with all my abilities. Now I'm in that role I used to make fun of. I'm accompanied by a very gorgeous nurse named Kait. She's five-seven curvy, a white chick, with long dark curly hair. She takes care of me all day, almost every day. She wears Daisy Dukes jeans, so short I can see her butt cheeks. Every time she bends over I think the most appropriate thoughts of a healthy young man. I'm thankful she's here. We get along great with everything. I'm still not breaking out, close to fifteen, wishing I could make a move, but too afraid and not experienced. Kait came to me on her first day when I was in one of my greatest fits of rebellion. I was kicking and screaming. She put up with me. She's lasted the longest, but I don't really see her as a nurse. Being completely off of the ventilator nearly an entire week, I feel my lungs completely exhausted. It feels like pneumonia. I can't really breathe, so I'm lying flat in my chair, tilted all the way back, in the living room. A quick call to Dr. Dettorre, then Kait and mom take me down to the emergency room at Johns Hopkins.

I can't believe I'm back in the same hell hole I was in before. This time I'm alert, with the head of the bed up more. I breathe into a ventilator with a nebulizer mask to my trachea. There's moisture-misted air for me to breathe. It's not exactly pneumonia. Even though I am congested, I think it was just exhaustion. I see Kait standing in the hallway watching over me. I see a poor little black boy, may be six years old, puffing on the same kind of oxygen mask and mist. His mother walked away for a break, so he's screaming at the top of his lungs with tears rolling down his cheeks. I tried to whisper to him that it's okay. I see other kids lying down, but this is the only one that sparks my memory, making me feel sad and depressed. I want to help all of the kids. All the images rush in and in about what I was doing the last time I was in this place. Kait is genuine. She is by my side and I can see her looking back, talking to my mother. At this moment I know I have some kind of a friend. My mind has just opened. I feel a connection like never before. I see her completely differently as my heart and mind now her presence and the importance of having her in my life. She is my arms and legs. She is the first nurse that allows me to open up. It is like love at first sight. Even though my emotions get the best of me, I am too chicken to make a move. She is about six years older than me.

The clanking bus jitters and chatters while I'm tied down near the middle. Only a couple of other kids are in wheelchairs. This yellow wagon takes every bump in Baltimore City as we go through detours every day in the worst and most interesting parts, then out to the suburbs to pick up two or three other kids. I pray to get picked up after all the others, which is usually what happens. Friends in the field watch me get off the bus, dropped off by a huge mechanical elevator, loud, old and rickety, announcing that Robert must be home, announcing my humiliation. All the time I complain I must be in the wrong place. The Step Program, STP they call it, is mostly young kids with mental retardation, most four or five years younger than me. We sit in a room singing about the weather and the news. I feel they scammed my mother giving her the wrong news and the worst advice for me to be here. Kait and I stare at each other most of the day, as she helps me eat my lunch in the elementary level classroom. Every day I take a mouth stick, and sit at the touch screen computer. I play card or board games with Mario Nintendo. It's the highlight of my day, hearing his voice, completely distracted, in my own little world. I am still so attracted to videogames. I like clicking on Mario's face. It's always a joy to me.

It's-a Mario. You want to play with-a Mario? The computer says.

They bring symbols and evaluations to me, pictures that are flipped over by the therapist who times my results. That's all people do for me now, to see my determination and level of intelligence. If they really want to help me, they should just befriend me. Nobody body steps up. I sit lost, all by myself, afraid to give wrong answers or show a bad attitude. They might recommend an even worse place than this, that's how crazy everything is. They have a little therapy room with a large mirror and a low mat for me to do some exercises, but that's about all they give me that might be somewhat beneficial.

I hear Kait talking about a videogame called Tomb Raider that she and her friend stay up all night playing sometimes. Kait also tells me there is a new gaming system out there called PlayStation. My curiosity is aroused. I get an arcade joystick and I'm testing it out on the PlayStation One. Using my ingenuity, I wrap a brown spongy material around the inside of a sterile water bottle cap. My fingers rest on the joystick. Using a mouthstick one foot long and a gold brass pole with a little vanilla rubber tip, I wear it down with my tooth grooves, testing every game. On baseball games, to pitch the ball, I push one button. I push another button to swing the bat. I've found my escape from boredom. This is great entertainment in my prison, that and basic cable. I spend hours upon hours playing, my left arm getting extremely tired. I'm barely able to push forward in some games that require it. I stick to baseball, some Madden football now and then, experimenting with Tony Hawk skateboarding too. Growing up with my brothers, I'd idolized all the great skateboarders. Now I watch ESPN a lot in see the first extreme sports X Games and the skateboarders coming back.

Carlo and I joke about the old days. We see Tony Hawk coming back strong so we play his Pro Skater on the PlayStation 1. It has basic controls at this early stage of this new technology. My joystick works almost perfectly, even though I can't push the button fast enough. Simultaneously pushing one input device with my mouth, I'm able to do flips, grind, and all the cool necessary tricks to meet the goals and even create my own little skate parks to use my creative ingenuity. Architecture is my interest also, but for the most part I spend days alone playing video games and the hours fly by. I'm oblivious to the pain, like headaches or needing to relieve my bladder every four hours. I sit still with the hospital bed table adjusted to the right height. My joystick is propped up on my Bible for angle leverage so I can push the buttons. I stopped reading the Bible. Instead, I visualize activities, different people and situations. I feel free and in control in this digital world of my computer screen. Time goes by and I get caught up in the graphics, the three-dimensional characters, doing tricks, sports, lost in the adventures of action adventure games. When I go to bed I dream about playing again, hitting the baseball, throwing the football for an interception or watching Laura Croft dodge dinosaurs, doing back flips shooting her double pistols. Before my injury I had Nintendo NES and only dreamed that three-dimensional graphics would be available. Even though I have limited function, I discover more challenges as the games become more technically advanced. This escape for my mind allows me to be fulfilled, something no one or anything else has been able to give me.

Little Robert comes over almost every day after school. Tomb Raider requires too much forward motion of me, so I watch him hunt for clues, shoot dinosaurs and go down caves, swinging on the ropes, like an Indiana Jones adventure. I am the navigator and he is the avatar. We are both thrilled by this game, going around creepy dark corners, not knowing who or what is going to jump out at us or give us a task to figure out. As I sit there I look around for clues picking up everything Robert can't see. He jumps around shooting, and together we both scream and our stomachs jump in our throats when a dinosaur jumps at us around a corner. We discover new challenges and get lost in this adventure. We play the game from beginning to end. It takes us about a month to complete. Saving our progress on the memory cards, Robert takes the game over to his house, tries to figure out the challenge and comes back the next day showing me how he beats that level. We even play Jenga together, stacking the blocks three by three with each row crisscrossing each other. We bring the hospital table up high enough for me to move my neck around, using my mouthstick to push each block out. Robert turns the blocks around for me to get underneath to pull from the other side. We have a lot of fun together after school each day. We spend hours sharing how faith has helped us and how His salvation has given me strength. I show Robert how much I care, watching him grow right before my eyes like a little brother, his big head with short hair and watery droopy eyes. I must make sure that he knows the salvation I believe in for eternity. I have always shared this belief with Robert. I don't know why except while growing up I've been taught that faith alone means that Christ will give you eternity after this world. I'm starting to actually see the hypocrisy in the church I go to. I attended Anchor Baptist a few years before my injury and still go regularly, but not every Sunday if it's too cold. I miss a few months because of that. Sharing with Robert is important to me. We exchanged Christmas gifts with each other.

Robert gave me the movies "Men in Black" and "Independence Day," just released on VHS. I gave him a rare videogame about helicopters and a small personal Bible. I had my mother highlight verses like John 3:16, hoping I wasn't pushing it too much. I know I'm not perfect, but there has to be some truth in a faith that gives me such a great opportunity to see my own future goals come true, even while I struggle so much to even get up each day to go to a school. I realize when talking to Robert about faith, I'm only trying to convince myself there's still something left to believe in. He tells me he believes that salvation through Christ is definitely true. I tell him I love him and our friendship means a lot to me. We remember jumping on the trampoline together and me teasing him about how his feet used to stink horrendously. We would jump on the trampoline in my backyard I would kneel down and smell the black rubber trampoline matt and look at Robert with my nose curled up in disbelief, exaggerating my overwhelmed senses. I remember his laughter, sense of humor, snorting, chuckling to himself, exhaling with a great burst of air. It took all my frustrations away and we would just keep laughing so hard. The more I kept talking about it, the more it just made him roll over laughing. We would jump on the trampoline all day and into the night until we both would hear our mothers calling out the back doors screaming our names. I would answer for him when his mother called, trying to be funny. No, it's the other Robert, not me, she was shouting for. The sound of those springs squeaking and stretching is a great memory and somehow both of us still are able to laugh about it the same way when I bring it up again.

Man Robert what is wrong with your feet? God, it's like something died and you smeared your foot all over it your stinking up my trampoline. You better clean your feet next time you get on it, I said to Robert.

It's my feet. I told you they stink. I don't know why. Here and look smell them, Little Robert said.

No way I'm not smelling your foot. Clean your feet sometimes man. My trampoline now smells like someone's ass or your feet. Your feet smell like ass, I said.

On my sixteenth birthday I am home in my kitchen with my brothers, my parents and my two dogs. Kait is now working the night shift from five p.m. to eleven p.m.. It's not the most exciting 16th

Life! It Must Be a Comedy

birthday I ever thought I would have. We all eat the cake after "Happy Birthday" is sung to me, the same old thing as the year before. I'm in my second year at Kennedy Krieger now, in the downstairs program with the supposedly, "normal kids." It's a square hallway with four right turns, not very long, and some of our classes we switch, simulating normal public school. I'm followed by my nurse and an assistant named Sheila. I have a really good group of people backing me. I'm being treated like I'm one of the kids in the program that have behavior problems. I'm still afraid to eat lunch with the kids in their lunch room next to the big hallway.

A guidance counselor sees me once a month and I get some physical therapy for my legs and arms. I'm surrounded by kids my age, some with cerebral palsy and some inner-city black boys with severe behavior problems, one step away from juvenile hall. The physical therapist made me a table to connect to my wheelchair. It's a clear plexiglass two by two square, with wooden rounded runners on the left and right and a bottom to hold my books. It's very sturdy, made out of black steel. While in class, I can actually read with no problem, no hurting my neck, no one having to hold the book.

While going from class to class, my home room teacher Ms. B, a stocky, short butch lady with spiky hair, seems to be watching over me like a hawk. She recommends that I actually be given my own assistant because my nurses should not be in class with me or helping me to eat. I go home every day from regretting I ever came here, feeling they are punishing me. They make all the students have each teacher at the end of class mark on a behavior paper, things like temperament levels, social behavior. It's like we are inmates for observation. Society guards people like me. If the state has to pay for me to live, programs like this are mandated and regulated to treat children like objects instead of human beings. The heart-wrenching tragic story of Frankenstein comes to mind. Instead of letting me flourish and giving me a real opportunity to live life to its fullest potential, people pretend to help us, grasping for answers, free to go home relax while wasting years of my life. I am marked one to ten about my behavior. I immediately complain to my psychologist and to Ms. B. to stop treating me like a threat.

Ms. B's assistant is one of my crushes, about twenty seven-years old, long dirty blonde hair, about five foot eight. Her name is Mrs. McKinley. I love watching her smile and laugh. Sometimes in the hallway when I'm laughing about all the stupid rules with my new nurse Summer and my helper Sheila I think she's laughing with me, looking through the glass square window in the classroom door. Almost all the classes have a one-way mirror in a connected room so parents and guidance counselors can monitor the kids without them knowing anyone is watching. The whole place has a very weird vibe to it. Secret rooms and secret rules and special conditions for each kid. It's more like a secret asylum where no one can hear me if I scream. If I do scream I fear they will put a straitjacket on me, adding insult to injury. Everyone's locked in. Being treated as if I have a behavior problem infuriates me. I struggle enough as it is to find my way in the world.

Ms. B. and her assistant Mrs. McKinley teach math class. Another teacher, kind of in her mid-forties, long, straggling, curly thin hair with a few extra pounds and tall teaches English. A tall extra pounds teacher with short brown hair teaches science class. The tech teacher is Mr. Durst. He's a tall, brawny man with short red hair, balding. His body hair sticks out everywhere. My favorite class is taught by a very genuine man, Mr. Alex Chancy. He carries himself with strong but quiet confidence and intelligent manner. He walks with a slouch, always wearing tight black T-shirts and tight blue jeans. He has short, black receding hair and is in his mid-forties. I like his squinted eyes when he talks. He's definitely a genuine American, very educated and cares a lot about kids. He's Greek and funny, a very witty personality. He teaches us history. I learn everything about all the presidents, some of their back stories. Mr. Chancy starts every class with a newspaper article that he reads and asks our opinions. He talks to me, not about me like all the other teachers. When describing to us where he came from and why he chose this job, he says he used to work for the ambassador from Greece, but not agreeing with some policy, he had to quit and come to this place. With all of his background and education he could have chosen any job, but he simply says he wants to help people.

He tells stories about his wife and the huge house he lives in and brags about his horses. He's the only teacher that I go to for inspiration. He gives me a pat on the back and leans over me, stands on my wheelchair, one hand on my arm rest balancing himself and holding his grapefruit for lunch, to get a ride down the hallway. To my surprise, I get straight A's in my classes. It's the first time I actually apply myself

since my injury. I memorize all of the answers for all of my tests. Two
other students in my history class, Jude and James, are like me, singled
out by Mr. Chancy, always getting one hundred and five percent or more
our tests. Somehow I don't know how they both do it. They always
manage to stay a couple percentages above me getting one hundred and
ten percent. James is a very tall, educated, verbal and descriptive young
man, confident, with dark hair. He reminds me a lot of Mr. Chancy in
his attitude and in his extreme intelligence. I'm always puzzled why he
is in the program, probably some kind of performance anxiety. He
always seemed perfectly normal around us. I see Mr. Chancy and James
in-between classes, going to the bathroom or coming back from therapy.
The two of them walk down the hall, while James is reading a book that
Mr. Chancy gave him to read. Mr. Chancy would give him private
sessions. Mr. Chancy walks with hands folded behind his back with that
little hunch he has.

*Hey James I see you're reading a book. Headed off you and Mr.
Chancy? You must feel fortunate having special treatment being the
smartest of us all,* I said.

No. Just you Robert, you're the smartest of them all, James
replied walking with Mr. Chancy, walking past backwards as he
turned around smiling.

Jude is quieter, slightly chubby, with a mohawk down the middle
of his head, dirty blond. He walks with heavy feet, wearing white tank
tops and very long shirts with a hunch. His upper lip hangs over and his
eyes are just a little bit droopy. I always see James and Jude having so
much fun in tech class where their homeroom is. I asked to be put in the
same home room as James and Jude, and I am. Discovering there wasn't
really much I could do, I watch the kids in the computer lab play first-
person shooter doom on Fridays when classes are cut short. Either
people watch movies, do arts and crafts or play games in the tech room.
Or, Mr. Chancy reads and works on some kind of play. Nobody wants
to be in Ms. B.'s room for after school Fridays. She is always so mean.
Sheila, Summer and even my new nurse Laura all know there's
something weird about that lady.

Sheila is very kind to me, a nice sweet Christian lady. She's tall
and curvy, with a great big smile, distinguished nose, glasses, and long
dirty blonde hair in a ponytail hanging over one shoulder. Her voice is
always so soft. I remember the first day she sat next to me in English

class. I was really curious why Summer wasn't allowed to sit next to me to change pages. Sheila arrives saying she was assigned from one of the other programs in the building. The first few days I'm uncomfortable and confused. Sheila witnesses my personality shining because of her kindness. I open up with Summer and Laura. We really click. Summer is a very skinny, petite, in her early thirties, with blonde hair and she has a little boy that she adores. She's always cracking some kind of joke. We joke about Ms. B. that she must be a lesbian or a dike. I'm still afraid to eat lunch with the other students. Mostly I spend my lunch time in one of those quiet little dark rooms with a two-way glass to see through both classrooms. I don't want people watching me eat. I feel like I'm a freak of nature. Sheila and I start talking to Mr. Chancy, so James and Jude invite us to eat with them at their lunch table. Laura is tall and always speaks her mind. Her personality and her beauty fortunately both mesh perfectly with me and what I need. She has long straight dark hair, long legs, a little upward nose and a smile that complements her tiny chin. She's a sweet Christian lady with a couple of young kids so her hours are weird. She doesn't live close by, so most days she comes to my house in the morning and then as soon as I get home she has to leave. I really dread the days I have to go home on the bus with Ms. Marcie and a couple of other kids, bumping around like a rock tumbler machine. In which even the hardest and roughest rocks take a pounding before becoming shiny and smooth. I've already been pounded into submission, but this bus is just another insult to injury. I must be smoothed and prepped for some reason in life, because this rock isn't changing form on the outside, but I'm definitely changing on the inside. Summer is great. She has a small little five-year-old son and spends most days with me, except for evenings when Kait is there to help me with homework. Everywhere I go I have to travel with a big blue bag, connected to the back of my chair, full of books, and a second one with medical supplies. The blue bag is my suction machine in case I get really congested. I hardly have to use it anymore.

Sitting in the lunchroom with my friends, even more crazy rules are being enforced. They won't let any of my nurses feed me, I thought they were joking about that, so Sheila has to come with me to the lunchroom to help me eat. Mr. Chancy shares his daily diet of ice cream and grapefruit. As he unpeels his grapefruit and then banana, I start joking around. For the first time I am actually laughing with everyone in the room, but instead of sitting with strangers, I'm with friends. I can see all the teachers staring at us as we laugh. It feels good to laugh about something when we all know the crazy rules we are under, it's as if we are laughing back in their face. We enjoy our time and don't mind them at all, for the moment. The prison guards and warden are always looking and listening. Instead of them being happy to see me coming out of my shell, Sheila whispers to me to be quiet about what she says, because Ms. B. is in the room and has complained about Sheila. This breakthrough moment for me at lunchtime lets me feel like myself.

Mr. Chancy why don't you try to fit that whole banana down your throat? I said.

Hush Robert they might be listening, Mr. Chancy said ducking his head in whispering quickly under his breath and laughing.

Oh yeah Robert, that's going to look really good. All I need is someone walking over here, and we won't say who, watching me shove this big cylinder shaped thing down my throat. I wonder what that's going to look like? Mr. Chancy replied.

I have a big smile on my face as I look around the room, not caring what anyone thinks. My close friends glow in affection as I come out of my shell. James, Sheila and Mr. Chancy grin at each other, looking at me and then each other.

The art teacher upstairs near the entrance of the building has hair like a poofy-poodle, and bright red. Ms. Claire has a pointy scrunched nose and red freckles, is average height and weight. I enjoy her class a lot. I have to use a mouth stick with a twist cap on the end. It holds art utensils through a little hole twisted tight. Art might be something I can do. It looks just like the mouth stick I use to play video games except for it has a different attachment on the end. I chew up mouthpieces just from the pressure. Twisting brushes and pencils, I'm encouraged to do some painting. I draw lines in a clay frame that I made. Using a pencil in the clay, I draw lines where I want someone to cut the pieces and put them together. I put a picture of me from eighth grade in it. In the photo, I'm standing up with a colorful umbrella over my shoulder wearing my starter Forty-Niners jacket standing outside of one of the classrooms in eighth grade. With assistance I painted the steps gold as if it was heaven. Someday I would walk up those steps, with pillars on each side and a Roman triangular roof.

The University of Maryland was having a competition and wanted the students in our class to draw something about brain awareness. I took my mouth stick home. With colored pencils and a black ballpoint pen an image in my mind came to life quickly. I have never drawn hands before, but looking down at my own hand, I start drawing a green squishy brain with a gold graduation diploma hat and a gold tassel hanging from it with the year 1998 on the end. The brain is sitting on a stool in front of a stage, while a hand reaches out in a blue business suit sleeve holding a white diploma. The people in the background are very tiny, one black and one white. The black guy has a gold hat on just like the brain and the white guy has a black cap on, as the brain gets rewarded. At the top I drew bold green squishy brain-like letters "Just Brain Smart" protruding toward the viewer. I accented minority students, which I think helped the judges give me second place. I asked for my drawing to be returned so I could keep it with me always.

After class, Mr. Chancy gives me a watercolor kit and brushes, a new mouthstick and a book of watercolor paper. He told me to take it home and do what I could with it. He thought it would do me good. I guess word got around quickly that I was painting with my mouth. Mr. Chancy is the only person who sees my potential. I'm not exactly sure what I'm going to do with it, but I'll do my best. At home I get my new table set up next to my hospital bed table with a styrofoam white cup cut on angle so I can get my brush into it and watercolors. There's a white

piece of paper napkin underneath of the cup to dab my brush clean. I
stare at the bonsai tree my mom got me and it's green little rectangular
pot with Japanese writing on it. There's a little figurine of a gold
Chinese man with a beard sitting next to a rock in the gravel. This tree
grows with a thick root around a piece of wood perfectly trimmed. It's
almost ten years old. I follow the contour of the tree, the outline of the
rectangular base and even the little man. The watercolor painting looks
to scale and each individual leaf is a great representation of what I see. I
can't wait to show this to Mr. Chancy.

My next challenge is going to be returning to my childhood
favorite drawings. I remember how I used to draw the Teenage Mutant
Ninja Turtles. My first one doesn't look very good. I try drawing a ninja
turtle from the waist up with turtle shell underbelly, Michelangelo. I
draw his shoulders, his big muscular arms, the distinct turtle face with a
mask around the eyes and nunchucks in his karate belt.

I'm not used to using the ballpoint pen yet. It looks like a Ninja
Turtle but the eyes and other lines are not straight. This time I'm trying
to draw just the face. I start with the upside down smile then the tip of
the nose and then go around a big circle left and right above that to make
the cheek. I draw a big upside down smile-shape line for the top of the

head, meeting up with the bandanna around the eyes, with the bulges above each eyeball socket and Chinese-looking pointed eyes. It looks almost exactly like what I used to draw.

I spend a few hours painting with just enough water on the brush, dipping it in to each of the little trays of color and then rinsing it off. My mouth reaches with my neck, as far as I can into the water, dipping it in and dabbing it again on the paper towel to make sure that my lines are not too wet. Now some of my favorite watercolors are mimicking how the water reflects the sunlight making stripes left and right, landing the sun in the water, the sky reflecting the orange in-between the rays, creating the sunset.

Now that I sit still, my mind seems to be focusing on school and on art like never before. I take medication now so I'm not even using diapers. Hershey Medical Center is helping my life be more stable. But as I sit longer painting, not moving, when I try to move afterwards I'm noticing my body is starting to shake more. I take medication for spasms. The doctors told me they might get worse as the years pass. In my mind I still believe I'm going to be healed. I am setting my hopes on three years. Maybe God will give me a sign and I will be instantly healed. I'm holding on to that for now.

It's time to graduate from this wretched place. If I learned anything from my time here it's that treating people the way you want to be treated means more when you actually do it. It's the only place I have to go and even if I don't want to, my mother will unlock my wheels and push me on that damn bus. I hope someday they will all realize that to be human also means to be treated like one. I have a letter from my attorney telling these people to stop treating me like a criminal, to take away the point sheet, or I will sue them. The amount of stress I go through every day is unbearable in my daily struggles alone. The people at this place could not be more inhumane. One day I see James and Jude in the hall.

Hey why do you guys not have your point sheets anymore? I asked.

Life! It Must Be a Comedy

We're not allowed to tell, they both replied, shrugging their shoulders, no more response, walking away.

My mom blows up at Mr. Durst the next day about the point sheets. He's upset. The teachers all seem to be in on the sheets. My mother storms in the room and starts yelling at him. She is so furious at him his eyes start to water in embarrassment. Summer and I can't help but laugh at him to each other. I should be out of here soon. I can't wait for graduation. I passed all of my state standardized tests with flying colors. The school gives huge trophies to the four students who scored the highest on the tests. To me it is a pathetic attempt to show they are sorry. It overwhelms me, because I've never seen a trophy this big awarded for even the greatest accomplishments. I never feel comfortable around a lot of people, but when it's my turn to speak I feel I have something to say. The one thing about my self image is this skinny little leather belt with a silver buckle. Summer tries to make me wear it, but we both laugh at each other saying how ridiculous it looks. My mother wouldn't let me go without it and my shiny dress shoes, dressed all in black. I feel very uncomfortable wearing a lot of clothes, but being dressed up, clothes tight up against my body and my waist showing that belt, my back is curved, I feel like I'm some kind of mannequin on show. Look at my manly confident walk, my belt shines.

My parents are sitting in the far back recording my speech on video. I know this is a great moment and even though the school has been challenging, it's still a very big accomplishment for me to feel confident speaking in front of people. With this big trophy, looking handsome, all dressed up, with in my speech taped to a four by four piece of paper on my arm rest, I pull up to the microphone ready to say what I wanted to say. I was frustrated about how I was treated, but choose to not react. I truly need to find another place to finish high school. I look deep inside, seeing myself on a long path that will help me discover who I am. My parents get a huge applause. I start getting a little bit emotional, seeing my mother sitting closer to the front, her eyes tearing up but smiling.

I would like to thank my family for giving me everything I need and supporting me. They sacrifice so much for me and they are here tonight. Mom and Dad, please stand up. Even though I have much further to go, I have accomplished so much. Thank you, Mr. Alex Chancy, for giving me some hope. Tonight for me is my miracle, but the miracle does not stop here. Thank you very much.

During the summer I have ventilator camp for one week. I try to get my trachea out, frustrated that Dr. Dettorre for not doing it yet. I attended the previous two years. I'm finished and tired of feeling I don't fit in at this place with these young kids. This year, at sixteen years old, I'm more a mentor. We're in the middle of nowhere in a forest this year, a new location, northern Pennsylvania this time. One of my friends has passed away. He was only ten years old, kind of heavy, a cute kid who loved to sing. He was on a ventilator twenty-four seven, with no ability to breathe because his spinal cord injury was higher than mine. I go quietly to the pond area where there is a little covered chapel outside to sit quietly, reflecting on my entire life and how I wish I could've shared my spirituality and discoveries about eternity with that little boy. Even though I don't have a lot of function, I am dealing with a lot of very hard realities about things I can't do at my age-things I should be able to experience and feel as a sixteen-year old. This little boy did not even get a chance to reach sixteen. He had a spinal cord injury at an even earlier age than me and died. My mind is storming more each year, every day wondering what the purpose of my life is, and hoping it's something great.

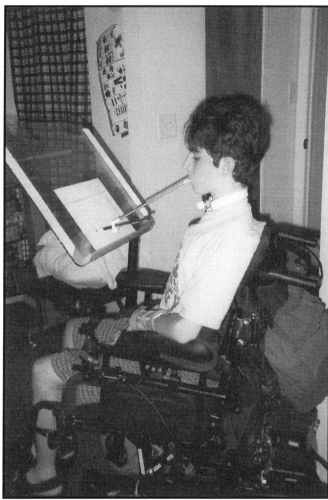

I flirt with one of the counselors who might be a nurse. That helps me pass the time. I try to cheer up and talk to the other kids. I ask that my parents come pick me up early. This will be my last year. I hang out with Dr. Dettorre, taking leisurely walks with the doctors, therapists and nurses that I've known from Hershey. I have one lady assigned to me this year. I can't go anywhere at home either without a nurse or one of my parents by my side. I remember the water balloon battle in the parking lot at the previous location last year with my mentor Ross standing on the back of my wheelchair as I would pop a wheelie. He'd throw water balloons at the other kids while they used their voice-activated water guns on each other.

I tried to keep my eyes on one of the assistants who's my age and extremely cute. Her name is Shannon. She is not much older than me. We write to each other a little through the years and I know she knows I have a crush on her. She has big rosy cheeks, long brown hair, brown eyes, a sexy curvy body, an amazing sweet smile, with a kind, soft and genuine voice. One challenge was for all of the campers to come up with a funny slogan or video commercial. I chose to do clean air and smoking. My helper is in her late thirties, not extremely attractive very skinny and smokes. She has black hair, stands butch strong and introduces me to the Camelback water bag that she uses to go mountain bike racing on the trails. I film her smoking, looking at a tall mountain in the background, while I narrate about clean air. I shown a company banner with its clean air slogan on a truck, as the camera slowly pans down the mountain in the far distance. I show Michelle smoking a cigarette, leaning against a truck, contradicting the commercial for the company. As I narrate the slogan and the campaign directive for the fake commercial she's caught in the act, trying to ruin the commercial as I yell "Cut!" and she runs away.

I don't exactly find myself when I'm at this place. I honestly think it's just a way for me to get away from home. My parents get a break. I have a reserved feeling in my mind. I never fit in or feel comfortable opening up, even though I have more so this year. It's more about me trying to feel like I can still be myself even though I'm extremely disconnected from my physical ability. I need to find my identity and comfort zone. I don't have that yet. In quiet times I create my own adventure during my six-hour drive home. Mostly I spend my time dreaming about my ideal woman. I get little flirting eyes at the end of this week from one of the nurses who wear's my sweater all day. This gives me a little sign of possibilities. I don't know if Michelle was just trying to get me to come out of my shell, but I really think she's cute. She looks like my dream girl, snuggled up in my green and brown hoodie. It fits her perfectly. When I see her sexy feminine shape and smile I can't contain my feelings. My heart is going to burst and my eyes are going to pop out of my head. Now I don't want to leave. I want to take her in one of the mentor's resting tents and strip her naked. I say goodbye to everyone, knowing that I won't be returning. I don't get a huge ovation goodbye. I think some of them are disappointed that I wasn't able to feel comfortable. There's only so much they can do for someone who is paralyzed. I'm sure there's more that can be done. I'm just not open to anything but girls.

I'm ready to look for more schools, hopefully a private school, as summer ends. The lawsuit with the pool company is coming to a terrible end. I need the fourteen million dollars to take care of me for the rest of my life. The court hearing at my house happens. Jeff's grandmother and grandfather attend with their attorneys for the pool company and my lawyers. Crucial questions will decide the outcome. During a five-minute break I see the attorney for the pool company outside my back door talking with his partner attorney and it worries me. It's hard to read their eyes, but what I think they say is "we do not have a case," then we all get back together and sit in a circle between my kitchen and my bed. I'm in the middle of a life sentence that will decide if I will be given a life of excellent quality, or have to struggle to make ends meet.

We sit down again and I feel unbearable, backed into a corner, and don't know what to say. My attorney and his assistant from Clown and Letgo Law Firm offer little help.

Did you ever say to your friend Jeff that if you ever injured your spinal cord diving into his swimming pool that you would not sue his family? The pool company attorney asked me.

Objection! my attorney shouts, standing up.

The attorneys mutter something to each other. The typist's fingers go fast, every letter pounding like a gavel of tiny but walloping judgment. I'm walking into a trap that I can't see with the worst tracking dogs leading me.

Something like that, I say.

In my mind I know I didn't say anything about my spinal cord because I had no knowledge about this type of injury before.

I remember sitting next to Jeff. Jeff was arguing with his dad about us riding dirt bikes and I told Jeff that if I ever got injured I would not sue his family.

After a few more questions everything was over. My words seal the deal. My attorney pats me on the shoulder and walks out quietly.

189

Life! It Must Be a Comedy

This is my life and my future walking out in business suits. I said the wrong thing. My attorneys did not give me advice like I thought they would. Every day my father tells me the money is coming, as if he knows something I don't. I see him holding on to every little piece of hope, and his eyes water when he smiles sometimes.

I pass the days playing video games feeling like I have good company with Kait by my side in her Daisy Dukes shorts. I get excited when she picks me up from my bed to the chair, seeing her wonderful breasts perking through her shirt. I use little things in my mind to dream about women. It is my escape. Still my friends hardly come to visit. Summer is so funny, Jasmine jumps around the room and Carlo goofs around with Summer, flirting with her.

With my straight-A report cards my mother finds a school in Marriottsville, Maryland about forty-five minutes away from my house. My parents would pay out-of-pocket tuition for the next four years for me to start in ninth grade and work myself through twelfth grade. Back to a private school, this time a Presbyterian Christian school. Mr. Kennedy is the principal for my grade. He speaks with a Boston accent, has salt-and-pepper hair combed back, a dark beard and a great big smile full of bright teeth. He's kind of short but taller than my parents, and for once I recognize a principal who speaks softly and means only good things for me and from me. He walks with silent focus and no fearful march. He has a great laugh and a quiet sense of humor. The school is huge. They have a gymnasium and even an elevator for me to get upstairs. Church services are held in the gymnasium (also chapel) once a week. I get a tour around the school by Mr. Kennedy with another kid. I'm on my best behavior, feeling like I'm back in a normal situation. It's just like the other private schools, dozens and dozens of them that I was recruited for it, rejected or simply not wanting to go. For the first time ever I actually want to be in a school. There are no kids except me with a disability. The greatest challenge is finding who I am, trying to be comfortable in a Christian atmosphere in the company of a higher class of students. My straight-A report card is something that the principal can't ignore. With my attitude and my drawings he says I'm going to fit in perfectly. The best thing might be that they don't have anyone doing psychological evaluations. He tells me there is an art class. My mother is extremely excited, she feels like this is God's plan. My mom had videotaped Josie Emerson Armada here, a motivational speaker in a wheelchair. This was Josie's school. When I was in the hospital room recovering, I rejected any possible destiny. If I could help others I would, but I only want to fix myself, if I can.

Chapter 11
Who Am I?

I am still being forced out the door every morning to go to a new school. I'm grumpier in the morning as my nurses arrive late, meeting me at school, forty-five minutes away from home. My mother and my father take turns driving. Mom picks me up using my new van. I've finally return to a normal private school. Chappell Gate Christian Academy is everything I've always wanted in a school. How amazing all of their sport programs are so perfectly set up with a great prep school mentality and a God-fearing teaching environment. I've been to so many schools even before my injury, and it's ironic that I end up in one that has every sport I want to play, but can't. I still don't know exactly who I am, struggling each day, discovering more and more about the person I am growing into, but still not sure what I am comfortably able to share with the world or what I am able to express. I'm insecure, trying to mask any sign that I am crippled, making sure my clothes look cool enough, not too tight against my leg or wrinkled around my thighs. My socks are always folded in the right way, while my shoes are clean and my shirt is always tucked over my belt, like a car seatbelt, hiding its red symbol. It's bad enough I have a chest belt going across and still wear an upper body brace to keep my back straight. Every morning I hide who I am, trying to project a confident mindset of a young man who doesn't need any help with my problems. My hair has to be just right every morning. It's clean-cut, combed back softly, and parted in the front with sides that wave back. I can't believe the image I see in my photograph for the 1999 yearbook. It's a kid that has been uncomfortably whipped into shape.

My school is huge, grades six to twelve. We travel the beltway every morning, arriving later and later, barely making morning announcements. My homeroom teacher Mrs. Hugin is short, but very kind, always wearing a skirt and a business jacket. She has short brown hair, past her ears, wears glasses, and reminds me of Velma from Scooby Doo. My nurses follow me around from class to class and the students don't talk to me too much. Some of my projects in front of the class don't get very many laughs or applauds. One kid fakes his laugh, as one of the students Carlie, acts out the play I wrote for a competition in our writing class. Carlie's mother is one of the Spanish teachers. The title is "Mad about Me" a spinoff title from the popular show "Mad about You" starring Helen Hunt. It's a play on words, with every character having a name like, the main character Itsme, with Notyet, and so on. The main character Itsme invites his friends over to watch his big screen television. The front desk lobby attendant increasingly gets frustrated as the friends with different names and similar usages arrive asking to talk to their friend.

I think the play is hilarious, but I don't feel like going to the front of the class because I'm so embarrassed by my appearance. I've come full circle in my rehabilitation, out of that insane institute and now into the real world where I left off the day of my injury. I've been to dozens of private schools, seen them all, and know the way they operate and how students respond to the way I act. I was always acting out loud and funny. I want to be myself again but without my hands and body I don't know how to bridge that gap. The teenage girls are pretty and I can tell they want to talk to me. Each student passes by me at the end the class where I sit near the door. We make eye contact and I look at them smiling at each other. I've become boring and I sit at the back of every class. Some students talk to me. Others who, are incredibly beautiful, just look back at me, winking their eyes. If I only had some courage of knowing who I am and could project that, I know I could have this one girl. She seems to be a sweet Italian girl, same skin complexion as my own, long straight brown hair, five foot three with a very soft personality, sweet and kind. She gestures *hello* and *goodbye* as all the students rush by at the end of the class. I sit waiting for my nurses to pack up my table connected to my chair, put away my books, write the rest of my homework notes. I try to talk to someone going past me. My nurses explain where my books go, getting frustrated that I'm not listening. The rest of the class walks past before I get a chance to connect with anyone.

Summer comes to me every day as my nurse. We joke around, becoming closer and closer. As I gain some minimal confidence in my classes by myself, she sits outside of the library doing her notes, waiting to meet me in my homeroom where I hide out to eat my lunch away from everyone. I do the same thing with Laura my nurse and any other person, including my mother, who I am embarrassed to have come with me when the nurses are unavailable. It's my own life I have to take charge of. I don't feel like I have any control. I learn more and more each day about the person I am. I am verbally stronger and confident person than I ever knew. My development is intellectual. The cool kid who would push anyone around is still in me, but only comes out when I'm completely comfortable with the people around me and the situation I'm in, to stand up for what I want. Talking with my teacher, some of the kids making up homework come in the class with me and eat their lunch. We actually get along. The cute Italian girl that I have a crush on comes more and more often to do her work. I never say anything to her, not much more than *hello* and maybe something about a class assignment. Her name is Jeanne and I'm attracted to her Italian beautiful, dark, long hair and her sweet personality. She is very soft spoken and very smart. Someday I will have the guts again to be what I need to be. I'll show everyone that they can be comfortable. Most importantly no matter what anyone thinks, I still feel depressed and hidden in my own insecurity. My teacher and I talk a little bit more now about everything I've been through, the amazing journey and how great it would be to share my story someday. I play around with the idea of writing a book about my life. Mrs. Hugin offers to be my shadow writer. I play around at home with my voice dictating software on the computer. I write down notes and thoughts about how I feel occasionally.

Bible class is the most interesting class to me. There is a tall, very pretty blonde girl, Carly, who I like to talk to and sometimes even flirt with a little. She sits next to me in class sometimes. Mr. Askart is my teacher. He's young, tall, with thinning blond hair. He wears glasses and spreads a rumor about being a famous BMX stunt guy just like all of the guys he used to ride with who are now on ESPN X Games. Sitting at the back of the class, I listen to all of the new things that I never knew about religion. I'm finally discovering how to pray and sometimes feel more confident in myself and my life after this life. I'm stronger and my hope is higher that God really is looking out for me. The Trinity and predestination are our main topics. Paul is also a great character in the Bible. With all of his faults, he still created a great following as a leader. My own faults give me my greatest strength. Through adversity I am a better man, and I'm starting to understand what it means to be human. I'm clouded by imperfection. Christ was a great healer, but not healing anyone anymore, especially not me.

Sitting at the back of the class at a table set up for me I find myself next to some of the kids who do not listen so much. There is a girl with long blond hair, who is a little bit rebellious and lazy. I have a flashback into the kid I was. I'm sitting beside myself and I want to shout that there is nothing wrong with her. Seeing this girl sitting next to me doing her homework as Mr. Askart requested, I help her understand some of the lecture. If she asks me for help, it's a great honor. I can see who I used to be. I feel a transformation that all of the hard painful memories I have might have some kind of a chance to change reality for someone else. I don't say much to her but when she asks me how to understand certain things in Spanish class I find myself talking to her more and more. Later, she grows more distant from me only sometimes saying hello with a friendly smile, passing in the hallway. What is more important to me is that I see the little things I said changed her reality. I wish I had someone that would help me understand, but my stubborn bull-headed nature was too strong a force. I could not hear anyone. My energy is different now. This girl is just trying to get answers. It doesn't matter. I'm just helping. Maybe I'll get another chance. I laugh at myself a lot, watching the kids walk down the hallway, messing with each other, how they interact in class. Most of them do not talk to me because my own fears project insecurity and wanting to be left alone. No one can understand what I'm going through. I can see so much more now. It's amazing.

All the popular kids in the school somehow seem smarter than me. This private school is in a richer neighborhood. Even the jocks are interested in their education. Sport events are a huge hang out for all the students.

Mr. Askart asks me if I want to share my story at Thursday chapel. I agree. I've talked in the library about my story for a couple of weeks. I think if I share my story with the whole school and put together some kind of Christian music and slideshow for my speech, some of them will understand and want to change their lives. I see that this could be my purpose. My teacher agrees.

At home my nurses help me with my school work, turning the pages and setting my computer next to my bed against the corner of my room and near my bathroom. My uncle made a corner cabinet with a white and black linoleum stone pattern for my wheel chair to go underneath. This is where I spend most of my days now, on the computer and outside with my dogs. I watch a lot of television, mostly comedy and a lot of action films. At night some of my nurses drive me crazy, like an older black lady who's a little bit senile, but still sensitive to my needs. My television is broken so I borrow my dad's little black-

and-white six-inch. Connecting the cable wire to it late one night, I ask her to change the channel with the little knob, getting some show. My greater struggle is dealing with my sexuality. I don't understand a lot about life, but at the same time I understand more than anyone should at my age. I don't understand how a loving God claims that he is such a great protector and healer, but does not just come down, talk to me, and take away all my problems.

I tell myself it's a great journey like all stories in the Bible, something to grow into, something great. All of it is a painful sacrifice. I vengefully curse at night against God. Fearing that something awful might happen to me, I start laughing, but then I think my words might come back to haunt me. I don't believe God will do anything to make my life worse. How could He? There is so much torture in the mind of a human being like me struggling, who cannot do anything for himself, my own feeling being completely gone. I want to pleasure myself. Every night I change the channel on the little TV and find the nude channels. I think this older night nurse knows what I'm up to, but changes channels for me anyway. I have to urinate in the middle of the night and watching her clean me off tortures my mind. I cannot feel it when she grabs me, but as disgusting as she is somehow I find that I need some release, some kind of sexual gratification. I'm watching these girls in a courtroom, fondling themselves while the judge talks. I need to go to the bathroom. The nurse walks over, inserts the catheter and cleans me off, with one eye on the television and then looks at me. I complain that I'm not clean enough and watch her clean the tip, up and down again as I complain, *it still isn't clean* and watch. She touches me on the face, smiles and says, *I like you.* In situations like this every day, as much as I wish that I could feel it, I clench my eyes closed tight, looking, then looking away, biting my tongue, grinding my teeth, cursing at God in anger and frustration. I need something back. I need to do something about everything I've lost, the pleasure that I really deserve.

I know it's not possible. I get into little arguments my parents and my nurses all the time. It seems so juvenile, but nobody seems to understand that I normally would be able to get up and scratch my nose, to clean something that feels dirty, or to put away some of my baseball cards. I'm more picky and ask for things to be done just right. I don't know other people that are in a similar situation other than Christopher Reeves, who I see on TV occasionally. Arguments come out of nowhere. Nurses threaten to quit, as Summer sometimes does. She gets along more with my brother Carlo, flirting all the time, and I suspect she's actually dating him. I grow more vengeful against her. Nurses have their little ways of expressing their attitudes, slowing down when it comes to my routines or making me stay in bed longer. This tells me whether they really care about taking care of me. I complain to my parents a lot about little things that are huge to me.

The day finally arrives to present my speech, sitting in front of the entire school next to Mr. Askart. As I talk about my life, he asks me questions, becoming more informal, inviting students to ask questions later. I can hear the drum roll and the symphony around me as my adrenaline plays to my imagination. I've never done a big thing like this, but I feel enthusiastic and energized. Something is calling me to do this. I've always been a great performer, ready to step into the lime light in front of everyone as the popular goofball or the baseball athlete. That must be it the reason I feel so comfortable. I'm nervous, but at the same time it all feels like when I would step up to the plate, swinging my bat, gripping my hands tighter and tighter, staring down at the pitcher, waiting for my chance to swing. I feel a similar energy rising right through me. I sit outside the doors waiting to go in.

Are you ready Robert? Mr. Askart says.

I am ready. Let's go get them, I reply.

Chairs are set up in front of the projector with a huge screen that's going to play the slideshow and Christian music of my life before my injury and images after. I know I have to give a great first impression. I watch my childhood from a baby, growing up to play baseball with my brothers and friends and me in eighth grade right before my injury. It makes me cry. The light is turned back on and everyone starts applauding. My microphone is turned on and I am still crying when I turn around to look at the audience. A student is kindly taking charge of the video recorder. Looking around, I see Carly, a different friend from Bible class, close by clapping but not really smiling. I wonder if I did the right thing, if I actually should be here. The questions start and I don't think anyone really knows I'm crying. My energy is not that high, my movements are very subtle when I react, as my breath is not that strong. The first questions come and everything changes. My attitude is uplifted and my message is clear. Explaining the accident, my faith, how I express myself, and how I actually get through the day is a powerful message. As I conclude my speech the last slideshow starts. There are images of my parents and me in my home therapeutic stander with my brothers next to me, pictures of some of my dogs, and some of the teachers and students in this school. The transformation of the new me is revealed to everyone. A few students and friends come down afterwards to pat me on the back. One particular girl I never noticed much before shows more of an interest in me. She's crying profusely, explaining that something similar happened to another one of her friends on the same day. I know I truly got through to some of them. Kids see me differently. I'm still approached with an awkwardness, but I'm able to talk to you on, not just cool kids. My role has changed. I just want others to open up and talk, give them a chance to find out who I am and, discover some good friends.

Mr. Askart told me one sixth-grader broke down in front of him, asking all kinds of questions about his life and how he can change some things. I hope I didn't scare him. Maybe he saw that we have a similar life that we are living. I've open up the eyes of a few other students. It doesn't last long. The end of the year approaches I haven't made any new friends. A few girls invite me to eat lunch with them. Some of the seniors who were not at the speech because of a field trip approached me after watching my video in Bible class. They asked me why I didn't eat with them in the lunchroom. The most gorgeous brunette in the whole school, a senior, showed some interest, but as soon as I said I was hiding because of my appearance she shied away. She got quiet, looked at me with sympathy and went back to her class and we never talked again. My bitterness grows inside against all the students, but somehow I still get up eagerly. I can understand intellectually what I'm being taught. I see all of the cool kids, and kids who are not cool, because that's all that I used to see. I can see right through their stubborn ways and immaturities. The teachers look up to me now as a role model, cutting me some slack if I'm late to class, helping me if I get behind. I don't have to make up some excuse which is a huge relief, because before I just simply would not show up or do any homework. Laughing inside like an epiphany, I see a side of school and life I never did before. I still wish I had the friends and the popularity and everything I know I will not be able to get back, like the sports and the girls I could have a chance with if I showed that I have confidence in my self. I can't find it yet. I know I have much more to offer than anyone else, but I know everyone only sees their own comfort; friendships they can have because of similarities. None of them live near my house.

Understanding so much about the world feels like a curse. The greatest power I have now is the ability to think. Maybe I do too much thinking. I have a good chance to discover more about myself because I'm actually in a normal school environment. It took me a few years to make it here. Even though I'm still struggling so much with everything I've lost, I see that my potential is growing. This side of life is a curse because I had to sacrifice everything I love. Even though it was an accident, sometimes I wonder if God caused it to happen. That's ridiculous. A loving God would never do that. The God I believe in restrained Himself from reaching out to His suffering son and stopping it.

I received a letter today that Cal Ripken Jr. is finally going to see me. This huge amount of good news comes just as I start wondering seriously about what God has to do with anything anymore. God must be listening because I'm finally going to meet my hero. I have thought about this moment for so long, but now that I'm actually going to meet him I'm not sure what to say. I have never thought about what I would talk to him about. It's late in the season and I've brought my black album with all of my favorite Ripken and Orioles baseball cards. I'm accompanied by my mother, Carlo and my mother's parents from Italy who are staying with us for a little while. I'm approaching Camden Yards Stadium and I can see it out my van window. I'm thinking of what questions I should ask him making sure I don't forget. I have my black and white striped turtleneck sweater on. I want Cal Ripken to see me as a strong kid. I don't want him to see my trachea because I'm supposed to be as good as he is. I was supposed to play Major-League Baseball someday.

It is fan appreciation Day and while walking to the lobby elevators the catcher, ace pitcher and first base players walk right past me. I quickly steal a photograph with the first base player while waiting for my elevator to go underneath the stadium where I will meet Cal Ripken. I'm underneath the stadium were no fans ever go, my family is following me as the public-relations lady guides us where to go. My heart is racing and I can hear all of the fans roaring above. We are waiting in a camera room where bases and balls are waiting to be signed by all the players. The room is very small only a ten by ten feet space.

Life! It Must Be a Comedy

Carlo points out between the small opening of the curtains that the left fielder is looking over some video. His sideburns are very recognizable. After waiting patiently for what feels like forever, Cal Ripken reaches his arms through the curtains and in one swooping motion he gallantly spreads his arms and stands tall before me. With a huge smile he starts shaking everyone's hands. He stares into the video camera Carlo is holding and shakes Carlo's hand too. Everyone is taken by his vibrant positive attitude. He is much more friendly and funny than I expected.

It's hard for a hero to live up to anyone's expectations because they are only human. My grandparents never watched baseball coming from Italy. My grandfather is a very short stout man who carries a mean and serious look about him. He slicks his white hair back and doesn't say a word. My grandmother always smiles but looks like her eyes are dipped in vino and when she talks her raspy voice speaks only Italian with a frequent curse or two. She is always laughing and making a comment or just nods her head in elation. I brought my baseball cards and baseballs with his face on them to be signed. Cal pulls a pen out of my grandfather's shirt pocket kindly asking to borrow it.

Cal sits down on top of a red wagon. He isn't worried about any awkwardness or that he is sitting lower than I am. I explain to him about my folder of baseball cards and all of the Orioles players over many years. Cal signs the baseball card with his childhood photograph on it and a 1983 TOPPS rookie card of his. I watch Cal go through all the images as he rests his knee down and his elbow on my arm rest. I point out the image of his father Cal Ripken Sr. when he was coaching the team along with his brother.

Cal stops and replies, "Really?"

We stare at them longer with smiles and we look back and forth at each other. Having Cal Ripken's hands piecing through the images my own hands once touched every day in admiration is too powerful for my emotions to hold back. I never thought I would meet Cal Ripken this way. My family is happy for me just to see me meet the hero every boy dreams of becoming. With every ex Orioles player Cal looks at I sense Cal's own reflection in his career after so many years playing.

Ripken points out one baseball card of Eddie Murray from the eighties. He has a huge afro and is standing in the Orioles dugout.

Ripken asks me, "Can I have this? I want to show this with the guys?"

Life! It Must Be a Comedy

Eddie is currently on the team but I can't part with any of my cards. I want to give the card to Cal but I'm too attached to them. I should have given it to him. Cal is late for batting practice but I could spend all day with him. I tell Cal Ripken I'm going to paint his portrait. Just like the way he has inspired me as an athlete, I'm going to take my artistic ability and inspiration I get from him every day to be the best just like him. Our blissfully meeting is over and just as quick as he appeared before me he goes back to the grid iron and where he came from. The legend of the Ironman is real. Even though we live completely different lives I still believe the greatness in Cal Ripken Jr. is the same thing I have in me. Cal goes back to his field of legends and mythology that will forever be written in the stars and the hearts of man. I sit in the best seats behind home plate watching the game. I hold my sign up proudly knowing Cal will be looking for it, saying "Hi Cal!" I look upon the field knowing it stands before me a place that identified the purpose of my existence. I've held the heart after the birth of this great fields star close by my heart my whole life. My own recovery now is stirring the cosmos for the birth of another star. The explosion is violent, but great in its own way inside of me shining very bright and far.

Life! It Must Be a Comedy

Later, after school, my nurse Laura and I attend one of the soccer games. It's a chilly day and the grass is incredibly bumpy. I see my classmates but they are on the other side of the field. At halftime some of the girls come over as we go to the other side where the team is. I cough up a little bit of mucus. Laura catches it, but I should look out for my lungs. Once the game is over, returning home, it's harder to breathe. Green mucus is showing up around my trachea. This is the first time I've watched my classmates play sports. I sense that I might be in great danger. When I get congested my trachea is suctioned. I dread that long skinny tube in my throat, sucking until it feels like I'm going to lose consciousness, as my blood pressure drops and anxiety starts. My mother drives me home. I'm coughing and barely able to breathe. My greatest fear is are also my lungs. I know what happened to me once in recovery and I don't want it to happen again. My instincts are usually right about my body. I cannot feel or move most of anything below my chest, but I know when something is wrong, like if my hips are sideways or my foot is slightly off. I always know when I have to go to the bathroom, because the skin on my head starts to tingle and I get hot and red.

I don't go a few hours without having to pound on my chest and suctioning more, as my lungs tighten in pain. The mucus is getting more and more green. Somehow I last through the night, but the nurse is completely out of it. She is crazy and not aware of my desperate attempts to catch my breath, trying not to pass out from lack of oxygen. She's not one of my regulars like Summer or Laura. She tells me all I need to do is rest and sleep and I will feel better. She doesn't do any work for me in the middle of the night. She sleeps and I have to desperately call for her, which wakes my parents and then they wake her up to do her job. Marilyn is so old and overweight, I can't stand being around her lazy African-American attitude. Most nights when I'm yelling I sing, *Mary, Mary, quite contrary, how does your garden grow?* I know she doesn't hear me. She stands over my bed as I roll my eyes, hardly catching my breath, trying to explain desperately, for anyone to listen. Summer arrives in the morning, takes my saturation, noticing my blood oxygen level is at 93 percent. Anything below ninety-five percent is extremely deadly. There must be something wrong because she calls the ambulance. Summer and my mother struggle to keep me breathing until the ambulance takes me out the backdoor. Fluffy and Jasmine are right by my side, not wanting to leave, as they usually sleep right under my bed, always loyal, faithful and concerned.

I arrive at North Arundel Hospital where my mother works. In the emergency room, I'm barely able to breathe as brown secretions are suctioned. My family has often found that the medical staff doesn't take good precautions at this hospital. I struggle to keep conscious, telling the doctors I'm really in trouble. They choose to put me in a recovery room until another emergency room opens up. Slipping in and out of consciousness, dumbfounded and distraught, I sit in the dark room with another patient and a monitor, with no nurses to suction me. I'm cut off completely. I scream out to my mother. She tries to pacify me. I grow desperate, fearing for my life, yelling at my mother, crying out to God, so tired. I cannot move and no one will listen to me. I am desperate. Mom tells me to relax, but looking at my blood oxygen level she can't ignore it. She goes out to the end of the hallway to get a doctor, and coincidentally walking down the hall sees my long-time pediatric doctor Dr. Rolling. The timing is perfect, he treats me immediately. He is surprised to see me. With his stethoscope around his neck, his skin folds and wrinkled face have never been a better sight to me. He greets my mother with his chipper smile, relaxed attitude and chuckling. He takes one look at me and immediately calls the nurse to get me into the emergency room.

Slipping into more and more respiratory failure, my greatest fear has become reality. The doctors cannot figure it out, so they tell me they need to actually go down with a long tube and small camera to suction out everything. The doctor makes the decision that there's no time to wait. My breath has become crackled and my secretions have turned solid brown and crusty. Any second now could be my last breath, as the doctors race to surgically suction out my lungs to keep me alive. I am so weak. I wake up able to breathe slightly. I have tubes down my nose and my trachea is attached to a ventilator and oxygen. A very kind nurse is there. I'll never forget her funniness, as she turns me every four hours, with chest PT, giving me breathing treatments, suctioning out everything to get me healthy again. I'm so thankful to be taken care of. I don't mind the excess fat and skin on her arm and all over her body, when normally I would be disgusted. After ten days in the hospital I get a visit from a couple of students. I guess I'm just thankful enough to feel happy that I am alive. I never got any respect from the students in school in the past, but somehow their bright smiles and attitudes cheer me up. I can't stop smiling and laughing. It's hard to breathe with my enlarged trachea (from surgery) that still bleeds a little. To my surprise they invite me to a huge party that they are throwing for the most popular kids in school. I get a few letters and they visit one more time. They are impressed that I go through something so hard. They see I am a really good guy. I'm so happy they invited me.

      As more students visit, it is my first chance to really see what these kids are all about. I stay home playing video games with Robert and Carlo. A group of guys my age who sit at the senior table come to visit me. The only teacher who really reaches out to me is Mr. Magnusson. We call him Mr. Mag. He's a jolly older man with white and black hair. In class he throws his weight around in a funny way as his neck slaps, the skin flaps, when he shakes his head in surprise to some of the student's answers. He speaks with a funny Maine accent, talking about eating lobster. When I get back to school work, I have one math class with him. He talks to me like no other teachers do. All the other students are frightened by this big misunderstood guy with a mean personality who cracks jokes in class, pushing the students to go farther than they think they can. He brings over a group of popular goofballs I've never talked to. We all take photos together. One of them takes one of my surgical gloves and puts it over his head than blows it up as large as possible. I show them my bedroom and my artwork. Mr. Mag says I sign my name with my mouth on my paintings better than some of the kids do with their hands. I have a seat at the popular table waiting for me when I come back to school. Mr. Mag singles me out to guide younger minds.

      Going back to school is not easy. I have made so much progress, but this setback embarrasses me. Tom sees me in the front lobby. I am definitely late. Coaxing me out in my van, I can see the look on Tom's face, he is surprised. I break down in tears. Dad doesn't know what to do, instead tells me to stop acting like a girl. He never talked to me like this before, he is frustrated. In Bible class, all the students give me a warm welcome. Carly is the first. Then I'm greeted by Amy, another sweet girl with a long ponytail and innocent personality. She doesn't talk much, but I can tell she's sensitive enough to be a friend. She had a repaired cleft palate. She has a little bit more sensitivity than most of the kids. She reassures me. I'm not grasping Spanish very well, but I try not to let it show.

My first year of high school comes to an end. The picture of myself and the kid with the balloon over his head makes the yearbook. It's been nice spending some time in the lunch room with them. Mr. Mag was definitely there, pushing me along. It's awkward having to ask people to give me my food. Some are embarrassed to do that. I try, but I just can't accept this is who I am. Until I can, I don't think I'll be comfortable relying on people or having someone help me go to the bathroom. When my friends hang out it's hard to ask them to do things for me. If I can't get over that, I'm not going to have the things I want.

Another summer passes. It's my favorite time of the year because of no school and warm weather and not wearing so many layers of clothing. It was a very quiet summer, kind of lonely. I play video games and get more interested in my art. Videogames are frustrating, but starting to become a source of strength. I'm still introverted. I continue praying for a sign or some sort of miracle. I don't think it'll ever happen, but I never give up hope. I don't know if God operates like that or if that is even right for me to think that. I still have so many questions. I thought maybe a lot of them would be answered this summer, but I guess I have to go through another confused school year.

The art teacher Mrs. Bonnell invited me to be in her class last year, but I was too embarrassed by my appearance. Mrs. Bonnell is no exception for an art teacher by her appearance. She has long strangling blond and white hair and walks very slow with the flow of her long dresses. She is a middle-aged woman wrapped around her own world of art. She might not be the first to cheer me up if I had a horrible day, but Mrs. Bonnell and I debate and talk about art a lot. This year I might try, without some of the turtlenecks hiding my trachea. Even a cool new haircut parted, colored frosted blonde on top, fading toward the front, could help. My hair looks just like I had it in eighth grade before my injury. Maybe this is who I am. I'm a cooler kid now, with an invitation to the cool kid corner and a great haircut.

The same nurses come into my classes this year. Mark is in my Spanish class. My teacher assigned him to help me with my homework and flipping pages. The year before when he helped me in class with some assignments we got along because we are both very quiet and don't

Life! It Must Be a Comedy

feel like we fit in. I thought he was funny and had potential to be one of the cool guys.

We are definitely an awkward pair. He has a lot of attitude that I try to help him actualize. Mark has no real style. He's one of the dorky kids with a button up plaid shirt and plain dress pants and dress shoes. He doesn't smile much and always has a serious but mild mannered look on his face, and his hair doesn't help him, short blond and combed forward. He is not comfortable in his own skin and doesn't want to be in this school. Mark is introverted, slightly overweight and definitely not one of the jocks. We goof around a little bit, talk about movies. It's refreshing.

I'm glad he agreed to volunteer to help me. We're both shy off to ourselves, glad we have each other. I've been around so many kids like that before. Those were the kids I used to always tease and beat up. I'm glad I get a chance to talk with him. I don't think I'll influence him much, but at least he knows he got someone that's a good friend. Lucky for him, because now he has a friend that's one of the cool kids. My new Spanish teacher this year Mrs. Flynn assigned another volunteer student for me and gave her class credit for helping me. Mrs. Flynn always has a big smile and wears her hair short and spiky. She's the friendliest Spanish teacher I've ever had and her generosity and good heart always makes me feel like I could do no wrong. The student assigned to me is the prettiest girl in school, the most flirtatious, and tall with lots of personality. Her name is Lindsay. I can't keep my eye off her, a pin-up model future, long blonde hair with highlights and perfect features. Her clothes push the boundary of acceptable private Christian school wear, black-and-white zebra stripes and short skirts to match. She looks much older, but is actually two grades younger. Mark and I just roll our eyes as we sit in the back of the class flirting with her. She leans over to turn my pages while I lean back and look at Mark with a big grin and he leans back, rolling his eyes, sighing and putting his hand over his face, tapping his foot.

High school is not too bad right now, even though I am getting there later and later sometimes not even showing up to home room. Certain things I can get away with, like wearing my long sleeved sweater on cold days with my hoodie up.

"Under the Bridge" Watercolor. 11 by 15

Life! It Must Be a Comedy

In my own awkward way I'm a small influence with kids who are shy, also helping the popular kids see things differently. I'm treated with kindness by some of the extraordinary students. I'm sorry for the way I treated some people when I was younger. Now I'm sharing who I really am inside.

I use my mouthstick in art class to draw flowers and a bench, creating perspective with my eye. There's music on during class while we all work on our projects, painting or drawing. There are a lot of seniors in my class. Being eighteen years old in tenth grade I feel like I am in the right class. Another girl was assigned to help me. She's a short dark-haired girl with a snippy attitude. My nurses Summer, Laura and Regina seem to have a lot of fun goofing off in art class. Sometimes they leave me in my class by myself while the teacher or another student helps me.

This is my time to shine. I practice at home with watercolor brushes doing ink on the tip of a toothpick to draw bridges over my watercolor landscapes. I illustrated the bridge Jeff and I were under in one painting. It illustrates us sitting under the bridge when the cop approached to question us.

We are assigned to do a self-portrait. At Kennedy Krieger I saw a video about a man with paralysis who painted enormous portraits on a huge forklift painting in squares. These little pieces of color from a photograph created an exact copy of a picture. My teacher drew a grid using an overhead projector using an eight by ten piece of white paper. Then she drew it over a photograph of me from a summer I wanted to do some modeling. I'm wearing my favorite Bugs Bunny hat backwards looking over my shoulder at the camera with a cute expression and water-drop eyes smiling. My trachea is hidden. I work my mouthstick, pushing stroke after stroke, filling in every little square, week by week, noticing my picture coming to life.

It is finally finished and all of our artwork goes up in the school lobby for a show. Everyone notices my picture is absolutely beautiful. The black mat and frame make it stand out. After school, as kids get picked up, their parents walk around and I can hear some of them talking about me and my drawing, describing how I did it with my mouth. They are mesmerized and give me smiles, patting me on my shoulder.

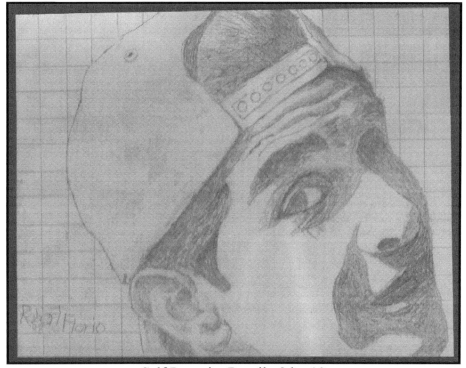

Self Portrait. Pencil. 8 by 10

A stranger approaches me while I am leaving school one day. He asks if I can raise my left arm very high. I can raise it a decent enough height. I feel extremely uncomfortable. He starts speaking to me very bluntly, as if he is only interested in examining me and not any kind of conversation. I began to feel extremely uncomfortable.

Why do you ask? I reply.

Interesting. I see your wrist is supported by a splint. You cannot move your wrist? the man askes.

No I can't move my wrist, I reply.

Oh. I thought you could move your wrist that's how you drive your chair. Anyway, I am a surgeon. I do hand surgeries on people to help them move their hands. People like you. People in wheelchairs, the man explains.

He does implant surgery to help quadriplegics regain function of their hand movement by implanting wires and elect roads under the skin called the Freehand System. In the back of my mind I have hope. I don't know if I am just being naive. His name is Dr. Edgslerman. He has three kids in my school, but I have no idea who they are. Maybe this summer I will have the surgery. I'm not sure yet.

My first meeting with this doctor is in the kitchen of his house. He holds my hand, explaining how supple my skin is, reassuring that this is the right surgery for me. He hands me a pamphlet and shows me a video of him in front of an audience describing the results from other people's surgeries. Maybe this is what I've been looking for. All my hard work and sacrifice, all of my faith is that this is a chance to regain use of my hand.

Sitting in my shower chair, hot water running over my head feels just like it always has. The prospect of more function, raising and lifting my left arm so I can reach something can be a reality if I get these electrode implants in my arm and wrist. I'll be able to open and close my fingers. My bicep is very strong and have a lot of dexterity and can keep my wrist from flopping around so easily. My right arm just hangs down the side of my chair all the time. I don't think it would be very functional since I can't reach things with it now. I fear losing any function, even though the doctor told me that I would have the same strength. That's very encouraging. Everything looks positive that the surgery would be a success, but I'm still not ready. I don't think I want the surgery just yet.

The school year is ending. Summertime returns, four months of hot weather for Maryland and me. I prefer hot to the risk of getting sick from cold weather. I'm dragging out my high school years, knowing that by the time I graduate I'll be twenty. Though my faith has reached a level of understanding from Bible class that reassures me, at times I break down and cry. It doesn't happen very often. I sit alone in my house, watching the Baltimore Orioles and Ravens play. I hope someday I can meet my favorite field-goal kicker Matt Stover. I am grumpy when I wake up, though I still have decent nurses to take care of me. They have common sense. Regina is a tall lady in her early forties. She's a huge horse lover. She used to train them and talks about them all the time. She's got curly, long dirty blonde hair and a tom-girl attitude. She usually wears jeans every day and shows some wit. She has a funny way of cursing when something doesn't go her way. My three nurses don't follow me around all the time, like others would; they understand what I need. Some days I don't feel like going outside even if it's a beautiful summer day. I watch Robert skate outside, watch TV, channel surf and surf the net or write in my journal.

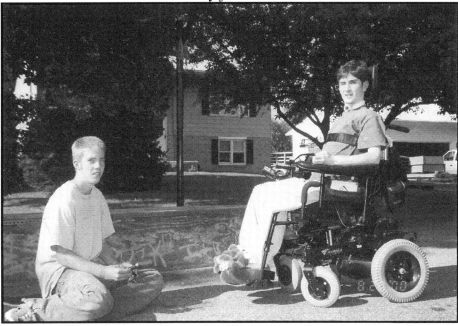

I still feel a loss of hope that I'll never walk again. It's in the back of my mind every day. I act like a strong young man trying to find himself, but I feel broken in pieces and never in control of anything. My dogs cheer me up, especially Fluffy who lies up against my chair, leaning his head back. He has soft furry cheeks for me to rub. I can't feel him anymore. No one has dropped by for so long. Often, I'm really mad. At least I'm finally off of that stupid bus and away from the crazy people at that school in Baltimore. I feel like I'll always have these challenges. The doctors don't tell me everything. Stem cell surgery seems hopeless because nobody has had a successful recovery yet that I know of.

I have no privacy because my bedroom is connected to the kitchen even though it has a door. Everyone hangs out there. My mother does the laundry in there. I have no room to move around either. I need money to make my life comfortable and we don't have enough. My dad comes home around eight p.m. and has something disturbing on his mind.

Well, the attorney told me today the result of our case, he explains.

Life! It Must Be a Comedy

*What they said is... According to what you said Robert...According to the judge...*Dad further explains.

What! What did they say? I ask.

Remember when they asked you the question about whether or not you would ever sue your friend if you got injured at his house?

Yes, what about it? I reply.

Well, the judge said that...Because you admitted you are aware of the risk of injuring your spinal cord, that we had no case to prove you are innocent against the pool company.

I can hardly catch my breath, horrified that my attorneys did not catch that trick question.

What! No way. There is no way, I say.

I'm sorry. I agree with you. The attorney should have caught that and explained to the judge that what you meant.

Dammit! You've got to be kidding! I never admitted I had any awareness of injuring my spinal cord. I only said if I ever got injured but I said, "something like that." I didn't mean that at all. I had no clue about this kind of injury. Those stupid attorneys for the pool company are slick. They knew they had me as soon as I gave that answer, but I did not mean it like that! I explain.

My attorneys at Clown and Letgo shouldn't say, "We fight for you," because they are the worst attorneys in the world, I say mockingly and furious.

All my hopes of having a secure future with money I need to live a comfortable life were taken away. I know my life will be a struggle, more than just physical. I sink into my own depression, the days press on my mind and spirit. I do not understand why God still just doesn't help me. I always feel screwed over.

On the weekend, my parents take care of me. Looking out the back yard glass sliding door I meditate to myself with my hands in my lap, knuckles over each hand trying to stretch my fingers out, just looking down into my palm, wishing I could squeeze. I think about everything I've lost. I pray and talk to God in a normal way that is completely one-to-one. I bring Him down on my level because I don't believe he knows what it's like to suffer like I do. When I curse Him, I fearfully ask for forgiveness right away so I don't get injured again. I laugh when I think about it though, how primitive and naïve I've been, believing in someone who calls Himself a Father, but never shows up like one. God wouldn't injure me anymore, would he? He wouldn't be that big a jerk.

God, I know that you have sent Jesus down to live, to sacrifice everything for us, to give us eternal life through faith. But do You really know what it's like to suffer? Do you help your children anymore? I don't think You do. We read your Bible and all of the preachers on TV sucker us into giving them money. You help them become rich and famous and successful. Are we to follow their footsteps? That is a bunch of crap. Don't You heal anyone like you used to do you? I am so frustrated and so tired of struggling. I don't even have the words anymore to ask You for what I need or want because I'm so tired of never receiving it. I don't know why Jesus waited three thousand years to come. I don't know why You let the Jews suffer for two thousand years before actually helping them. Do you enjoy watching us suffer? Use the power You have and your love you claim You have for us, like our Father. I know my father would never let me suffer. In fact, my father would trade his life in one second for me to have a better life trading places with me. If you claim to be my Father why don't you do the same?

My emotions get the best of me, breaking out, releasing fear like I haven't in such a long time. The tears roll down my face with my exhausted hiccups of breath. I look up at God directly, my soul reaching out like a shining beacon through the clouds, straight through the space in heaven to be acknowledged that my prayer was actually heard. *You will hear everything that I have to say. I have to be answered. If You do not, You are not my God. I believe You will answer them in time. Why not now? I don't understand much. There is so much to understand. We were created in this flawed body, supposedly to be perfect. You put things on this earth that would always tempt us. It's Your fault that we suffer. You can't give a human being a conscious mind then say "it's in your image," when everything about you is fake. You deserve to go to hell, not us. You can't sit there while we suffer and not reach out and do your job of healing. The human race is no longer going to stand for that. I don't know why we keep our faith. I know now why people choose not to believe.*

But You have showed me a different side that is very beautiful. I am the only person who can see it this way. My brothers aren't willing to see it because they have their bodies. They don't have to think the way I am forced to think.

This is my prayer. I am asking You now to answer everything. Always be there for me and always lift me up and give me strength. You owe me at least this. I will be your strongest and greatest ally if You let me. Maybe somehow make these years and months go by very fast so that someday if I am healed it feels like a minimal amount of time. I don't want to fast forward that much, but I honestly believe that You will give me everything I want from now on. Rather, You will give me what I need. If my life will be a struggle for money, if money is what makes this world go round and I cannot have it to make myself live comfortably then I only ask you to at least let me know You were the one who answered my call.

I release one last yell at the top of my lungs with all the strength my half-paralyzed diaphragm allows me. I pray Christ's name. I stare back through the clouds as far as I can. I am seeing straight into heaven, straight into God's eyes. *I will not be ignored anymore. I will be a force to be reckoned with.*

I debated whether or not this surgery is for me. After trying to grab a pen with my left arm I have coordination to maneuver it to the edge of the table. Getting it into my fingers, but not being able to squeeze is what made me decide. I will have this surgery. After more consultation at the doctor's house and another at the hospital, I'm still nervous. The doctor tells me he is, *"ninety-nine point nine percent sure and confident that the surgery will be a success."* I am ready. This must be what God had planned- the sacrifice, and now, the reward. The night before the surgery, I call Joyce the therapist who works with the doctor. I know she can tell from my voice that I may not show up the next morning.

I do show up. I'm prepared for surgery. My mom signs the papers. The doctor gives with me the final paper giving permission for him to perform the surgery. Then I'm sent to anesthesia. In seven hours we'll see whether my life will change by being able to hold things again.

My eyes open. The doctor is leaning over me asking me if I am awake, telling me I will soon be in the recovery room and can have the tube taken out of my nose. My last-minute request before going under was concern about plastic surgery--hoping the scars around my arm and my chest would not be too obvious. I was reassured that the doctor's precision is as good as a plastic surgeon's.

I wake on the table and I can feel a sharp pain behind my left shoulder and I say so. They assure me everything is fine so I fall back asleep still in the operating room, waiting to be comforted later by my mother in the recovery room. There is something sticky on my eyes and my left arm is in a brace, straight out, to keep my fingers and blood flow corrected for optimal healing. Has something gone wrong? I don't know. Is this what I was supposed to wake up to? I don't know.

I have a gut reaction, a sick feeling that this was not supposed to happen. I slip into fear and anxiety. I begin to cry and shout out for someone to wipe my eyes. They are starting to burn from whatever liquid is covering them. After an hour of shouting and crying for someone to get my mother I realize the truth. I have been tricked. I have severe discomfort and all of my dreadful memories from when I first was injured are starting to flashback, the same feelings I had in that hospital room, paralyzed again for the first time. I cannot believe that in this environment of health care professionals no nurse has come over to help me. I'm wondering where am I and why this is happening. This is torture. God, why have you set me up like this? I get a feeling that something has gone terribly wrong. I trusted You God. With my eyes closed for what seems like hours, I'm afraid to open them because of the burning sensation. I'm crying and screaming for help. This must come to an end. I open my eyes but all I see is a blur and the stinging gets worse.

What is wrong Robert? A man says.

My eyes are burning! I have been crying for someone for an hour! I need a wet cloth to wash my eyes please! I pleaded.

Robert I am not a nurse, the voice says.

What! So?! You can still help me, please!

I do not know who this person is. I hope it's not the doctor. My frustrations are filled with hatred from his misleading words of comfort. Finally someone washes my face and my eyes with a cool wet cloth. I open my eyes and see a blur of a shadowy figure. After another hour, Mom arrives and I explain all these frustrations and delays. The doctor said it was all going to be fine, and he would even let me have this tube out of my nose.

Life! It Must Be a Comedy

I was calling for you, and nobody would come help me. My eyes were burning for an hour. What the hell is going on? This fucking doctor! If I could I would choke him. They said they would not get you for me, but they wouldn't help me themselves! I cry.

We wait three days in the hospital for the swelling to go down and the pain to decrease. I ask for and received more morphine. The Benadryl on top of more morphine makes it impossible to relax. My mind is sensitive and paranoid to every movement in the room. My muscles can't stop twitching.

Even when the doctor shows up to explain the progress with my tendons and fingers, he disappears quickly, giving me the impression something has gone wrong with the operation. I'm lying in my bed and a throbbing pinch is coming from the back of my left shoulder. Summer and my mother lean me forward to see what I have been complaining about ever since waking up in the operating room. They pull out a tiny metal staple that is lodged under my skin. It must have fallen behind me on the operating table during surgery, but I have no idea what it's from. Every day I heal reveals more of the debacle that this surgery has become. It might be naïve of me to put so much faith in this surgery, but it's all I know and I've thought about for so long. It's been a few weeks and the electrodes are turned on. The therapist guides my hand as I raise and lower my right shoulder. The sensor joystick sends a message to the wire circle taped over the implant in my left chest below my collarbone. My hand is opening and closing and shaking from fatigue, which should get better as the muscles warm up from the electricity and build stamina. Trying to grab an upside-down plastic cone my fingers stretch around it.

This is the moment of truth, what I have waited so long for. My hand closes as I lower my shoulder. My fingers are around the cone as it gets narrow at the top and wider at the base. This is the standard test all patients with this implant take. The doctor watches. His arms crossed, quiet, in his scrubs looking through his glasses with blood on his shoes. I wait to see his reaction. I anticipate a sense of failure. He says nothing. The therapist tells me to lift my arm. As I bend my elbow I feel something different. The tendon transfer has transferred too much of that strong muscle. The doctor was so proud that my strength would never be less, to keep my wrist from falling, because it was so strong. My elbow hurts. Every day my arm quivers from the pain in my elbow and the loss of function from the tendon transfer in my wrist created.

My elbow pops, it pinches all the way up my arm down through my fingers, and I've even started losing dexterity in my forearm muscles. That muscle is too weak to bring my arm up. My fingers have slipped right through the cone. My hand comes up, but I am unsuccessful, not grabbing it. I try again and again. Joyce is frustrated, but does not give up, with the doctor looking over my shoulder. She sighs and pats me on the shoulder. The doctor mumbles something about what might have happened during surgery. As he walks out of the room I can feel his disgust, but his arrogance doesn't allow him to show much emotion or any concern that the surgery may not have worked.

Weeks go by with no real progress. I keep looking for a simple explanation or show of concern, maybe a show of confidence and support that he won't give up, but I don't get that from the doctor. A simple sign of looking forward to my progress to see what comes from this surgery, to gain my trust and confidence in his hands, but nothing ever comes from him. He walks away, silent and cold, like a vigilante or the superhero who doesn't want to get caught in the act of helping someone but really making their life worse. Afraid to admit he was wrong, not concerned for my body or respect for my life, when a simple explanation is needed. I'm left in the dark. I get more frustrated as my fingers get worse, no longer staying straight. The tendons were tightened in my fingers and thumb including a pinched tendon in my wrist to keep them all straight so I can reach around objects. My fingers start deforming and curving unnaturally, skinny, as the green sutures pooling the tendons are seen through my skin on my knuckles.

I have more therapy as the adjustments are made. I'm sent to another rehab hospital to help my hand open and close and my thumb to get more electric stimulation to fine tune the pinching grasp with the computer to the implant in my chest. When summer ends I return to school. Each visit with the therapists and doctor at the rehab hospital I am more vengeful toward them. The pain I have experienced from my elbow and loss of function still continues. I have to learn how to reuse my arm with compensation. I sacrificed one thing for another. I put the device and shoulder position censure and switch on almost everyday, brushing my teeth with it, but hardly able to figure out how to do anything else. It seems simple enough, my hand opens up and I close it with two computer programmed grasping positions, pinching and one for grabbing cups. The fingers don't extend far enough to reach around an object, and every time I hold something to it put in mouth I can't rotate my wrist, I crush the object or it falls out. I look at my fingers; they are deformed because the tendons were tightened. What have I become? The attempts I have made to better myself have instead left me bitter, lost, frustrated and not sure of how to look at this positively. I know the risks and benefits now, and some of them outweigh each other, but from everybody else's eyes (who are not in my position) it's hard to understand my loss. I put my faith so high in God and in this doctor, for what I wonder? Maybe I'm looking at it all wrong, but hopefully someday I'll understand the sacrifice. Right now I couldn't be more determined to fight back. The angels and demons on my shoulder are playing for the same side. Everything that is up is down and I can't see how this makes sense, because I've been given an opportunity, I just wasn't told I would be responsible for what happens on the ride. I'm blindfolded and told to find my own way through the trails and tricks. The guide I've been given is not easy to follow. I look to higher powers and even myself to decide what decisions to make, but my body is malfunctioning and so are the powers and I look to. No one knows how to fix the mechanisms of my mindful heart, but me.

      The new school year begins. I try to find my dreams in art more every day. I amaze people with my portrait of Cal and still I'm bothered. My attention is now on my hands. Sitting at the lunch table with the other students, I am now able to hold my sandwiches. I began to laugh to myself. I look around the room. I know the doctor's three kids, three daughters and one son. I now know their faces and see them when we pass by in the hallways. His oldest is his daughter who is in my grade. My thumb has pinched straight through the sandwich. I can't get the shoulder sensor to open my hand. It crumbles in my hand and falls in my lap. I'm extremely frustrated with the results of this surgery. I sit at the end of the table with the cool kids, and they hand my lunch to me placing it in my shaking opened grasp. No one says any words or any comments about me being able to open my hands. I am least happy about it not working. Sharp pain continues to pierce through my elbow and up and down my arm. I have no idea what they see or think but we don't open up to each other and I feel more disconnected from them. I can never relax and be myself. I am consumed by the doctor's guarantee of success because it has been a lie. My friends stare at me. I'm filled with fear and start searching for an attorney to sue the doctor.

Cal Ripken Jr. Pencil. 11 by 15

Rumors spread through the school about my disappointment. Even the doctor's wife is upset. No one ever says anything to me, I feel paranoid that his daughter and family see me using my hand. Frustrated and sad, I'm paranoid that they are talking about me. I would not want to live with the kind of man who is running my life. His children are quiet, very book smart. His son looks exactly like him with the same arrogant look on his face acting like the cool kid in class.

After thirty attorneys, nobody is taking my case. It has become an obsession. I no longer sit at the table with the other students. Even my relationship with Mr. Mag starts to deteriorate. One day we have a guest speaker. As he is introduced, my jaw almost hits the floor. It's Matt Stover, the field-goal kicker for the Baltimore Ravens. I've watched him in his number three jersey kicking for a horrible team. His famous fingers point straight to the sky thanking God after every kick. Listening to Matt talk about his life story is so encouraging. He says it's

221

all a blessing from God. I want to ask him a question. Maybe I'll get some answers, have some fun, and maybe become a friend. I sit by myself in the gym for Chapel. I raised my arm and Mr. Fry, the school counselor, holds the microphone to my mouth. My comment is funny, but not very well received by Mr. Fry. He stands quite tall and lengthy, skinny with a very short haircut, balding, with a cracked smile about my comment. The students start laughing.

I have a question. Are you that kicker on the Ravens who scores all of our points and who set the record on consecutive field goals made?

Yes I am, Matt replies with a chuckle.

Wow, that's you? That is so amazing. My dad and I watch every game. We keep saying to ourselves that the Ravens really suck. If it wasn't for you we wouldn't win any games.

Well thank you. I really appreciate that, Matt replied.

I speak with Matt after chapel and get his e-mail address. I think a prayer came true. He could be that great friend that I need. I keep in touch with Matt through e-mails. Occasionally he buys tickets for my father and me. We go to one of the opening games. Being a Christian, Matt has expressed that he is definitely blessed and someday I could have the same thing, if God guides me. I don't know about all that, especially with what's going on in my life, but I always keep hope alive, believing that God looks out for me always. Someday I'll have everything I ever wanted. I do believe that.

My good friend Matt Stover gives me some encouragement every once in awhile as we e-mail back and forth. It's so much fun. He gives me passes to watch him practice at training camp and for a couple of games this year. After training camp I get my football signed by the entire 2001 Ravens as they were running past the fans and I stood in their path. After practice, Matt and I talk about football and the Ravens, anticipating a Super Bowl run. Brian Billick the coach walks over. Matt tells the coach he should bring me on the field with them and the coach looks at me. I smile, hoping he would say yes, but we share a friendly conversation instead. We won the Super Bowl this year. I am friends with possibly one of the greatest field-goal kickers, if not the greatest field-goal kicker in the history of the entire NFL.

The year is almost over. It feels like one big joke. Laura sits with me occasionally as I eat lunch now at the little table in front of the library, with a few of the other outcast dorky kids who joined me part of last year and all of this year. Laura asks whether I think I should graduate or just get my GED and get the heck out of there. I see her point and it is tempting. I know I don't belong in school anymore because I don't want to be twenty years old when I graduate. I'm taking summer classes at Anne Arundel Community College for drawing. All my friends have abandoned me. I'm feeling neglected because of the hand surgery. A rumor is spreading that I am suing the parents of one of the other seniors. I speculate more in my mind.

Traveling the hallways, Summer and I are interrupted and grabbed aside by the librarian, Mrs. Breen, an older lady with white curly hair who always wears long dresses and reminds me of a fairy godmother. She's distressed as are the students gathered around the television set in the library. It looks like New York City is up in flames. One of the tallest towers has smoke pouring out. We're horrified in disbelief. Some sort of Biblical happening is in our minds since we have Bible class and go to a church school. Summer's jaw drops. Everyone is quiet. Before my eyes, in a blink, a second aircraft slams into the other tower. The newscasters are shocked. All the channels are broadcasting this. Students start pouring out of classrooms calling their parents and walking into the gymnasium. We start to pray. *"Today is September the*

11th 2001," the broadcasters continue to repeat on the television. Today our nation is forever changed. The stations repeat these visions. They are replayed every day. I see people's faces as they run away from the tumbling towers that are crushing people. I will always remember where I was, just like everyone who witnessed this event. Perhaps I can choose to be happy, feeling like I have some security in my life, even though the entire nation is emotionally demoralized.

I give up my cool guy haircut. I'm ready for graduation. I don't know what I'm thinking but I definitely don't like my new cut. An old friend of mine, Curtis, from Odenton (we used to ride dirt bikes every day together) has been staying with me for more than a year now. He is just about to fly back to home to Florida as I realize that even though he's an old friend, the entire time he has been there he has ignored me, and hardly hung out with me at all. He skateboards with Robert and his friends, even flirts with Stephanie next door (which makes me mad because I've always wanted to get near her and couldn't). Curtis hangs out down the street with the kids in the neighborhood to do drugs, getting in trouble so he is kicked out of my house. He moved in with Adrian when Adrian bought his first house. Both of them got kicked out at the same time for some dumb thing I don't remember, except Curtis hid a huge stash of what looked like marijuana, trying to explain that it was only tobacco though it didn't smell like it. It was important that my friend came to stay with me, but I realize now that he is not really a friend. Curtis is still Curtis with his goofiness and never being serious. We had some good times. I would follow him and Robert to some local schools, holding my gigantic camcorder on my lap, recording them doing skateboard tricks.

Curtis and Robert would also play in my bedroom where I'd set up my arcade joystick to play video games. I found my greatest outlet away from school, besides artwork, was playing Tony Hawk and getting the new versions as they came out each year. My wheelchair is Curtis's barrier, as much as it is mine, but I'm a completely different person. I say that to myself, but I feel the same person inside, shut off somewhere I don't come out. The good old times when we would ride our dirt bikes, smoke marijuana and cigarettes and drink beer were long ago. I'm almost twenty years old now. I still do not know who I am. I've had all the heartache from my surgery. I thought things would be the same, but something's missing. I've never had a girlfriend. I don't know if I ever will.

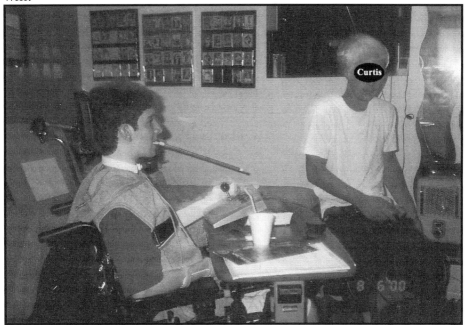

I thought I was graduating this year but turns out because I didn't take enough classes each year, to make it easier on my schedule. I have to go through with one more year. I thought I would graduate before I was twenty, but the joke is on me. I spend a lot of my time at home not doing any homework, mostly playing video games and meditating. I'm definitely falling behind in trigonometry. Mr. Mag lets me pass most of my tests by giving me a lot of help. I sit right next to him and he gives me pointers on how to finish the equations. Our friendship is not the same, but my attitude toward school and grades has completely changed. I only took two art class in my second and third year. I showed some of my talent in my English and history classes, drawing some relevant material for a story or a project. I have definitely gained a lot of respect as one of the best artists in school. The end of the school year comes. In the yearbook I am voted the most artistic. On our senior trip I chose to talk with two not very popular girls in the bus ride home from that trip. They don't talk to the popular senior girls arguing with one of the popular guys. I give nerdy kids a voice and show them that they are special to me. Even I can shine as one of the most popular kids in the school and give less popular kids the respect they need. It's a nice trade-off.

I don't care about popularity because I've seen exactly what all that means. They look up to me because they weren't accepted in the lunchroom. We are all really comfortable with ourselves. Students are not allowed to get lunch outside of the cafeteria but because they are sitting with me, they can. I watch authority figures like Mr. Kennedy walk by and say nothing as we sit with each other. I know they think it's totally cool.

The senior girls in charge of raising money for activities ask me to help raise money during the, rent a senior for the day, Senior Chappell fundraiser. Mike grabs a chair, one of the twin brothers in my class, and Midas helps set up an office chair with wheels. I could always find them two in the computer lab. Even though they wore glasses, didn't play sports, and carried their weight will there are always cool. Mike holds onto the back of my chair with wire and we show off my hall surfing trick. I'm last to be presented and one lucky, skinny and goofy outsider sophomore wins the bid with one hundred dollars. Keith said he was going to bid on me while we ate lunch together outside the media center. They saved the best for last and all day Keith and I get to surf through the halls and show off. The halls are clear and Keith grabs the handles on the back of my chair for better grip with his feet placed over my wheels. We race past Mr. Limanstuer (the senior Bible class teacher) a tall, slender and curly headed man who's always laughing. *Coming through!* I yell while Mr. Limanstuer is sitting in his empty class with one student. He laughs and shakes his head with his arms crossed.

Senior Chapel at the end of the year is always a special occasion. This year I was asked to be the senior to give the speech to the rest of school. A perfect opportunity for me to finally express the way I've been feeling. Somehow I have this desire to tell everyone that even though I have been going through so much recently with this surgery, I can speak a message of encouragement for everyone. There is a lot of hope in why I was chosen. The whole school looks up to me as a spiritual, positive attitude leader. I think it's because I'm in a wheelchair and I do such great artwork. I shine with potential, so others around me see me as a beacon. I have been carrying this attitude for the last four years, even though the surgery didn't turn out to be all it was supposed to be.

I sit in front of the whole school, speaking about the challenges I have gone through to get to graduation. It's a huge accomplishment and honor to be able to express my struggle. I am a strong person for it. All of us fall short in something. Somehow I express my underlying disappointment about my failed surgery, looking right at the children of that doctor. I know it's not their fault. I describe how my hand surgery leads me to believe it is God's plan. I describe how the arrogance of the human mind can disappoint all our hopes and dreams. They don't know I'm directly talking about the doctor. I feel like I finally got it off my chest. Some kids had ruined one of my art projects of Martin Luther King in the hallway. I did not deserve that. I suspected it was the doctor's son Jack, who is three grades below me, when going past him staring at the poster tapping his pen against his teeth.

I go down the hall and just as he starts tapping his pen on his teeth and glares back at me as we cross paths, I turn the back of my chair fast and ram into and over his ankle. I can hear the bone cracking and his voice screaming for help and lashing out at me as if he was mad. Grinding my teeth I look down at him with the white of my eyes piercing through in rage. I back up and go forward again crushing his fingers back, while he screams "sorry!"-- That never happened, but I think about it a lot. The Robert I know inside would have never hesitated to slam him up against the wall and pound my fist into his face. Later that day under my picture was written, *"I'm so vain."*

I add love for animals in my message. I find a Bible verse to quote, something with humor, saying be kind to animals and remember that without hope our dreams cannot come true and without perseverance and trying our best (though the odds may be against you) you can shine, a symbol of encouragement for others.

I'm on my way to get my senior picture taken, but before my father and I go to the photographer's house, we stop by the nursing home where most of my family is visiting my grandfather. Pappa Carlo Florio, my dad's father, is days away from his ninety-ninth birthday. He was walking around, always hunched over, and can barely see, but whenever he hears anything that sounds like music he starts to dance. I don't know where he gets the energy for life. His wife passed away in the nursing home a few months after my injury. Pappa was crying the last time I visited him. He was walking before he injured his back. He was looking at me and touching my leg, feeling sorry about what happened to me. I've always been afraid of nursing homes because my grandfather doesn't have any money, and it isn't much of a life. The quality of life at those places appears to be very minimal.

Carlo Florio
(June 2, 1902 – August 15, 2001)

Life! It Must Be a Comedy

Even though there's not much you can do for some very old people, at least the environment should be happy and the nurses should care more about peoples loved ones. We are all visiting Pappa, my brothers and I, my mother and father, uncles and aunt and a few cousins. Pappa lies on his back staring at the ceiling. He is very skinny, with a decent amount of hair left, completely white. They combed his hair to the side and he rests, lying down slanted and his head slightly falling off the side of the pillow. I made a comment that his neck must be uncomfortable, because when I lay like that my muscles are so relaxed my neck hurts.

He never talked much before but now it's a more solemn last visit. My father and I leave early for the photo shoot. A few days later my father and I are enjoying a lovely summer day when we find out that Pappa passed away in his sleep. My father has always been there for me and I apologize to my dad that we had left early. I have to work hard every day and make a good living so someday, with whatever progress I make physically, I'll always be taken care of. I live with my parents and the state pays for all of my care. I know I can always rely on my parents, but with my injury I have to wonder how I will afford the life I deserve. My father assures me that it was OK we left early, because he was happy to take me for the photos. With my dorky haircut, I sat in a chair in front of a wooded area. I can't help but see my grandfather in the photo of me. My grandfather saw many things. He was one of the first to see an automobile and he was the person who walked on stilts to light the candles in the city. He even worked in a graveyard digging holes. I am very proud of my grandfather for coming to Ellis Island from Italy and bringing my family to the United States. I hope someday I'll have a family of my own with a beautiful wife. I will instill the respect and honor a strong Italian family deserves.

My mother and father are at my graduation with Carlo, but somehow Adrian could not make it. My uncle Sandro and Aunt Mabel, cousin Alessandro and his wife Shri also attend. Summer and her son Nick are in the audience and one of my mother's good friends, Ms. Lani, who she started in Mary Kay with some seventeen years ago. My name is called as Mr. Mag accompanies me back stage to the ramp. He's trying to keep me close and under control so I don't say what's deep down inside me, because I know that doctor is sitting in the audience watching his daughter graduate. He says to me to not say much because I said a lot at Senior Chapel.

I receive my diploma, shaking the hand of Mr. Kennedy. The high school principal, Mr. Van Ness the Headmaster does too. The two principals have beards, Mr. Van Ness's dark and Mr. Kennedy's white. My baby picture and my graduation picture are projected on the screen along with my announcement, made by Ms. Bonnell's voice, as a incredible artist, someday to be recognized among the greats, an entrepreneur since I sold my watercolor paintings on note cards the year before raising over one thousand dollars from parents, students and teachers in the school. I'm also a videogame designer and film student, knowing I want to design games to help people. I didn't add becoming a malpractice attorney, but I smile and thank everyone. I thank my parents and Mr. Kennedy for helping me attend school.

When I sit down it's time for hats to be thrown in the air. The funny kid in our school, Joe, sits next to me with his huge afro and his dark complexion. A petite blonde girl next to him, I'm sitting on the end, and she says she doesn't want to do it, but Joe grabs my hat and throws it straight in the air. I thought I had some friends, seems no one has common sense, but Joe just smiles and I look straight up. My hat goes flying coming back. I hope it doesn't hit me in the head. I thought I had good friends, being a role model and all. I need to get out and discover who I am. I do not care anymore about people like this. I don't care if it hits me back in the head. All the students know I am defenseless. I really haven't met any good friends. It's a lot to ask someone to step out of their own comfort zone for someone different. Nobody did and I didn't step out to show them.

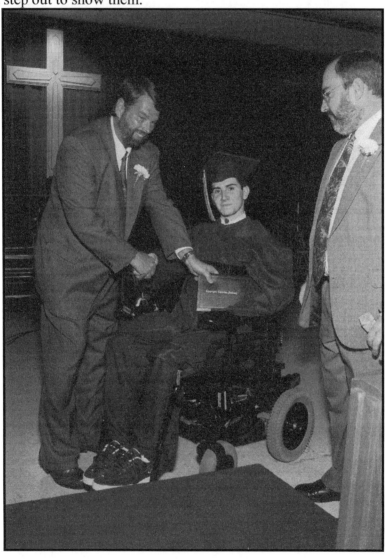

Life! It Must Be a Comedy

I look forward to summer and I look forward to college. I can't wait to get out of this school. I know who I need to become and that person is finally going to happen. I can feel it. I hope college gives me that opportunity. A world without boundaries, and a world without immature students, people who can be themselves. High school was still a time of being treated like an immature and irresponsible kid. As the ceremonies ended, there is a surprise guest speaker by video projection. Her voice is heard loud and clear. It is Josie Emerson Armada, the quadriplegic who spoke at this very school when I was in rehab and the person who e-mails me. I got the honor of meeting her and I'm kind of her friend. She said she was she sorry that she couldn't be there in person since a lot of people know her. She grew up in this area. I feel so embarrassed as she mentions my name several times as being a good friend of hers. She brings a big smile to my face. My parents were as surprised as I. All of the students grew up reading her book. This solidified my stature as the person I am now. I can accept that.

I know my role is to be an example of strength. I see it in the hope I give and in the talent I have, showing it to Josie when I met her in person. Her encouragement turned on a light about who I could be. I'm not a preacher like her. I can share my strength and hope. The artistic side of me shows me who I am and who I will become. I can make the future what I want. College is a new venture. In high school, classes were chosen for me. I feel a sense of relief and elation. My future is limitless even though I have a physical barrier. All of my pain and suffering prepared me to be someone that I want to be. I choose to be successful. I choose to find happiness. There is such desire built up inside me to do something great with my life. All of the little steps of schooling have led me to my own path, and I will find it, with or without God guiding me. What will I do and who will I become? I know my confidence level is higher than it ever has been. No one will hold me back now.

Chapter 12
The Passion

I look forward to the choices I have. I know I cannot change the past even though I think about it often. There is a fire inside me now, burning hotter and brighter with every struggling moment. My mornings are filled with frustration, with a nurse in my face. I'm in their hands as they help me to start my day. Little things cause me to be impatient and down on myself. I take time to find clarity in solitude, meditation and prayer. I see my possibilities, desires and passions for the person I want to be and the position I want to be in some day to help others.

I know I have overcome the worst days now. I'm twenty years old, continuing at Anne Arundel Community College, taking drawing classes, a few other prerequisites, acting, and psychology among others. I now have a choice. I had a dream of being an architect in my childhood. When I was very little I carried a yellow plastic suitcase with my connector toys, building structures, having a notepad and drawing on it, scribbling sentences as if it was part of my job. That dream is a possibility. I want to do something that is fun. No one in my family has ever taken on the challenge of college classes and four years of studying. I can do this, but I'm waiting for my heart to tell me what I really want.

My father and I watch the Orioles on TV. Cal Ripken Jr. is my idol and boyhood hero. There is a new player, number 25, with a strong swing and a bulky muscular stance who impresses me more than all the other players coming to bat. His swing and the concentration in his eyes strike me impressively. Cal Ripken Jr. is near retirement now. The Orioles need a new hero. I have not felt this connection to another player except Cal. A young twenty-five-year-old redheaded guy with a stiff arm swing powers through a pitch like slicing through butter, left-handed and strong. I watch the ball soar over right field at the Camden Yards scoreboard, between the flags and over the fence, nearly hitting the Orioles outfield warehouse. This is the guy I cheer for when I hear his name shouted from the screen. It is 2003 of his major-league rookie year. Jay Gibbons, stands almost six feet tall and speaks very softly. I'm impressed by his power and uniqueness. When I hear him speak I know he is special. My passion for connecting to athletes through my art, showing them what they have to cherish, is a dream I hope to accomplish.

Lord I know that this person is someone special and I pray someday you will let me meet him and let me show Jay Gibbons my talent and share my friendship. I know Christ was always a friend to a person first and then would share a life lesson. I believe Jay Gibbons can bring me a similar opportunity. I don't exactly know what the purpose is, but I know I want to meet him. I think this is what I'm waiting for. In Christ's name I pray, Amen...

My classes continue at AACC. I meet some other people in wheelchairs around the campus and go to a Disability Club that my guidance counselor Mimi introduces me to, since she is the chairperson. I have never been with a group that promotes a better quality of life. The current president of the club spends a lot of time keeping it going. We lobby around campus quietly, looking for inaccessible things that need to be improved with a door switch installation, mirrors around corners, and a bridge between sides of campus that goes across a heavily wooded ditch area. The wooden planks are bowed from weathering and pressure, creating a bumpy ride in my chair.

I now take a much higher dose of spasm muscle relaxers. My spasms have increased. I try to fight the side effects of drowsiness. I try to keep my spirits high and motivated but it is very difficult. Every little bump in my wheelchair or in my mind or even someone touching my leg makes my entire body shake like an earthquake. I play along, humming a tune jokingly, as my stomach and lungs muscles tighten and I belch out a quick high-pitched squeal to be funny. My nurses giggle at me while holding my knees down, helping me to quickly get my hand off of my joystick so it doesn't clench around it and my arm straightens threatening to send me off a cliff someday if I'm not careful.

Ah, ah, ah, ah. Dammit! Holy shit-for-buckets! Ah, ah, ah, ah. ... WHEW! I repeat when I get spasms as my body tremors, and my voice vibrates.

I continue painting, starting with two oil portraits of Fluffy and Jasmine. I read an oil painting how-to book on landscapes (my mother gave me for Christmas) from front to back. I take a large photo of Fluffy and Jasmine, draw on to an eight by ten flat piece of white canvas and free sketch exactly what I see and paint Fluffy first. Painting his fur blue instead of black-and-white I find a new passion and talent in my artistic ability. Everyone is amazed that it looks just like the photograph. Fluffy lies on his side in the picture. I do a close-up of his nose, slightly larger than normal, his face lying on its side, very narrow in the background and ears flat, almost disappearing in his long hair. Jasmine's portrait is the complete opposite. She has her mouth wide open with a pink collar and her funny, cute smile. I put a blue and yellow spinning star in the background and texture her fur colors, black, shiny and silky smooth. She looks exactly like her photograph too. I know I could paint Jay Gibbons just as well.

"Fluffy" Oil. 8 by 10

237

"Jasmine" Oil. 8 by 10

This winter, my days consist of homework, a couple of days of school at the campus each week, watching Orioles games and talking with my parents. Fluffy and Jasmine follow me everywhere I go, always my loyal little friends. I do not feel any more pressure like when I was in high school. I'm still a little confused about what I want to do with my future, but I'm comfortable at college, having my classes paid off with a Social Security voucher. I continue to pray and discover in my mind and my heart what the next step might be. It's the little steps that get me where I need to go. It's the little things I accomplish, that are allowing me to train for something bigger someday. Not receiving that money that could have made life so much easier has been a disappointment. I believe soon God will send me a message like He always does, just what I need, that little bit of hope and encouragement, the next mentor on the journey for me to connect with, to learn from and grow. Waiting for these opportunities strengthens me. It's a twisted feeling and a reality of life, to see the positive happen as I struggle for bigger things to come. God might be listening. Answering little things gives me exactly what I need. God has a sick sense of humor. He watches us fight Him in the systematic maze that He chose for us to live in. There's an unspoken agreement about the nature of this world, created with a flaw. I struggle in my mind about how a loving God allows me to suffer, but I laugh at Him and to myself when good things happen.

I'm off to Best Electronics because my little sixteen-inch television has gone down. I used to sit perpendicular to my television, with it about chest high, hitting the buttons with my knuckles on my left side to change the channels. I have worn off the buttons. Adrian and his pregnant girlfriend Coral come along with my mother and I. We search the store. I love the 50-inch television. I choose a twenty-seven-inch Sharp, but the box has a big dent on the corner. I have to get it checked out before taking it home, but it's the last one and I'm too excited to leave it.

I look back at the fifty-inch and see someone else looking at it. My heart dropped and I can't believe my eyes. It only takes me a split second to see my opportunity. I wheel over toward the man who is looking perplexed, staring and studying the television. He is fairly tall, wearing sandals and a long black windbreaker, pants and a T-shirt. I take a deep breath and the whole room seems to go silent. My face starts to get flushed and my mind goes completely blank. He turns slowly toward me stars at me, as I collect my thoughts to speak. My anxiety gets the best of me as I try to introduce myself. I know who he is but I'm frozen, my mouth is open but I can't say his name.

Excuse me. Hi, I say to him in a long pause.

Hi, the man says back.

You are, umm……………………umm……… umm…. umm…. umm.. umm… Jay ---right! I finally say.

Yes I am, Jay replies.

I knew it! My name is Robert. I'm your biggest fan. So what are you doing here? I ask.

I'm just looking at this television here, Jay said.

My dad and I came in the other day looking at the flyer for this fifty-inch flat screen and we did not see the other zero, I say.

You know what? I think I must've done the same thing. I thought this was twelve hundred thousand dollars not twelve thousand dollars myself, Jay said, and we both start laughing.

Hey you're not injured are you? I ask.

No, no, Jay explained.

Oh, OK. I just glanced at your feet I thought your sandals were somehow a hospital shoe for a foot. You know what I want to ask you? Would you mind if I painted you? I say.

Hey, sure, Jay says.

I am an artist. I paint with my mouth. Can I give you my card? I ask.

Sure, no problem, I would like that, Jay said.

Can I introduce you to my family? I ask.

We chat for a couple of minutes. I am in complete amazement. What were the chances that I actually met Jay? My family approaches, thinking that he is just an old buddy from high school or something, having no clue who Jay is.

I want to introduce you to somebody, I say to my family as they slowly walk our way.

This is Jay Gibbons, I explain, as Jay shakes their hands.

He plays right field for the Baltimore Orioles. This is the guy I was telling you all about, I explain to them.

I seem to be the only person completely amazed at who I have met. I try not to overwhelm Jay with my star struck attitude. I quietly thank him and give him my card with all my information on it, hoping we can e-mail back and forth when I finish the painting, to give it to him. Later, Jay is in line, standing quietly, with a smile, his huge muscular stature standing out. I can point Jay out anywhere. We stare at each other. I smile and give him a nod and he smiles back in quiet stealth mode. I don't give his star presence away.

I'm anxious to get home. There is already an e-mail from Jay for me. We keep in touch once or twice a month through the off-season. Waiting for the new season to start, I give as much encouragement and insight into life that I can to maybe help Jay grow as a person and a player. I secretly hope that my influence will give him a better chance of success. I search around for a good photograph of Jay. A customer at my dad's barbershop brings in one for me to paint from. My dad always comes home with barbershop talk. His stories always start with "This guy…"

This guy came into the barbershop today and gave me this photograph. He said for you to use it. That was really nice of him. You see that God has put everything in your way. First you meet Jay and now you have the perfect photograph group. Thank you Lord. I can't wait to see it finished. I bet when Jay sees that portrait, he's not going to believe his eyes. When are you going to start? Dad seems as excited as I am.

I always listen to my Dad's jokes. Uncle Sandro just rolls his eyes at the corny ones. My dad also tells me the history of anything and everything. My dad does all the talking at the barbershop. My uncle keeps things more serious, but they still crack each other up. Whenever I have a bad day, Dad always comes home with a smile on his face, even when standing on his feet all day and skipping lunch, trying to keep up with the speedy fingers of my uncle.

I have now started Jay's portrait, set up next to the bed in front of my new television. I watch every single Orioles game. The season has started. Dad, Mom and I cheer Jay on, I get closer to the completion of the portrait. Our friendship has grown. As I paint with my mouth, a strange feeling comes over me. Seven: thirty p.m. on weekdays and one p.m. on Sundays I paint and watch the game. Jay comes to bat. Jay is having an amazing second year hitting home run after home run, scoring RBI after RBI, with amazing glove work in the field, accurately throwing anyone out at home. He shines. Though our connections seem small, I've gotten to know Jay through our e-mails and a couple of phone calls. I feel like we are truly becoming buddies.

The brush pushes paint along the canvas, as the life of my hero builds in layers, like our friendship and the life I have to take control of. I have drawn to transfer grids on my canvas to get the exact perspective and color detail. I hear the crack of the bat and Jay's name announced every time he comes to the plate to do something spectacular. My heart races. When he's up there, I'm cheering Jay. I missed the opportunity to play for the Orioles, but now I have a connection. My friendship with Jay allows me to imagine what it's like to step on the field, step up to the plate and swing the bat. My dreams are more intense, as I feel my hands perfectly wrapped around that wooden bat. It is so light. I am very strong, effortlessly swinging at the ball. I am running or walking. It takes concentration and willpower and a very strong mind to be able to sleep and be aware that you are dreaming and take control over your thoughts and desires again without waking up. This is my world. When I sleep I can control what I do. I choose to be everything I no longer have. I struggle in my mind, fighting who I really am when I wake. It pulls me back down into that chair, making it hard to imagine all those things again. I don't have to imagine that I'm playing baseball for the Orioles or swinging the bat when I am awake. Through Jay's hand and our connections, it's real to me.

With my service to the accessibility group, I am elected president. I have even met Anne Arundel County Executive Janet Owens at our Disability Awareness Day. I ask her for an opportunity to show my artwork if she knows a place. The public would become aware too. It's still in the works.

In Advanced Figure Study Classes I draw the body as a beginning artist, to master all the intricacies and delicate detail, studying the human body. There is a meeting being held in the media building where I take my Figure Study Classes. I'm going to class when I see Ms. Owens walking in the building right next to me. There is a very tall man with her, a reporter from the Baltimore Sun Newspaper. He is intrigued by what I'm saying. There is another meeting with Ms. Owens. I remind her of our agreement. She's surprised to see me, but both her assistants seem intrigued by my idea too.

Different people accompany me to my night classes for drawing. I can't be there by myself. Someone sets up my table and sharpens my pencils as I draw the nude model for each class. It is the class I look forward to the most, for obvious reasons. I get to study the nude female body, which is of the most interest to me. Summer accompanies me, but she is not always able to do it. Big old Marilyn or my Dad go with me sometimes. Adrian and Carlo both have also volunteered.

This one particular night my dad is my assistant and the female model is a little overweight and her voluptuous breasts are jiggley. I continue trying to get my dad's attention, laughing to myself. He continues to stare at the naked woman. It's too much of a huge culture shock for him. He is always joking around about "sardines" being beautiful women. When he sees her naked in class, it's overwhelming. He is standing there holding my mouthstick, just staring at the lady, looking her up and down, acting like he is studying her also. She opens her eyes. I desperately yell, under my breath. She starts to laugh, all of her roles start jiggling. I can't stop laughing.

Dad, dad, dad, dad, dad... Dad! I say as quiet as I can.

Whaaaaaat!? Dad finally turns around as if nothing happened trying to be funny.

Come on! Look you're making her laugh. You keep staring at her. Stop it! Come on it's too funny I got to concentrate now. I said.

Whaaaaaat!? I was just studying. She's used to people staring at her. This is some, shhhhhhit! Hey, when is that other model the skinny sardine going to be the model? He says, shakes his head smiling and laughing.

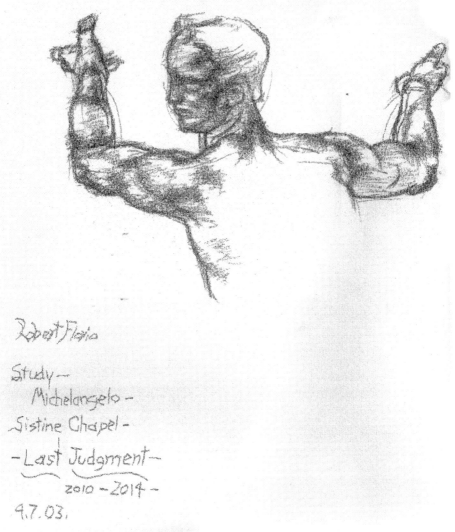

Robert Florio

Study—
    Michelangelo—
Sistine Chapel—
—Last Judgment—
    2010 — 2014 —
4.7.03.

"Last Judgment" Michelangelo Study. Charcoal. 8 by 10

Carlo is assisting me a few days later. This time it's a very flat-chested skinny woman who's not attractive at all. She lies eye level on a table. We are studying foreshortening techniques. She turns her vagina facing me. I'm face-to-face with a vagina. The most horrifying, open ended, spread and loosened vagina I've ever seen. I ask her to turn around. I love studying women, but I can't pleasure myself. I have a hard time getting the image of beautiful women out of my head from class. It's amazing seeing them live. It's a curse and a blessing, but this is not one I want to fantasize about. Carlo and I start laughing to ourselves. My dad just got off work so Carlo can go home. Dad walks across the room not sure who is lying on the table. He does a double-take. I start laughing. I've never seen his eyes so big. I can only imagine what he must be thinking. Every class has either been a beautiful woman or a voluptuous woman, and he was imagining there would be a sardine tonight too.

This is some, shhhhhhit! Dad whispers, and stunned at what he sees.

Robert Florio

10.17.03.

"My Eggs" Pencil. 8 by 10

Finally an e-mail comes that my art show is going to be set up at the County Executive's office at the Maryland State Capitol in Annapolis, a half-hour from my house. A reporter Ryan, with the Baltimore Sun, e-mails his interest in my story too. He tells me he is so impressed with my boldness in approaching Mrs. Owens. My show is set up. The front page of the Maryland Gazette says, "Taking Control of His New Life." There's a picture of me and my parents with Mrs. Owens giving me a Citizen's Award. On page two there's a photo of me and my dog paintings displayed in the lobby and people admiring them. It captures a few of my watercolor landscapes as well on the walls of the lobby of the County Executive's Office Building. I received a letter in the mail from The White House. The letter said;

Dear Robert:

Congratulations on the recent exhibition of your art at the Arundel Center.

Your determination to overcome difficult circumstances and to focus on the positive is an inspiration to all. By setting high goals and working hard to achieve them, you demonstrate the heart of our Nation.

Laura and I send you and yours our best wishes for a joyous holiday season.

Sincerely,

George W. Bush

"My Hand" Pencil. 8 by 10

Ryan comes to my house now a few times a month as I continue working on Jay Gibbons' portrait. The end of the baseball season approaches. I have never been questioned in detail the way Ryan does with all his intimate, deep concepts. He brings out my amazing story, but the same time my emotions are so intense. Even though I'm not comfortable, I must tell my story. It's hard for my parents to be in the room when I answer. Ryan becomes a friend, writing an amazing story, hinting that it might make the front page of the Baltimore Sun paper.

Study. Charcoal. 8 by 10

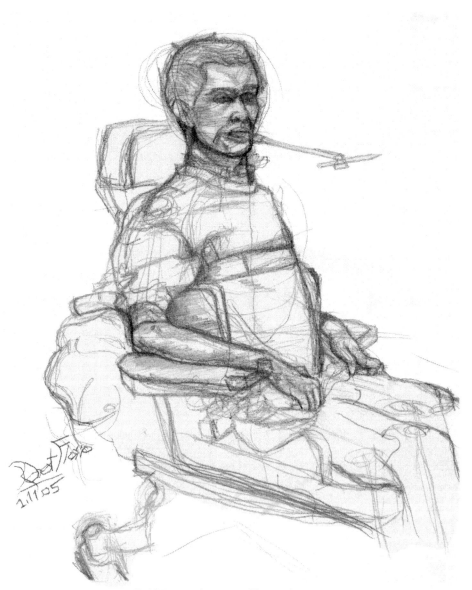

Self Portrait. Pencil. 11 by 14

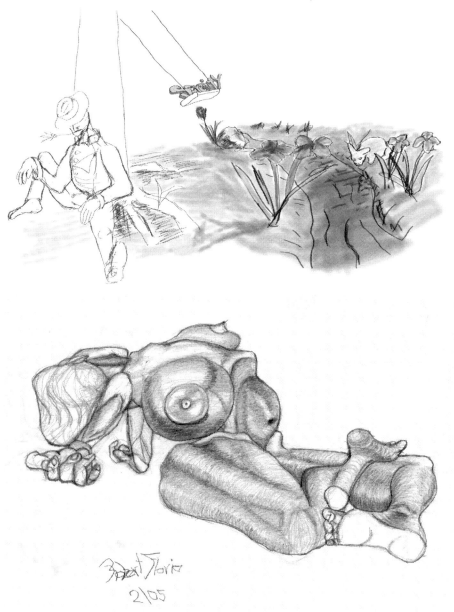

"Abstract Woman" Pencil. 11 by 14

Jay Gibbons could have easily set up all sorts of media for me to get that exposure, but I got this media on my own.   It's a great chance for me. The painting is wrapped up in paper bag material, with a black frame and an orange and black matte. The sixteen by twenty inch oil portrait of Jay Gibbons is about to be unveiled. Jay invited me on to the field during batting practice near the end of the season. The photographer arrived to capture the moment and Jay walked out of the dugout giving me a black bat signed by the whole team and another signed by him with his branded signature and, "To my buddy Robert. Thank you for showing me the true meaning of life. Your Buddy." Before Jay came out the second baseman Jerry Hairston Jr. gave me a bat of his own and signed it as I chatted with Jerry Hairston Jr. and Brian Roberts. We were in our own little triangle huddle behind the batting cage on the right side of the field near the Orioles dugout. I truly feel like one of the guys.

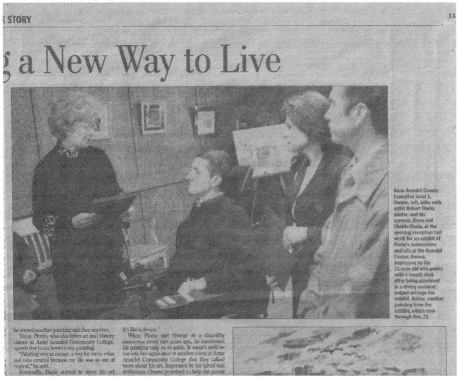

STORY

15

a New Way to Live

Anne Arundel County Executive Janet S. Owens, left, talks with artist Robert Florio, center, and his parents, Elena and Ubaldo Florio, at the opening reception last week for an exhibit of Florio's watercolors and oils at the Arundel Center. Owens, impressed by the 21-year-old who paints with a mouth stick after being paralyzed in a diving accident, helped arrange the exhibit. Below, another painting from the exhibit, which runs through Nov. 23.

he started another painting and then another.
Today, Florio, who also takes art and history classes at Anne Arundel Community College, spends five to six hours a day painting.
"Painting was an escape, a way for me to relax and take control because my life was so out of control," he said.
Eventually, Florio started to share his art.

It's like a dream."
When Florio met Owens at a disability awareness event two years ago, he mentioned his painting only as an aside. It wasn't until he ran into her again later at another event at Anne Arundel Community College that they talked more about his art. Impressed by his talent and dedication, Owens promised to help the young

We go in the building, going down the tunnel to the lower reserves directly behind home plate, talking to the ushers. They point at me as if I am some sort of famous person, joking around, welcoming me. No fans are in the stadium yet. I pal around with Jay. My mom holds the front-page story of the newspaper. I ask Jay if he's read it. Jay gives me a few Xbox games, a signed game-worn jersey and a signed hat. He opens the portrait. His mouth is wide open, unable to describe how amazing the painting is. Ryan notes everything we say. Jay signs one reproduction copy for me to take home and I give him the original and another reproduction for Jay to put somewhere else.

Life! It Must Be a Comedy

You got everything perfect, Jay says.

I had looked into Jay's background and birthday on the Internet before the game. My heart starts skipping.

Jay I need to tell you something that I think is absolutely amazing, I say.

Yeah what's that man? Jay asks.

I read on the Internet that your birthday is March 2. That's my birthday too, I say.

The Yankees come on the field for batting practice. We look at each other in a brief silence just smiling.

Well, it must be meant to be then, Jay says.

It must be. I could stay on this field forever, I reply.

Stay out here as long as you like Buddy, Jay says.

I think you're going to hit a home run tonight, I say.

That would be amazing, Jay says.

No pressure buddy. Thank you, I'll never forget this day, I say laughing a little and smile.

My mother and father are on the field with me. Adrian and Carlo are both in the stands close to us and Summer and her ten-years-old son Nick sit quietly. Jay heads back to the dugout to get ready for the game. I wait to put on the Jersey that Jay gave me. I have perfect seats, directly behind home plate.

"Jay Gibbons" Oil. 16 by 20

Life! It Must Be a Comedy

It would be amazing if Jay hits a home run. How much better could this night get? I eat my hotdog, put on my jersey. While Jay's at bat, my head is down. I look up, hearing the crack of the bat. I should have been looking at the swing, but it's only the first pitch. The whole stadium rises in joy and bursts into cheers as the ball goes toward right field. Jay slowly trots toward first base. He hit a homerun on the first pitch. It's like something that only happens in fairy tales. It feels like everything has been rough, but for this brief moment I'm enjoying every minute. With my short gasping lung capacity to yell, my voice doesn't travel, but in my heart and in my body I want to jump up and down screaming as my mom gives her high-pitched yell and Adrian, Carlo and Summer all look back at me with big smiles.

Jay's father Jim is sitting close to us and walks over to give me a big high five. He's a very tall man nearly six foot three inches with the same nose as Jay, but with dark hair and a deep froggy voice and quiet smile. Jay does his normal homerun trot with his head down, looking straight forward. He doesn't look up at me after touching home plate. I seen him hit so many home runs, twenty-six for the season, and over ninety RBIs for his career major-league high. He's only been in the Major League Baseball since 2001. I know I picked a good friend. Jay finished the season with twenty-six home runs and one hundred RBIs becoming the team's most valuable player of 2004.

As the baseball season winds down, I find myself sticking with my classes at college. I'm closer now to a decision. I think I know what I want to do. I want to learn how to create videogames with art. It would be fun and get me close to my goal of helping other people in rehab using these games psychologically to support them. No game company has been these needs. I have the best ideas, so I'll be that person to do it.

There is a cute girl in my psychology class. A young skinny boy with blond hair and glasses volunteers to copy his notes for me. After class, I notice his sister and we start chatting about the new movie, "The Passion of the Christ." I can't stop looking at her. She's got a very sweet, innocent look, blonde hair like a large-breasted curvy angel. Her full lips and swooping downward nose with blue eyes catch my attention. She is just a little shorter than me. She sees me checking her out so I get courageous and ask her to see that movie and she agrees.

Life! It Must Be a Comedy

Her name is Chastity. She and her twin brothers go to the church I used to go to before my injury. It's a very strict Baptist church, one that I don't associate with very much anymore because of their crazy rules.

I show up at the movie theater and she's a little shocked to see me without my nurse. The movie makes me cry a little bit. I think of my nephew Nathan, recently born, Adrian's son. He reminds me a lot of myself. I think of how my mother was there when I fell. My mother is practically raising Nathan. Nathan is the happiest child, with a great big smile on his face always laughing and in good spirits. I try to protect him, knowing the benefit of being loved. His sister Melissa, on his mother's side, is a tuff sweet little four year old girl and I always give her all the love and understanding she needs. I always have her in my heart too. Suffering the cross on his shoulder, Christ falls down and looks at his mother. The screen flashes to when Christ is a young boy and hurt his knee while his mother comforts him. We both become a little emotional during the movie, so maybe we have something in common.

Life! It Must Be a Comedy

Chastity and I hang out more and more now. She sits next to me in psychology class, taking my notes. I see her during lunch and she sees me after acting class. As school winds down for summer, I learn that Chastity has a secret. She has multiple sclerosis. I ignore the red flag in my mind. I give in to her big eyes winking at me. We set up more times to see each other at my house.

My brand new chair arrives, allowing me to lay completely flat and even go up like an elevator to stand on my own two feet with a knee brace. My body is no longer a fourteen-year old frame. It took the state Medicare Program two years to approve this thirty thousand dollars wheelchair. I now see the world from a standing perspective whenever I want, trying not to let my blood pressure put my system into too much shock. Standing upright with my girlfriend, and we can get close to hug or passionately kiss.

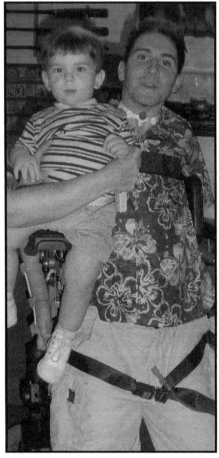

Life! It Must Be a Comedy

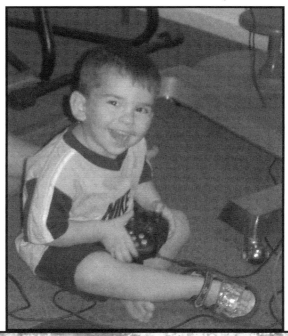

Today I'm visiting the church down the road from me that I have not been to in several years. The preacher wears a Hawaiian T-shirt and shorts that I like. Afterwards, I see Jeff, who I have not spoken to in years. I've held so much anger inside of me toward him and hoped to never see him again, because he abandoned me when I needed him most. We both stand still, like being caught in headlights, not making a move. I can tell we both have nothing in common anymore. He comes over and says *hello* and I say *hello* back. Somehow I find the guts to actually say a few words that I really wanted to. Jeff definitely has gotten taller. My heart was broken and it still is because of the lawsuit.

Where have you been man? I say with more disdain than friendly with a mix of emotions.

Yeah, I know we haven't seen each other since that last time when I came to your house, Jeff says.

I guess a lot has gone on for both of us, I say.

Life! It Must Be a Comedy

Before I get too emotional I break off the conversation agreeing to someday meet at my house. Jeff's fiancé is the pastor's daughter. Somehow God most of brought us together today. Otherwise, Jeff would never have set foot in that church.

A couple month later my girlfriend and I getting ready for Jeff's wedding. He visits my house so we're able to catch up on some old times for Nathan's second birthday party. Everyone says that Nathan looks and acts more like me every day. Nathan plays with my sister's six-year-old son Ezra. The two of them are the exact opposite. Nathan is short with a big smile and muscles and very friendly, and Ezra is skinny and tall and quieter. Nathan looks like his father, especially when he shows that angry face. Jeff's fiancé has come along too. She is a girl with dark hair, who has soft pretty features, pregnant. My parents joke that they're both too young to get married. Jeff and she reply, *everyone says that*, annoyed, saying they know best and disagree. The conversation gets a little bit more serious as I share with Jeff just how I felt that I didn't have my best friend when I needed him. To my surprise, he says he lost his best friend at the same time because we were separated from each other. Jeff reverted to a life of drugs and alcohol while I went through my days suffering paralysis and loss of feeling. Maybe I would have been even worse off than I am now. I still have disdain, but maybe we both went down paths we couldn't control.

We watch the wedding from our table, and then the food is served. I see Jeff hasn't touched his plate. I sneak out after Jeff's wedding, getting out early, saying it was good to see all of Jeff's family that I hadn't seen in so long. To be honest I really didn't care anymore and was just there to support a friend who invited me to a special part of his life. I had to respect that. The life I left behind is frozen in time. I can't return there. I would change everything, making the future the way I think it should be now, but that's not reality. I have learned firsthand how fragile we are, how cruel fate is. The only good things we have sometimes are the choices we make.

Chastity and I sneak off to my car. I lay back as she sits with her head on my shoulder with her raspberry lip balm teasing my senses and I joke around, asking if I could taste some of that. It took eight years for me finally to get a kiss and it is so soft and gentle that my heart is racing and my mind is floating, while I think of nothing but her and being together all the time to kiss even more and more, as much as we can.

Life! It Must Be a Comedy

The tongue was absent but the lips were very gentle and sincere, innocent but sweet.

Lying in my bed at night, I wish I had more privacy in my room, since my nurses and parents all come downstairs to do laundry or sit at the table. Chastity and I pretend to be sleeping under the covers in my skinny twin bed, as she tries not to fall out, hoping that they will get the point and leave. We always laugh to ourselves in those situations, and part of my excitement and relief is because someone finally sees past my wheelchair. It makes me more turned on and attracted. She has beautiful blue eyes and a really cute Indian shape flat nose. Being a virgin myself, I thought every girl who goes to church must be a virgin. I think she must be one. I'm expecting her first experience must be with me, because I have never been this close to anyone before. There's no way she has ever been with anyone other than her ex-boyfriend. She talks about him, but in the back of my mind I put it aside, because everything is happy right now together.

The sweet touch of her gentle fingers caresses me as she straddles over my face, turned around as my tongue enjoys everything I can feel making the senses I have ten times filled with passion and desire. I cannot feel intercourse and even though I was very experimental or explorative I should say before my injury, I can look in her eyes and I can see the pleasure I give her. I know from some of her words that because I can't feel it and she can't tell what reaction she is giving me, that from her movement that some part of it is bothering her and in return starts bothering me. *How do I deal with this*, because I have no experience. I try not to cry and I tell myself this is a very enjoyable experience and I'll never be able to feel it so I have to get over this and not be afraid. I could go for hours kissing her with my lips on my tongue feeling every part of her body and caressing her in her most gentle place, as she sits over my face giving me a vision of beautiful delight. It's incredibly warm, moist and a lot of skin folds to maneuver around with my tongue. I have no idea what I'm doing or if I'm kissing the right spots. It's a lot more prickly than I imagined. I guess we both were not completely prepared to be in the mood to touch her down there for my first time. It's heaven for me. I have dreamed about this for eight years over and over again, and for me her pleasure is my pleasure, so everything I do I want to make sure makes her happy. I know I need to find ways for me to share that I am receiving the same pleasure.

    I am finally ready when before our way of making love was not going all the way, but now I know it's something I want. It seems like a crazy concept, of course it's something I want! Not knowing the right time in my own mind was holding me back, but I know for sure I can and will be good and confident that it will happen. I have to watch in order to see what is happening from my perspective to visualize where it is and feeling every action like a man doing my job. It feels too good, there is no way I see this as wrong. I am going to be the best from this moment on, feeling every movement and committing one hundred percent. I am a natural, regaining my talents as if someone has healed me and let me show the abilities I knew I could perform. Sex is the closest thing to feeling restored, more than anything ever will. I almost feel like crying and frantically do, savoring all our moments together while turning up the television louder and louder to mask our sounds.

Life! It Must Be a Comedy

This is it, while my parents are at my uncle Emilo's house eating dinner. I just got out of the shower. I am naked sitting on top of my chuck pads after going to the bathroom so that I do not accidentally make a mess. We push tongue to tongue as I push and she goes down and as I pull out she goes up. She puts the condom on, and I watch her make it larger. My heart starts pumping faster releasing adrenaline and endorphins. It goes in slowly as she sits over my pelvis, the sound of the condom and the moisture between her lips. We touch faces after I watch her arch back so I can visually see the pleasure of intercourse. The noises being made and the words being said are very passionate and probably not something that a man would say so intimately in love or should say during sex. I know I do have experience in that area but my passion and my desire bottled up for so many years, everything has to be expressed until I am fulfilled and making sure she always is. We make love for hours, until my parents return. I have her turn on the fan to mask some of the smell, but we both know even though we can't smell it's not going away. I make her climax two times, but I still don't know how to make myself do it. I don't know if impossible, because only twenty percent quadriplegics with my same condition (according to the Internet research) are capable of ejaculation. I'm not worried about not feeling it, because this is so new to me, even though the orgasm would be the most pleasure I've ever had. I fight that concept the entire time of lovemaking, feeling sad and happy, even though this is the happiest moment of my life. I have the world's biggest smile, but I'm very confused.

I found the school that I want to continue my education with. I have found the online division of the Art Institute of Pittsburgh. After

Life! It Must Be a Comedy

seeing a commercial about the Art Institute of DC's animation program and visiting the DC location, I learn that they have a Game Art and Design Bachelor degree program. This is it. This is what I have to do. Being accepted in the school was the first challenge, not knowing if someone who draws with their mouth and keep up with the other students, but I get accepted immediately after my application and drawings are filled out. I'm beginning to see all the things that I've ever needed are right here in college. My classes are not exactly set up the way they should be. I immediately recognize that the professors need to pay attention more to the quality not just the quantity of work. I join the first-ever Student Government Association as a representative for the game design program.

"Jack Smack The Bounty Hunter" Digital Painting

Game design is an amazing field. I do all my work online studying the intricacy of developing a team of programmers, artists and designers and managing that from scratch. All the things that one needs to know about designing games, even the animation, art and advertisement are available. I am preparing myself for exactly what I need and what I want to be. The state has a program called DORS, Department of Rehabilitation Services that allows me to afford going to school to train me to be in the workforce. I have to plead my case and prove I am worthy of the expenses and show the outcome will give me employment. They sent me to Baltimore before school started to do testing. I scored above average and off the charts on some of their tests The DORS program is a lifesaver, but I have to fight to get benefits, because the state has strict rules. A fire is lit inside of me. I get frustrated with state workers, because if I don't speak up for what I need to survive, they will not stick up for me. I switched to a different counselor, and he is more than willing to help me. My heart goes out to people who cannot speak for themselves, because I don't know what they do to survive.

The adjustment has not been too smooth. I spend most of my time from ten o'clock in the morning until eight o'clock at night almost every day of the week trying to adjust to this new strange schedule of classes by quarters that online school has set up. I submit all of my work through photographs or scanned on the scanner and verbally texting with voice dictation software. I can read all of the lectures and all of the answers and questions from all the other students, making it very easy to learn.

Finding time apart and trying to schedule intimate times with Chastity is getting harder and harder. I learn that Chastity is not a virgin. I wanted to hold her to some standard. I should not be nagging her. It's pushing her further and further away. It causes arguments and I try to work them out somehow, making it into a happy situation, making love either in my chair or in bed. It's exciting for me and I think of her as we escape to my room and everyone else's in the other room or my parents are sleeping in the room above me. I turn up the background music playing Maroon Five to set the mood and block out any noises. It is embarrassing at the same time very exciting to get away with something I haven't done before in my parent's house, but I know we both need more. Chastity and I are growing apart.

My heart continues to become broken as I reflect on what we once had. We e-mail and talk on the phone more than in-person about our problems. Chastity stays out weird hours at night with one of her guy friends and doesn't find anything wrong with that like I do. Our intimate times become more and more awkward as I bring up certain things about her virginity or an ex-boyfriend at the wrong time. His name was also Robert and that makes me feel more jealous. My insecurities and sexual frustrations, over the years, have put a barrier in my mind and it's hard to enjoy being with her. I see in her eyes that I say the wrong thing, but my mind cannot get rid of visuals. I lack experience, but I thought I was capable of handling something like this. We begin to break apart. My heart and my mind are not able to make sense of it, as we continue pushing each other away.

We have lasted almost six months but the last two months have been muffled by a few close intimate times together. I know the time has come now to finally confront her and tell her that it's over. I don't understand the concept that there are more fish in the pond when my heart has been waiting so long to be with one. I have to wait again for the pain to stop for me to acknowledge and understand that better times are coming. I realize that even the things I have control over in this world will fall apart in my hands. Love is not something that I can control and as much as I thought. It will definitely take someone even more special to give me the things to grow and accept that things change.

For the first time I have discovered that it is possible for me physically to have children. It has to be done in a fun way with oral sensual massage, but the process is possible. She is pleasuring with her hands, her mouth and we make love. We both are learning about my body, because to me it is the first time I try to orgasm. Every night we are together is a new experience and a revelation, a discovery for me, but to someone normal it's just another night. Not me, my body starts to straighten, when out of nowhere because I can't feel my penis, pressure builds up in my head and my blood pressure goes up. Holding her mouth over me, she mumbles that, *it's a lot,* but I just want to know what's going on. In every part of my life, I have to ask someone what my body is doing. This is one thing that is a miracle for me, a elation and euphoric escape even without feeling, the rush my body experiences, is unimaginable. I can imagine it is possible to be a father someday now. Each time I try to orgasm it is a workout for her, but my nervous system creates too much pressure in my brain, and with every climax the headache is worse. I hold a lot of reserve resentment toward the love that I have found mostly because of my inexperience and that sex is against the church's teachings. It seems that even Chastity's two twin brothers and mother think I'm not right for her. In the back of my mind I know someone with multiple sclerosis is only going to degenerate in time. That's not fair of me since I am in a wheelchair, but I would really prefer to find someone that allows me to have a long relationship together with at least one of us being as healthy as possible. I sense the change that needs to happen and the incompatibility between us. Conversations are almost gone. We talk more about our feelings on the telephone than in person and sleeping together seems to be a result of fighting.

Love has entered my life but another kind is slipping way. The life of a dog in short, but what they offer in return is unmatched by any other creature or human I have ever known. Fluffy has gotten very old and is deteriorating quickly. I've been too preoccupied with love to decide what to do with him. I know what I must do. We take a few photos with my family together and I watch Fluffy walk around the corner of the back of the House with my dad, through the path. He looks back over his shoulders as if to say he knows what is happening. I start crying as we make our last eye contact. Like any connection I feel with someone close to me, seeing him walk away is the last time movie together. I sometimes feel like a child, no matter how old a person is, this life always has something to experience and teach us. I know I'll never see him again, except for my prayer and wish that my reward is to have Fluffy beside me in heaven. My tears are uncontrollable as we all start crying together for a long period of time. I know the next two weeks I will be thinking if he had any pain. I carry his memory every day of looking at his brown eyes. The reflection and acceptance that we shared gives me strength.

Chastity is off to Germany. It is two weeks since we broke up. Whatever my suspicions had been for her new friend visiting, she has just taken off for two weeks to stay with him in his dorm room in Germany "to visit the country." Chastity traveled with my gray long-sleeved shirt with a number seventeen on the heart patch. It's her favorite shirt so I give it to her to take with her, secretly keeping my intent hidden. I know she has returned. I leave a very long heartfelt broken explanation of my feelings, investing everything I can with her and releasing everything I feel before the machine is full. I wait for her hateful reply.

She parks in front of my house. I follow my path to the front yard and meet her in the driveway. Holding the long shirt I let her borrow to give it back to me we are both silent keeping something in reserve, I'm not sure what. Maybe it's just my inability to recognize all the signs that have led me here. Part of me knows what is true. The other part knows the girl I fell in love with gave up a long time ago on trying to make things work. We speak in quiet explanations, slowly rising with more temper and frustration. It's hard for me to make eye contact with her. Why do I try to look for that passion once more and let her know that this is what she gave up, someone whom is willing to work on it even though we broke up. I am trying to project that. I am confident and know what I believe in and stand for and it's much better than anything she might find without me. I explain why I think it didn't work as I hear Chastity reply, rolling her eyes with a deep breath or two and snippy word expressions.

I know why it didn't work, I say.

Why? Chastity says.

Because it was all your fault. Everything was your fault. I love you. I was trying to tell you the things you did I did not like, but you continue anyway and shoved it in my face telling me, I was wrong, I was insecure, while you did nothing to work on the situation, I explain.

Whatever! It was always something with you, either I was not skinny enough, or I wasn't enough of a virgin, or I had an ex-boyfriend! No one else is going to want to be with you! Chastity explains.

Staring into each other's eyes, Chastity gets up and puts the sweater on my lap, walking over to her driver's side door, holding the door, and looking right at me as our eyes lock and no words are spoken for what seems like minutes. Reflecting on all the memories and the things that will never be. I say one last thing before she closes the door and takes off. With my eyes about to tear up, but without crying, finally it is over and she drives away while I watch as the car goes down the street.

Life! It Must Be a Comedy

Goodbye Chastity. If you truly love me you will be back, I say.

Waiting for a half hour to see if she returns, I summon my mother, pleading for a lighter and then I watch that shirt burn in front of me in the grass where her car took off. The destiny of the shirt is the same as my heart. I delete her number from my phone and months go by. Occasionally I receive phone calls as my story makes headline news across the state and I post all of my news on my homepage website. I never answer any of her calls and when I think it's Chastity disguising her voice I know. I vow never to speak to her again, thinking this is the only way for me to ever get over this feeling. Her last phone call comes. I quickly hand the phone over to my mother having her explain that I am congested and my voice is not good so I cannot speak. Everyday I have those memories. I know I can't get them back and I don't want to continue the love I have with this person, but it still hurts to walk away. I don't know how many years it will be before I find love again. I am determined to change and take what I now know to be a stronger man the next time around.

"Able Hearts" Digital Watercolor. 11 by 5

The 2005 baseball season begins. I speak with Jay at the Orioles Fan Festival at the Baltimore Convention Center. He tells me he wants to help in some way. I spend the whole year working hard in school, fighting for the state to continue paying my education, while learning as much as possible about the art and design of videogames, excelling as a model student in every class. I am always the one student who asks all the questions and make sure that I get all the answers. Sometimes I feel so alone in my computer room with my new computer desk, with my dot on my nose, sipping and puffing to click. I swear sometimes I'm the only student in every class that has so many technical problems.

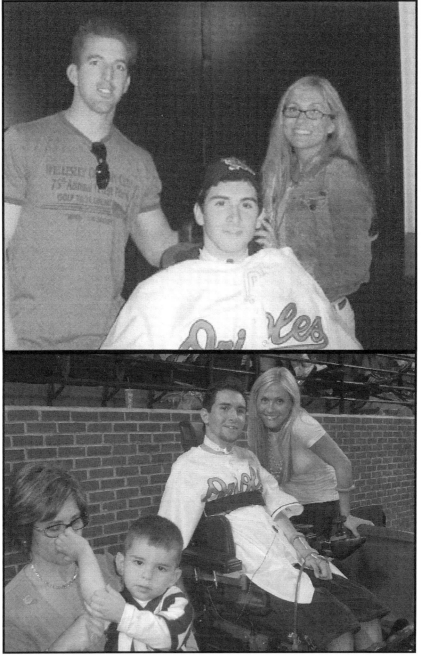

Life! It Must Be a Comedy

It is the end of the year now and Jay Gibbons has helped me raise five hundred dollars for every home run he has hit. We're on the field reenacting the meeting when I gave him the painting as Jay invites local big-time sports broadcast personality Steve Davis to do a radio and television cover story about us and the fundraiser. It airs on the television as a cover story that is unlike any Steve Davis has ever done. I make friends with Steve himself and also have some benefits from being in the public eye. I am starting to see my dream of being a famous artist can actually come true. Steve is the friendliest reporter I've ever met. Steve is a straight forward quick thinking man with compassion always on his heart. I've had other reporters ask me deep questions but Steve is different. He smiles after every question and tries to understand where I'm coming from. He isn't afraid to offer his ideas and help me whenever he can with his radio and television shows. He is light on his foot, hands at his waist, with dark hair sharp and quick to find out more information. Often I'm alone staring at the painting of Jay Gibbons. Emotions run wildly in my efforts to silence the beast inside. Every brush stroke of a new painting, including this one takes me a way. Sometimes it's hard to believe that I painted what I did, but the reality is sweet and bitter, spiritually, and physically my heart is connected to a spirit I struggle at times to believe still exists.

I still pray every night. Every little setback feels like a mile last, but I wipe the sweat from my brow and walk down that road. I push and roll my way through all the negativity around me, forging my heart, mind and spirit, tougher and harder. I refuse to let my heart get tight and my exterior impenetrable. I must keep an open mind. I've learned the smile is my shield and my paintings are my sword. Watching Jay hit all those home runs, being in the stands in my favorite seat and high-fiving his family and fiancé Laura was so exciting. She's a polite blonde girl with a big heart and a bright smile. She is always so cute, wearing her black-framed narrow glasses. We all become good friends, allowing me to become as close to that professional ballplayer experience as possible.

I am flying to California after writing a letter about all of my dreams and ambitions. The cover story by Steve Davis is nominated for an Emmy award. The radio interview wins an Associated Press Award. I am President of my school Student Government Association, with front page stories with dreams of a videogame scholarship. I was accepted as one of twenty-five students out of three hundred applicants to the world's largest game design conference in San Jose, California. I am accompanied by my mother and Gina, spending nearly a week and meeting up with the International Game Developers Association and all the other winning students in San Jose, filming my process along the way, having an experience like never before. This experience opens my eyes to the world of game design and seeing for the first time the path I need to take to reach out to people with similar disabilities by using videogames to heal. I meet with my mentor Michelle Hinn is was assigned to me. Shc is heavily connected in the game accessibility design world. Michelle is sitting at the table with the other mentors and greets me with a smile. Michelle's short red hair, big green eyes, bubbly and energetic personality molds perfectly with my ready to go attitude. Whenever we meet up we are buddies, standing out with her green tight short sleeve shirt, satchel over her shoulder crossing her chest and me in my single-handed wheelchair in a sea of legs. With Michelle by my side I feel unstoppable. She is the perfect mentor. Michelle's chronic pain brought her to the world of games to distract her mind from her body. In this way we are the same and I'm no longer alone. It's a perfect opportunity for me to reach my goals.

I go to a lot of the sessions with other game developers, who give their advice about different aspects of the game design world, trying to learn everything I can before going home. Being charged up with these reinforcements, I use this opportunity and my story as a beacon to inspire the world. I start reaching out to people with different challenges to use the game design world. It could have helped me when I was injured and depressed. Millions of other people need this. I must develop games like never before. I am saddened that the world has not accepted people with my condition, designing games for my needs, but I am in the perfect position, never giving up, trying to accomplish this goal and dream. My injury has led me to believe I must fulfill some significant purpose in my life. It might be a personal goal but I cannot ignore the feeling, the connection I have, to help others suffering. I am left overwhelmed by the lack of support by the game design industry, clueless, with no heartfelt connection to any other perspective if it doesn't have a huge dollar profit connected to it. It might be true that there's not a big demand for helping people with disabilities, but I disagree. What happens when a gamer (God forbid the developer) gets a disability and can no longer play their favorite game? The business motto should be, protect the investment by allowing customers unlimited access and control of their favorite games no matter what happens to the gamer physically.

Ever since the invention of a projectile flying through the air to be used as a weapon for war, the advance of armor plating soldiers bodies somehow never became conceptualize until after the Vietnam War. How can that be? I don't believe anyone believes human life is dispensable. I am a fallen soldier in the field of gaming, and I know longer participate in purchasing my services. I have to arm myself as one of the fallen. The challenge seems large, but the changes that can be made to help people play games are so simple. Allow videogames to be adapted directly, connected to the equipment already being used on computers. Thinking a little bit outside the box even makes the game easier to play for the casual gamer. They demand a certain market and always get frustrated by complex controls, detailed displays, tutorials, of the most challenging but most entertaining games that everyone wants to play. It's the condition of the human mind, wrapped in greed. Every person questions why we exist, and what the purpose of life is, but it's only when our condition deteriorates that we appreciate what matters most.   I know life is difficult. I believe people can change, even if history has proven that people advance but always fall short of being human.

I met up with my favorite developer, David Perry, before going into a conference room with the brightest minds of the game design industry. The session is called Experimental Game Play. David Perry, developer and creator of Earthworm Jim and all of The Matrix series games and so is the creator of The Sims. I question David about my concern for accessible videogames. I can play his game with my mouth controller, specially designed by quadcontrol.com and I conquered it. Surely David must have an answer to this challenge. David shares an interest, telling me he completely understands, but I'm disappointed that he doesn't create a strong initiative or that there isn't already one. In my excitement I can't help but ask David about The Matrix, and if he knows if the character Neo will ever return after supposedly being exhausted or wiped out, but nobody knows at the end of the last movie. David signed all of my Matrix game covers, and even The Matrix art book. I consider him a great friend. The way our paths have crossed will be inspiring to me forever.

Even though I have frustrations from the industry, this was the greatest experience I could have ever asked for. In the session Michelle asks, *"What can developers do to make videogames more accessible?"*

We both are shocked from their response. The one young developer suggested giving Third World countries used cell phones so that they can play video games on their phone. He could not have been more off the topic. Their hearts and minds appear to be completely disconnected, even though a few designers that work for some big-time companies approach us saying, they wish they could do something to help.

I've been home for a few months and I've been fighting off a few sinus infections and I have returned to therapy for my body. I'm coming home from the spinal cord rehab program at Kennedy Krieger Institute in Baltimore. I need to keep my body in top condition. The program is directed by Christopher Reeves' Dr. McDonald. Summer and my mother strap me in my chance take off. I see my mother's face, white and somber. She says a good friend of mine has passed away. It's the Robert I grew up with, our next door neighbor. I don't know how it happened. We all sit quietly while Adrian explains some details to my mother on the phone. She wasn't told much only that Adrian was there with the family at the hospital.

The last time I spoke to and saw Robert was a few weeks ago. Summer got his attention in the front yard yelling for Robert to come in and catch up with me. He came downstairs to visit me in my computer room. He lost a lot of weight. He was wearing shorts and a tank top but didn't stay long. We even made plans to go to church the next Sunday. He was excited to go, commenting that he was going to straighten out his life. I didn't know what he meant by that, since we haven't hung out in a while. It was great to see him. I gave him a bunch of my business cards and he was eager to share them with all of his friends. He looked around my room, and saw my artwork and newspaper clippings, acting impressed and proud of me. He put his hand on my shoulder and I put my hand over his arm and we said goodbye. He ran back up the steps, pushing open the glass door turned around and waved. We never went to that church the next weekend.

Preparing for Robert Cherry's funeral I have to accept that life can be horrible, but in my experience, if I can speak in front of everyone at the funeral I can offer some sort of peace or hope for those who need it. I don't know why life surrounds some of us with tragedy and hard times. Everyday of my life I am shocked and surprised about what has happened to me and how unbearable it is. No matter how much I overcome it, I cannot accept that this is just my part in life. I have accepted that more than most people ever will. In an imperfect world, ultimately I must know it's far from perfect. In that realization I've found peace and harmony, realizing the meaning of life. We must live happily, in spite of negativity, to fiercely face every challenge. Robert lives in me now. I push myself further when I feel down. Keeping Robert's memory alive gives me strength. When I speak I can share a glimpse of how beautiful life can be. I look one by one at each of his family members, sisters and nephew, mother and father then staring at Robert.

I offer a chance to see the beauty that this moment brings to our life. I'm thankful that sometimes this kind of things in our life can bring people closer. When I mention his name in my speech, I can't help but cry. Somehow I pull myself together and finish my speech. I try to offer some kind of peace not knowing if it will help. Robert was like a little brother to me. When I speak, I keep everything in the present tense to show that he is still alive somewhere, waiting for everyone, where we'd someday meet again. I speak about salvation, and the modern-day

version of God's promise. The conflict in my heart and mind about faith
and God resolves in me more every day. I speak about faith very
expressively and passionately.   I see the good in myself more and faith
only as a guide.

I know the years have been hard but we have laughed and we
have cried together. My parents make me laugh and I appreciate them so
much more than ever before. All of my nurses have now left. I wait for
months for the nursing agency to find the right match for me. I never
know who the new one will be, but still I am picky in choosing the right
person who fits exactly what I need. No one is Mercy, and she has a
laugh that is contagious and friendly with happiness. She's only a few
years older than me. She has curly scratchy hair pulled back, rounded
face, a cute little scrunched up nose, and common sense, thank God, she
just gets it. She's the simplest thing I've been looking for. It's funny
how I rely on the hands of others not my own, laughing when we get
along well, like we are connected in a special way. Many people before,
unlike those who have helped me most, where people who just did not
get it.

My story has reached the ears, eyes and hearts of some local
people in my area as I complete a portrait of Baltimore Blast star
Denison Cabral, who's also a friend now. Amazingly, that all came
together when a fan named Don heard the story of Jay Gibbons and I on
the radio. Don has come in my life, a cheerful man, bald, tall and a little
stocky with a deep raspy voice, who said, *I just want to help.* Tonight I
speak at the Babe Ruth and Sports Legends Museum at Camden Yards to
unveil the portrait donated by the winning raffle recipient, on permanent
display alongside Jay Gibbons' painting. I give a speech for Channel 2
News, covering the story alongside Denison Cabral and Jay Gibbons as
they both speak about their friendship with me and how we have been
able to help each other. My life has been an example to these great
athletes, inspiring them to a world of possibilities, through perseverance
and not giving up. Every opportunity like this makes me look at what
people say about how great I am for what I've done. I never thought I
was that great a long time ago, starting from nothing but believing in
something back then. Their words strike true in my heart. Jay speaks
first, then Denison. I wait to speak last. I hear their strong words, but
the ones that stick out the most, will always live with me:

Denison Cabral. Oil. 16 by 20

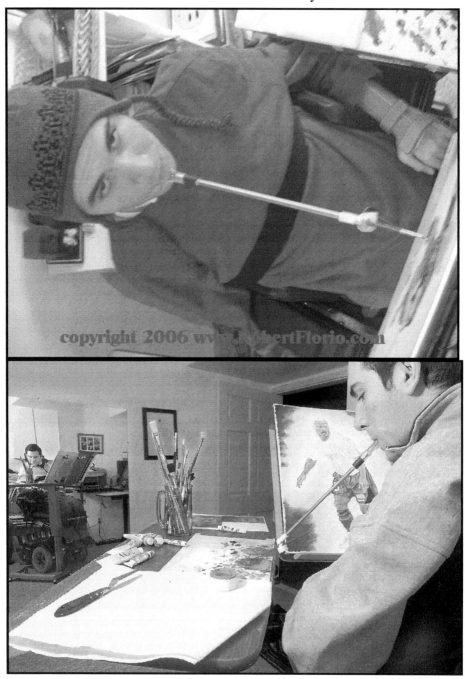

*From the day I have met him Robert has changed my life, totally!...I look forward to many of these events with Robert...His true gift is his ability to express to people...I believe he has only begun to scratch the surface, of conquering this world...Knowing Robert, he is going to...*Jay says.

Why can't we be like Robert...He doesn't complain...So whenever I have an injury I always think of Robert...I think that's why he came to our life...So we should listen, Denison says passionately with his Brazilian accent.

*I prayed for God to give me something, to push me, because that was something I desperately needed...I look back at the sacrifices my parents had to make, and the sacrifices that I made...Not one prayer has not come true that I truly believed in... Jay Gibbons is a true friend, a godsend, an angel on my shoulder. Without him I would not be where I am today. My dream has been to be like the greatest artists someday. To have my paintings in this museum makes me feel like I have that honor...These paintings I have created, and many more that I will create, will be the fingerprints that I leave on this world...*I said.

It has been almost four years now and I'm nearing graduation. I have been pushing my inspirational story through the years and my parents and Jay Gibbons have been my greatest friends, like angels on my shoulder, opening up every door and possibility and the beginnings of my dreams and goals to be accomplished. I have recently seen defeat before I'm about to speak in front of a group about game accessibility. I've been invited to be a speaker at the Games for Health Conference in Baltimore as a key note speaker representing an online accessibility awareness group called The Accessibility SIG.

Before attending this speech my life has been bombarded first with pneumonia after one of my nurses. She's from Africa, young, slender and airheaded. She carelessly dumped my breathing treatment all over me and didn't pick up on my worsening condition. It has been a short stay (only a few days) recuperating from pneumonia and I thought I was doing okay. Shortly after coming home I spend fourteen days in the hospital with unbearable pain. I have overcome it, discovering that autonomic dysreflexia, the results of my digestive tract being backed up, causing my blood pressure to be unbelievably high. For a quadriplegic it can be deadly. I have just experienced it for the first time this severely. While my body tries to adjust, headaches pierce my brain. Only the most powerful pain relievers give me any comfort.

I'm ready to get up in the morning. I'm all dressed and have my hoyer lift pad wraped around me while lying in bed. Mercy pumps the lift to put me in my chair, when instantly pressure builds in my head. My head feels like it's going to explode. The pain is out of control as Mercy presses down, cupping my forehead in the palm of her hands while I'm screaming for more. Nothing is making the pain go away. My head throbs off and on in front and back. My mother rushes downstairs to hold my head as Mercy gets ice and calls the ambulance. I have no idea why this is happening so I empty my bladder and relieve five hundred cc of liquid. Several minutes have passed when the ambulance comes to my backdoor I am cathed to relieve my bladder again, and another five hundred cc comes out. The pain is so horrible that I am ready to pass out.

His blood pressure is two hundred over one hundred and twenty and rising. What do you think, should we take him? The one paramedic guy says to the other paramedic guy.

What!? His blood pressure is how high!? Are you crazy? With his blood pressure being that high he could have a stroke or die. You better take him! My mother demands furiously and in shock.

The paramedics look at me and I look at them like they're both crazy.

You have to take me now! I need something for the pain! I say.

I'm pushed to the ambulance. Mercy holds my head in the ambulance and they're trying to put in a PICC line but can't. My mother stays behind comforting my nephew Nathan and gathering a few things to meet at the emergency room.

Robert wake up, don't fall asleep. I need you to stay awake buddy, the paramedic says to me as we are on our way.

Aren't you going to turn on the sirens? I say after almost passing out from the pain.

No, we only turn the sirens on for emergencies, different kinds, the paramedic explains.

What the fuck is this!? I say.

I'm shocked they wouldn't turn the sirens on. I'm in so much pain and I can't imagine something that would be any worse that wouldn't qualify for hitting the panic button. I'm furious they are acting so stupid. I arrive at North Arundel Hospital in Glen Burnie screaming for pain medicine. They leave me in the hallway in the emergency room for fifteen minutes with no one assisting me. After an x-ray of my abdomen I'm given a fleet enema, Percocet and told my stomach is full of stool but I still don't go to the bathroom. Without any more concern the doctors have no clue what to do with a spinal cord patient and they send me home. The pain goes away but only as the medicine kicks in. This hospital has always been so horrible. They are known for wrongful diagnoses. I heard of this happening to people with spinal injuries, but I never knew what it meant or how serious it was until now. Sometimes I wonder, what the hell could be next in my life? I just need to get laid, that was my biggest worry until now. At least for a little while things had been going okay. When all this is over I hope my luck starts changing in that area.

My mother holds my head in each hospital. I'm finally relieved at a third hospital. Good Samaritan Hospital in Baltimore reveals to me where I belong in life now. My local emergency room at North Arundel Hospital misdiagnosed me first after arriving in an ambulance. The next day I went to Johns Hopkins, and see my surprise, the supposedly "world's greatest hospital," also told me to go home. They kept me a little longer and put in an indwelling catheter. I can't even relieve myself without the pain being triggered again. Three days later when my Pulmonary Doctor Steiner at Good Samaritan Hospital admits me. I'm taking laxatives and going to the bathroom as often as I can and every time I have a bowel movement, the throbbing returns and my mother holds my head as I seriously think my time in this world is over. I'm introduced to a spinal cord specialist who answers some of the questions I never knew I should've been asking about my condition. For years my belly always looked distended and I'm had trouble consistently having decent bowel movements. That was my first warning sign but I didn't know how to take it serious, like keeping a healthier diet and monitoring the fiber I eat. It's a never-ending story of constantly monitoring my condition and reading the warning signs my body tells me before it's too late. Amazingly without being able to feel most of my body, I'm always right when I know something is up or how to take care of myself. When I have to urinate the AD makes my blood pressure rise and my head gets tingly like Spiderman's spider senses. It's the same when I need a bowel movement or if something on my body is in pain making me hot. I say *my spidey senses are tingling*. If I don't monitor my body the pain can be unbearable and fatal. With a black turban around his hand and a dark beard, he speaks with an American voice. He is kind with a polite smile, tall and a tad stocky. Doctor Sandeep Singh takes me to the spinal cord rehab floor and treats me.

I have just been discharged, barely able to keep my head up and losing my breath, too dizzy to speak with my full intent and passion about the challenge I have in life. Fate has put me in a humble state to recap my life. Mom takes me straight to give a speech I have prepared months in advance. I have tried to advocate about helping people through video games. I speak at the Games for Health Conference in Baltimore City, volunteering as part of my game accessibility online advocacy group. I present my findings and thoughts to fifteen or so people, introducing myself with a recent Fox 45 news cover story by reporter Amber Theoharis to grab their attention. I met Amber after Steve Davis invited me to a Baltimore Ravens special training camp at their private facilities. Amber was quick to befriend me, and I couldn't wait to talk with a beautiful blonde. Amber is the prettiest reporter that ever followed my story, she gets very quiet when listening to me talk and constantly tries to pin down the key most interesting talking points. Her lips and eyes clench as she listens to me answer questions on camera. We quickly become good friends and we keep in touch. I could tell she was interested in my story as Ravens star linebacker number fifty two was looking at the artwork I brought, especially Jay Gibbons' portrait and her video cameraman captured the moment. Ray Lewis said to me, *you painted these with your mouth? I really want you to do mine!* The story reveals who I am and the event at the Sports Legends Museum, highlighting my goals for game accessibility. Somehow I last through the entire speech, trying not to pass out and eager to go home.

I was invited by David Perry himself to be part of a secret volunteer videogame project. Not only did I get to meet my favorite game developer in San Jose but it wasn't long after I got home that he invited me to design a game. The project has been going on for more than a year and we have created an amazing new type of racing game with animals and characters who train and race on beasts. I have created a completely new control interface for people with a physical disability like me who can't use their hands. The game is made through Acclaim

Games and directed by David Perry. I have used every bit of knowledge from my Game Art and Design bachelor's degree program, how to manage a team, animate, create characters, levels, and game play all for a massively multiplayer online racing videogame. Almost fifty thousand people signed up to be part of the project and immediately it dwindles down to less than three hundred people throwing in their ideas as the game becomes more and more complex and specifically directed and designed by David Perry choosing the best ideas. We meet twice a week on the phone and I constantly push for game accessibility but it feels like I'm the only one with this driven innovation to reach out to a new demographic. I'm very pleased to hear David Perry personally saying that he wants the game to be accessible specifically so that I could play it. Another volunteer and I work hard for a game design document for accessible controls.

It's very simple. By using the mouse click and movement, a player can move the mouse forward for speed, down for slow, left and right for turning and clicking once or twice left click and right click to access and fire weapons, including jumping. The idea is to have a heads-up display in the middle of the screen that is transparent and when the mouse is near the sides or middle the selections can be made. This is all created and documented in theory and design but never made it to actual programming and game play. The process has been amazing. I have learned so much. The game is close to an end. There have been twenty-two volunteer designers left standing who have qualified for an award, a recognized letter of recognition directly written and signed by David Perry and announced on the official Project Top-Secret web site the finalists are listed. I'm one of them. I have pleaded my case for accessibility and made sure that when the game needed adjustments I addressed it. In my attempt to share my passion for game design I even wrote a multi-page risk analysis, breaking down the resources realistically about what should be designed to save time and money. At times I saw the project screaming out of control, on a huge epic scale with only a handful of novice (and just a few experienced) designers. I know for the future, when designing a game, that the best solution is the most obvious and simple. The bottom line is, is the game fun? I now know what it means to be part of a team and design every aspect of the game from scratch, work with the director and the people in charge, and specifically have the idea of accessibility accepted. The fate of the project is unclear but I commend all the people who worked on the project diligently. I'm honored to be part of that experience and be one of thousands who made it to the end and was recognized by David Perry.

Life! It Must Be a Comedy

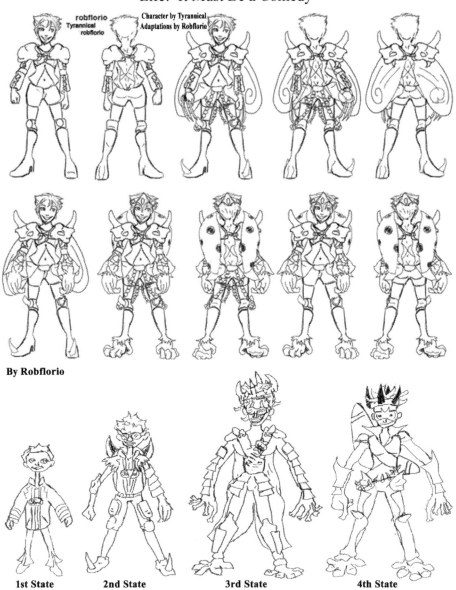

By Robflorio

1st State   2nd State   3rd State   4th State

290

Life! It Must Be a Comedy

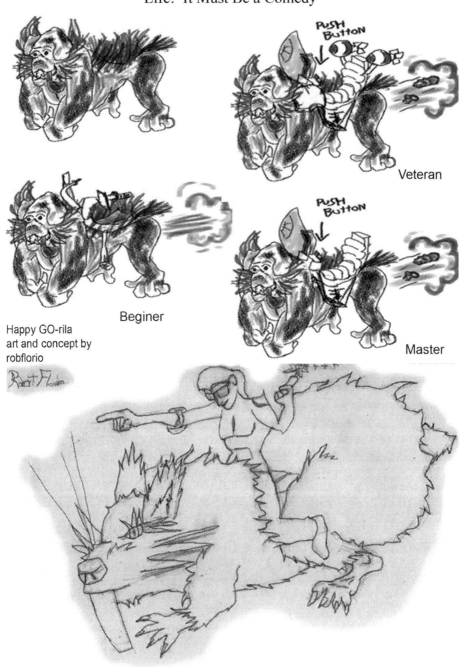

PUSH BUTTON

Veteran

Beginer

PUSH BUTTON

Master

Happy GO-rila
art and concept by
robflorio

Life! It Must Be a Comedy

by robflorio

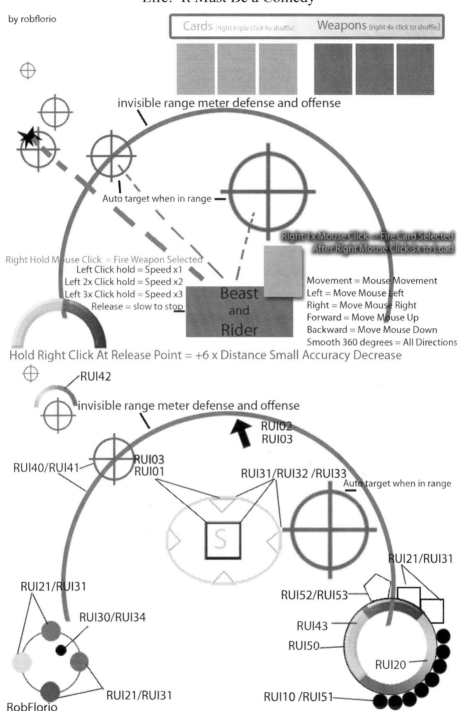

Cards (right triple click to shuffle)   Weapons (right 4x click to shuffle)

invisible range meter defense and offense

Auto target when in range ——

Right 1x Mouse Click = Fire Card Selected
After Right Mouse Click 3x to Load

Right Hold Mouse Click = Fire Weapon Selected
Left Click hold = Speed x1
Left 2x Click hold = Speed x2
Left 3x Click hold = Speed x3
Release = slow to stop

Beast
and
Rider

Movement = Mouse Movement
Left = Move Mouse Left
Right = Move Mouse Right
Forward = Move Mouse Up
Backward = Move Mouse Down
Smooth 360 degrees = All Directions

Hold Right Click At Release Point = +6 x Distance Small Accuracy Decrease

RUI42

invisible range meter defense and offense

RUI02
RUI03

RUI03
RUI01

RUI40/RUI41

RUI31/RUI32 /RUI33

Auto target when in range

S

RUI21/RUI31

RUI21/RUI31

RUI52/RUI53

RUI30/RUI34

RUI43

RUI50

RUI20

RUI21/RUI31

RUI10 /RUI51

RobFlorio

Life! It Must Be a Comedy

by robflorio

Hold Right Click At Release Point = **+10** x Distance Medium Accuracy Decrease

Hold Right Click At Release Point = +6 x Distance Small Accuracy Decrease

Hold Right Click At Release Point = +2 x Distance Excellent Accuracy

Shoot Weapon Distance / Accuracy Meter = Hold Right Click 0x

Steering

The mouse movement outside of the selection area in the center of the screen allows controls on turning left, right, forward explorationand down for down deceleration. You are free to move the mouse in these areas to control the direction of your Beasts and Rider..

Forward acceleration speed

Current position mouse above the sensor for forward acceleration. Acceleration speed is sensitive mouse movement up.

robflorio

Life! It Must Be a Comedy

Turning Left And Right

You move the mouse left to the left side of the sensor to turn left. Sensitive to angle of turning.
Similar for turning right you put the mouse across the screen to the right side of the sensor selections space. Turning angle is the same sensitive function.

Deceleration

you place or move the mouse position below the sensor selector. Deceleration declines beat insensitive to the move-

robflorio

296

Sensors Selector Function

The sensor selector is the red oval shaped in the center of the screen with the black box in the center. This Heads Up Display HUD is the device for selecting your cards and weapons.

Function

The outer red oval with the four arrows allows you to scroll through your selections and your mode of play for cards and weapons.

robflorio

Sensors Selector Function

The black box in the center of the sensor selector displays the options available to be activated for use in the game.

During Gameplay

You will notice during gameplay this sensor selector will be transparent and if visible at all to not impede in the vision of the gameplay. The sensor selector centers the mouse position in the middle centering all your actions into one spot.

robflorio

298

Life! It Must Be a Comedy

Sensors Selector Function

Activating Sensor Selector

You can move the mouse over and through the sensor while steering alldirections. With the mouse function,, you **Left** click over the area to activate the selector. Steering functions are still active but in this selector becomes more visible and active.

Hovering the mouse over the four arrows scrolls through your selections. The square box will display your selectable options. The scroll arrows turn yellow.

robflorio

Life! It Must Be a Comedy

Sensors Selector Function

You can activate your chosen option by **Right** clicking on your mouse. This reduces the time it takes for you to make your selection while still steering.

You can now **Right** click to use your selected weapon or card on your opponents. After making your selection the censors selector deactivate to not impede your vision for gameplay.

robflorio

300

Life! It Must Be a Comedy

Two years have passed and the goals I have set upon myself are closer than ever before. The Baltimore Sun published a front-page story titled, "Hues of Life Stir After One Dark Day," on December 4, 2007. It's a big spread and the oil painting of Babe Ruth I completed in it titled, "The Golden Bade."

"The Golden Babe" Oil. 18 by 24

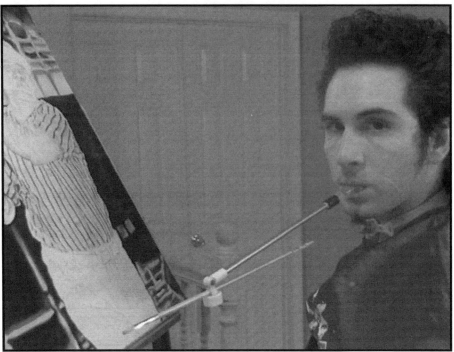

I am very conscious about the image I project, thinking someday if more people hear my story they might see the handsome man I am, but at the same time I have fun with presenting myself with style. I cut my sideburns past my ears thinly shaved to a point, and mohawked my hair to the back and front spiked, sides straight up with my little chin goatee to a thin point on my chin. I get my inspiration from many places, but some of the most tranquil deep inspirations come using music to visualize my accomplishments. I can hear the lyrics of Linkin Park playing me on, "Crawling in my skin, these wounds they will not heal, fear is how I fall, confusing what is real!" to the stage of life. When I create art or have a challenge in life, I have always turned to my faith and the creative drive that comes from music and movies. After years of staying true to my appearance, the image I see for myself, to mess up my hair for this occasion, I am proudly going to cover my hair in a graduation cap. December 13, 2007 is that moment in my accomplishments, as the marathon I have traveled in life ceremoniously rewards me with results from all my time spent fighting for what I want most. I am the first in my family to graduate college.

I prepare to walk across the stage to receive my diploma, a bachelor's degree in computer science specializing in Game Art and

Life! It Must Be a Comedy

Design from the Art Institute of Pittsburgh Online Division. From the airplane I'm accompanied by my parents, displaying my talent of accomplishments during the assembly, hours before graduation. The time has come. I sit in front of all the other students I have never met before and even the instructors I have never met in person, the select few online game design students scattered all over. We see each other now for the first time. I'm not sitting in the crowd with the students, instead I've been chosen as the guest speaker as I sit on the stage next to other honorary students.

I am receiving the first ever Dean's Merit Award, created for my accomplishments as a shining model student with a three point eight GPA. As I sit here listening to the other students speak I see the past twelve years of my life flashing by. Wearing my black robe and special honors yellow double sashay rope, I look out into the audience. I smile reflectively, realizing the time spent, the years of hard work, trouble and sacrifice, justified by this award and knowing that my goals are right at my fingertips. My parents get an ovation when I introduce them and describe everything they have done for me. The program director of my school game classes, Jeannie Novak, and fellow instructors are attending. The vice president of the school introduces me and she describes all the criteria required for this award. I get an ovation too. The room is filled with clapping and admiration from so many people celebrating my accomplishments. I've been down a hard road. This is one big celebration that I have done it with a passion for life and inspiration that a man named Christ has given me. With the support of my family and friends, even through the darkest hard times, this day takes all the pain and sacrifice away, as everyone can see I have won the prize of my meaning-filled education.

I receive my diploma, going across the stage and having my picture taken as my mother runs to the front and my dad struggles with the camcorder. My hair is slicked back on the sides and duck-tailed in the back, straight up in the front up like comic book Wolverine, with long pointed sideburns, covered up by my graduation cap. I shake the hand of the President of the school and receive my diploma and go to the end of the stage. This moment is filled with shock and appreciation, of living in the moment, of so many years dreaming of being on this stage, heading toward my diploma, of pictures and videos in my mind of how athe future might look, but now actually being here and accomplishing what I said I would.

My speech had ended with gratitude and reflection in a poem by Robert Frost called *The Road Not Taken*, showing everyone the meaning behind the path I have taken. Carefully expressing my emotions, I pause to speak with full intent as I say the last words:

> "*I shall be saying this with a sigh*
> *Somewhere ages and ages hence:*
> *Two roads diverged in a wood, and I---*
> *I took the one less traveled by,*
> *And that has made all the difference.*"

The journey has been long and it has been hard at the very start when most of my ambitions and dreams were shattered. I still look for love. I am waiting for the dream girl I have always envisioned to enter my front door. We met a few weeks ago on a Match.com web site. When she does, I know I am in love. She stands five-ten, with long beautiful blonde hair. She's a model with an amazing cheerful personality with a great big smile, perfect teeth and beautiful blue eyes. She comes to me dressed in white leather Italian boots to her knees and a beautiful letdown ponytail to the middle of her back. Her elegance and sophistication is a sight to behold as my eyes satisfy the years of waiting. My long, arduous dream has just become reality.

Life! It Must Be a Comedy

I enjoy the pleasure of her company at night a few times a week, and most weekends, we are together. Instantly I knew, seeing her, as my heart felt like it was pounding out of my chest. She is real, her name is Candy. My love is pure and very passionate holding on to so much, blissfully realizing and releasing my desires more than three years in the making. Every situation in my life is awkward. I'm about to make out with her and make love in my bed. Not only has my girlfriend met my parents on our first date, but my mother was the last person to handle my penis to prepare me for sex. That's the difference. The time with her is fun and the time is rewarding and I can't help but think of so much that I still cannot feel or do, but looking in her eyes and knowing she is fine with knowing my inability, having the attraction for me equally makes me gain strength and confidence. This woman is so beautiful there is nothing that will stop me from enjoying the moment so I will put that to the side and not allow myself to ruin what has finally come true. So many years thinking I could not have a girlfriend. I didn't approach anyone, but finding her and being together is exactly what I've been longing for. We celebrate Valentine's Day at my favorite restaurant, The Rusty Sea-Dog, in Baltimore's Inner Harbor. Both of us can't wait to finish our meals, speaking words of passion in anticipation of the romantic night to come. I look into her eyes, surrounded by the beautiful city, hovering over the water, as she whispers to me, to be taken home and made love to. Kissing her, everything is larger because of her beautiful height, her lips, her legs and hands against me and we pulsate for each other. Her desire for me is surreal. We celebrate my twenty-sixth birthday together, but the only gift I need is what I have and I am happy.

I watch her leave me in the mornings, and come to me all the time, as we lay in bed. I have a makeshift convertible new sofa bed attached to my bed, so she spreads out with plenty room. It's all coming together now in my new spacious apartment. Rejuvenation green walls and one reddish chocolate wall behind my bed surrounds us. The light comes in the morning from my five tall windows and the French doors out the back and an extra door on the side. I have plenty of room for my exercise bike, to keep my legs strong and my heart pumping. It sits in the empty corner at my bedroom door waiting for me to ride. I wait for stem cell research to finally give me back the control I long for. The future feels promising, as I watch her flaunting her naked body, strutting down my double wide sloping ramp that goes to the other room. She moves her body erotically to the music, while holding on to the railing. Her body is illuminated and the fans keep our bodies tempered.

We make love spinning in circles in the open room in my chair, having plenty of room equal to the entire space of my old living room, kitchen and bathroom combined. My apartment is recreated with a brand-new kitchen, yellow walls and tiles with a red stripe all the way around, continuing through the slanted tile work on the back splash. A fundraiser has given me a long-awaited gift for renovations for this new apartment, complete with a dark brown and sandy ceramic tile floor in my room. A lighter color stained stonework pattern leys throughout the rest of the basement and my computer room down the hallway. Where I sleep is my place to escape, outside surrounded by five-foot wide concrete walkway and a ten-foot walking extension off the back. The motion lights outside pickup every movement, beautifully lighting up the white shingle exterior walls. Each of our movements, kisses, and thoughts are entangled. We watch TV in my new living room, surrounded by a computer desk, couch and my artwork on the walls beautifully lit up. Her beautiful perfect body is slender with just the right size breasts. She's three years older than me and is an angel in my life. Like a pill of relief from so many years of missed opportunities. I feel everything now in this one woman, holding back nothing, sharing everything. In my attempt to remove my trachea tube under supervision of my doctor, I feel the sweet kisses around my neck as the taped on patch closing the hole temporarily allows me to caress my skin in places never before, from gentle wet soft touches as we make love. Together she feels my eyes of pride and her beauty reflected by her actions, movements and words.

I see my vision leaving me, with no real explanation. Candy is distancing herself, and my phone calls are not being returned. Her body is a prize and her mind is appraised, she is sold only on the idea of becoming a stripper. My fleeting heart and beaten mind stretch to conceive the idea. At first I am surprised, but I realize I'm in a wheelchair, and a girlfriend who is a stripper would be the most amazing sacrifice I would ever have to make. Her anxiety and last dashing hope of making a lot of money at thirty years old, she waits to get the job and I lay back and wait for her to come to me. I'm intoxicated and blinded by this beautiful vision before she runs away.

Life! It Must Be a Comedy

Candy and I attend an unveiling at the Babe Ruth and Sports Legends at Camden Yards Museum, for a painting I was commissioned for of Babe Ruth. Her girl friend comes along hoping to meet a guy. I have the great opportunity to talk with Johnny Unitas' wife. He was a quarterback legend of the Baltimore Colts. Also there is the manager of the Baltimore Orioles, Mr. F. Mr. F is exhibiting his hand that he sculpted wearing his Baltimore Orioles World Series 1983 championship ring. Johnny Unitas' wife Sarah is there honoring portraits of her late husband. The curator of the museum, Shawn, introduces me around. Shawn is always responsive, permanently enshrining my portrait of Denison Cabral. He is a tall man with a dark full goatee. He's very knowledgeable on every historical subject and eager to tell people about every detail. The entire museum is crowded with people. Sarah and Mr. F can't believe that I painted Babe Ruth with my mouth and with such great detail and skill. We all talk a little bit and I try to convince them both to buy my portrait of Babe Ruth. It is truly an honor to be standing between both of them in a great museum honoring the greatest ballplayer ever.

After the ceremony, television reporters film us opening the exhibit. I can't keep my eyes off of Candy. She is standing beside me in her tantalizing long black, fur jacket, and miniskirt and high heels, with her hair pinned up with the long wavy ponytail. I steal glances at her all night back and forth. I'm proud she is by my side. We wander around the museum drinking beer, eating hot dogs, getting caught in the elevator making out. We have what feels like a lifetime of things in common, our personalities are sharp and our thoughts are positive. I could watch her smile and hear her laugh all day, walking around me with and without clothes. Her walk is equally unique the way she sways and steps casts me further in love with everything about her. She steps first on the heel of her foot, then steps high off the ball of her toes lifting her body up and down and side to side. I'm tantalized by every movement, gesture, smile, thought and words. She looks into my eyes, lying naked on my bed as I sketch her portrait from head to toe. Her green shirt with a number on it is pulled up, and her breasts are exposed. Her undershorts are pulled down below her cheeks, she rests on her left hip and her back is flat with her bottom exposed facing me. I finish her portrait in less than two hours, and to her amazement it looks exactly like her. We look into each other's eyes as I'm drawing and we whisper the desires of our thoughts.

Life! It Must Be a Comedy

Any woman would be lucky to have you. When I look into your eyes, as you draw me, I can feel your passion, Candy says.

We full around while I lay my chair flat and into standing mode. We make love standing up. She gets excited and arrives. She's amazed that she could do it standing up.

I only speak of the greatest things that have affected my life and that I have waited the longest time for. I know there are so many people in my position who have always wanted that one thing to come true. I have so many more dreams that I want. I fight for the greatest answers, to give me the best quality of life every day. It is real, my discovery or mirage, a vision of beauty and desire, leaving me reluctantly, to choose that job in her lust for money. Now I stand alone while the echoes of her promise piercing my heart. I let go, feeling like a man. I stand by my love. I watch the sweat drip down her back with the long vine tattoo of two lilies at the top of her back, all the way down, like she grew from me. The honey from her sweating lips, quiver for my touch, never tasted sweeter. She is with me one last night, standing in her beautiful silhouette naked structure. *Will I ever see you again?* I say. She's standing in front of my dresser. *Without a doubt baby,* she tells me. I fall asleep while she gets dressed for work. I feel her sweet kiss on my lips and I wake up looking into her eyes. I don't want to stop looking at her, then slowly she walks out my back door like every morning to go to work. Holding her bags, in her tall boots with her long hair extension clipped on down her back. The door is still open and she peeks in, closing it, waiting for one last look, and she smiles, blows me a kiss and says, *I love you.* I get up and go to my computer to find a piece of paper with her lipstick kiss and, "I love you," written on it. She has faded away, and I'm left to wonder. The dream is over. I have now just awakened.

The man that I am now is someone strong, unwavering and reassured through my faith and determination that this life will not hold me down. I get great inspiration from movies and music. The music soothes the rhythmic pulse, beating inside me, as my passion races, as my conscience sometimes tries to rip through and I try everything to lift my head again. I don't kid myself I know the harshness of life, but in defiance of the system we live in, I choose to survive. I have unveiled the desires and losses in my life, facing them head on. I sang out loud, regenerating my spirit to live and inspire.

Going on, I express what I cannot feel. In my journey my hands are strong, as I reach out for hope, to share what I have trained myself to feel. I have seen the prayer that I send out continue to echo through the heavens, out through space, as far as this galaxy and beyond to its destiny. I know hell is right here on earth, but I don't know where in the hell heaven is. The ears and the eyes of the all-powerful knowing Creator are somehow laughing as I slowly discover the truth for myself. Watching as I stumble, thumbing through pages in a book that I was writing myself. The rules that I live by in this world are the stepping stones to allow me to grow. I look up as if some great vision hovering above me is now leaving to ascend out through the sky, clouds, space and time searching for the next person that will be its catalyst. It is my story and my journey that I have witnessed with my eyes, experiences in a world that I never knew existed.

I wait for the next journey in life, hopefully to keep me safe and healthy with love right around the corner. I take a few experiences and opportunities to grow from, looking for success that I'm now prepared for. Along the way I hope to inspire and spread courage, peace, hope and strength, continuing to master my abilities and gifts. I will always look back at that fourteen-year-old boy waiting for the next great thing to come his way, while fearing the misguided mind I had, not sure what I wanted to do, fearing all authority, wanting to be free and full of passion. Somehow, I have fulfilled some of that for myself. I have seen the beauty of the world through a sea of tears. I believe in myself. I'm blessed because I don't have to see to believe, but I believe what I see. I will heal the wounds that only time can heal. I hear mockery and laughter from the greatest powers that be. My human experience is not a feeble tale, but it's from the world. People choose to do something greater with their lives, holding on to the little miracles that do shine through from the best parts of humanity. It is at the exact moment when success is reached, after facing failure on the road that no one else has traveled, revealing God's sense of humor that creation seems to echo in life. The fragility of our lives reveals the harsh nature of this world and the little things that mean the most. I don't think I'm the only one thinking about the choices I've made. My faith has always been the most constant thing to rely on. When all is lost, faith will let me rise above anything, because of His promise. I realize now it was the result of my actions, because I chose to live. It is my willpower that gives me great strength.

My journey is like a rock concert, with success in mind, winning the battle against negativity, and being cheered on. I wait for my wounds to be healed. I step up to the front stage to shine my light for everyone to see. Whatever forces I believe in, I know God is a guide for everyone who chooses to believe. I found my own way and other people can too. I take an arsenal of abilities to be my weapons, with confidence, forged in that faith and rising above the hardest times, to win my fight in life, creating my dreams. My faith will guide me, and my willpower and self-awareness gives me strength when all else fails. I choose to look at life and believe in myself, as the pictures of my past rise up and the face of time stares at me revealing, it's my choice to make all my dreams come true. The passion and Spirit of life lives in me, like a dragon, as beautiful and preserved, revealing the power of my heart and mind through my abilities. I will never give up the fight, stepping up to the plate to swing as hard as I can.

Cal Ripken Jr. "My Hero" Watercolor. 18 by 24

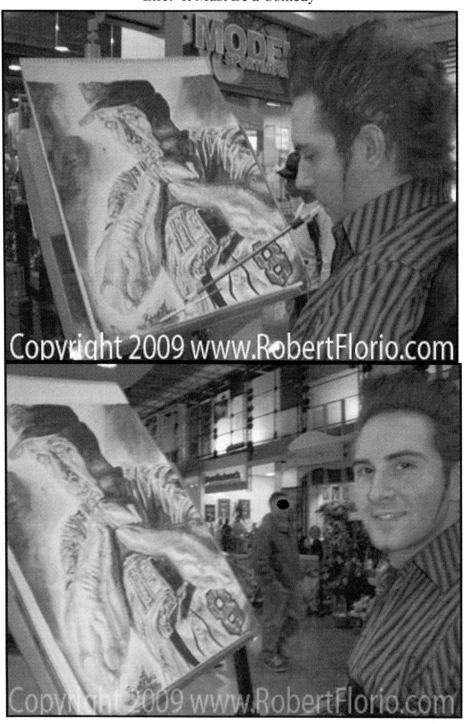

Cal Ripken Jr. "Ripken's Last" Digital Watercolor. 15 by 11

Chapter 13

13

I'm surrounded by beautiful women every day. My life is tough, but I realize I have more women assisting me in my private life than most men dream is possible. I am always a gentleman with people who help me, but a huge part of me smiles because to be with beautiful women was one of my biggest dreams when I was fourteen. I have a great group of girls my age, or a little older or a little younger, taking care of me. For the first time in thirteen years I have people who fit into my life beautifully, and all my hours are covered for the first time. It takes patience and a lot of explanation and time to find the right people. Not everyone is a gem. It's hard to not fall in love with the right one by time spent together and connections made, but I try to be myself, smile and be positive so that maybe someday I can have the best of both worlds. I've come a long way trying to understand the way I am and how different every person is who comes into my life, so when that special person comes along she will know I understand what it is to be a man and to be there for her.

I know what you're thinking, because I'm thinking it too, how open-minded can I get? There's just so much space now in my heart and in my mind, because I've emptied my cup to accept everything; now I need to fill the empty space with someone. Yes, I'm tired of my cup being half full or half empty. I'm either half full of myself or half left empty, thinking my fate lies in decision of other people. To be determined in life should not be a judgment in the hands of anyone who stands in my way. I know exactly what I want and where I'm going. It's not necessity determining my future, but the necessary means of my actions and my own determination. No one else will fight for me, so I must fight to survive. Every person has to take control of life and that is precisely what I'm doing. My art has expanded into the realm of exploring possibilities, expressing beliefs and sharing experiences. My expression goes further and into the beauty shared across cultures and across beliefs. My art is the expression of my life. I am a life form, but it's the way I form life that makes life worth living.

My most prized possession has always been my affection for a physical relationship with a woman. It's not that I haven't suffered enough, with the loss of feeling and movement and being able to pleasure myself. I'm on my way to a Linkin Park concert. It's a warm and relaxing July night. Mercy and I are preparing ourselves in my room. I have the bright idea to use a new indwelling catheter I have never used before, with a blowup balloon, it's red and soft. I never use indwelling catheters because I straight cath every four or five hours. Upon insertion everything seems to go okay and some urine comes out. This is great because if it works I won't have to use the bathroom the whole concert and I can have more fun drinking. The second insertion I feel a little tingle in my head and she blows up the balloon to keep the catheter in the bladder and not coming out. I notice some blood coming out of the bag, and it's no ordinary little scratch.

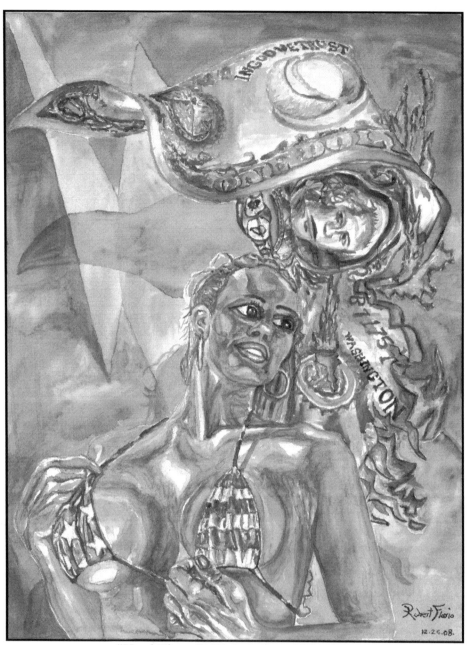

"Hard Times" Watercolor. 18 by 24

"Through Whispering Eyes" Watercolor. 18 by 24

My mind is racing and as the catheter is pulled out some more blood around the tip of my penis is showing, but as soon as the catheter comes out, blood starts gushing out like a fountain. Immediately I scream to call the ambulance and my mom walks downstairs acting like it's not a big deal, but as soon as I take that towel off and release pressure the fountain comes out thick and strong again. This can't be the way I go out. I punctured my urethra. The ambulance shows up and I'm sitting next to my bed and then lifted and transferred onto the stretcher. I'm sitting in the ambulance about to takeoff. The sirens are screaming as we get down the road. I plead not to take me to North Arundel Hospital, now called Baltimore-Washington Medical Center, because I give them the story of my last visit to that place. The only thing I can think of is to protect my family jewels.

If I pass out, will you please tell the doctor to save my penis!? Save my penis, save my penis! I panic and say hysterically.

The paramedic outside the ambulance starts shaking his head and laughing to himself. The ambulance takes off and I'm patched up at Harbor Hospital. Four days later I leave the hospital and a better indwelling catheter has been inserted, attached to a urine bag, to avoid any scraping of the area and for it to heal. I'm all healed up after three weeks and that catheter is no longer in me. I'm ready to go and good as new. I have accepted that my penis must be a superhero, because only a superhero gets less action and more abuse than me. I must be waiting for that special woman to be my Lois Lane.

I have taken you through the journey of my life, from the beginning and through the most horrible situation possible and out of it into realization of who I am. If you take away anything from reading this book it should be what strength you found in yourself, and by using my life as an example, I hope I have inspired others to laugh in the face of adversity. I've had my trachea patched over for one year and now I'm ready. It has been thirteen years and today on April thirteenth I'm finally going to surgically close the hole in my neck. I thought this day would never come. In the spirit of laughing in the face of adversity, I have no choice but to keep the date scheduled even though some people say thirteen is not a very fortunate number. If I'm going to do this I couldn't think of a better day to randomly be selected. It's as if a huge weight has been lifted off of me and the omen of this day will stay infused in my spirit forever as a thorn that I will finally pull out, left with only its scar. I'm finally ready, prepared through many sinus infections that I have overcome, pneumonia and many pills and treatments that all have trained me to take care of myself and my lungs with this trach finally out.

"Amber Waves of Hope" Watercolor. 18 by 24

Self Portrait. "No Fear!" Watercolor. 11 by 15

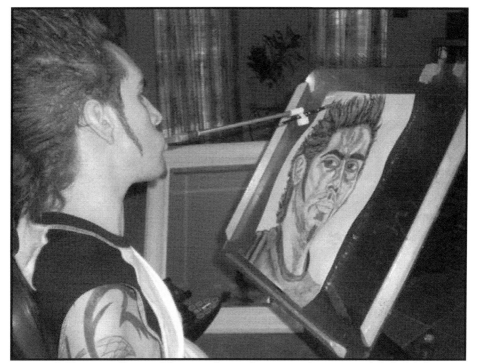

Minutes after waking up from the operation my spirit is high. Even though my neck hurts, I inspire my nurses to dance with me down the halls and in my recovery room as I bop my head and lift my arms, smiling and celebrating. The surgery has healed. I head for the hot mist of my shower, the light on the inside to enter pillows of mist blissful gates, and the dark surrounding it; it's majestic and powerful, welcoming me to my new life. I feel rejuvenated anticipating the hot virgin water, and its sensual intoxications of enlightenment which I never thought would return. My full appreciation of my skin could not come without thirteen years of tribulation, desire and longing for a piece of connection to return to my body. The water on my neck doesn't go into my lungs, as if I've been baptized again every time I take a hot shower. I sit in the shower tilted back in my shower chair with the water massaging my head relieving my itchy scalp. The hot water runs down my face without me choking. It's something I haven't done for thirteen years. The sensation is overwhelming the first time I feel the water on my face and down my neck. Every time from now on will forever feel amazing. The soft kisses of a woman's lips on my neck on that spot are like a climax of release and pleasure.

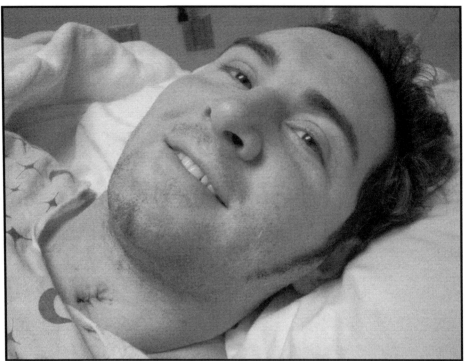

I'm finally free from its burden and never again will I underestimate my own ability to overcome a challenge. I'm never going to know all the answers about life, and you know what? That's OK. I'm tired of beating my head up against the wall and speaking to an invisible Being Who claims to have so much power and love but never actually does anything with it. I wouldn't exactly say I don't believe, in fact I think all beliefs should be looked at perhaps equally across-the-board. Cynical as this might be, as a person who has spent half of my life with a paralyzing injury, and reading promises of physical miracles and inspiration of moving mountains, I finally realized, ultimately it was my own actions and what I choose to think every day that results in positive living.

Maybe believing in all the beliefs could be a free meal ticket to the afterlife? They will ask, *"how did you get here"?* When I get to whatever there is to get to after this world and life I'll be able to say to those people, *"I just believed in them all. I figured one of them had to be right".*

Everyday when I wake up I have a smile on my face, why? Because I choose to! My life has been an experiment maybe to the gods, or maybe a simple test of what life really is; it is what you make it. The process of believing in something and believing in yourself are two different things. I choose to believe in myself. I've lived with faith, religion, and I've seen how the closest people to me, can judge a person like me because I believe different.

Self Portrait. "Freak Me" Digital Watercolor

It's difficult living with a paralysis because it's easy to have my back pushed up against the wall. I can't change my physical world when up against the wall, but my heart and mind must always stay free. Physical freedom and psychological freedom almost always depend on each other, but for me I have to find another way. There shouldn't be barriers from stopping me to find what makes me happy if something can be done about it. Living with my parents has proven to be one of the biggest challenges in my life. My mother and father strive every day for what is right and what matters most. They are strong and loving parents. I love my parents, and I am blessed to be with them, but I have needs. No one can ever know exactly what I'm going through, but I must find my release somehow. In every way I strive to be independent and be myself, but I'm still like every other twenty-eight-year-old guy. I always have to put my life in perspective. I realize I really don't have it that bad, because after all, Jesus was only thirty years old when he moved back in with his dad.

It turns out Jesus might be able to support me in any part of life, because maybe He can relate. It's hard enough living with parents sometimes, but I can't imagine what it would be like having God as my roommate. With God it's never, maybe, the answer is always, yes or no! I know because I've written Him many letters, to the North Pole, and you don't see me walking. I believe Jesus truly wants to heal people, but if God gives one person a healing, it's just like my parents always said, then everyone will want one. No, we can't have that now, can we? I look around at people and women my age and wish things were different, especially as I get older. I have come out of this experience a changed man. I'm not afraid to challenge my own beliefs. I have expanded my experience outside of faith, and it has made me a better person. I'm not fearful of something or someone to be dictated by rules that contradict the human condition. I've seen results that have shattered my expectations and heart. I have also seen very impressive and unquestionable results in my life. I always say the world is a beautiful place because for each person the mind wants to believe what the heart feels. The real world is harsh and impossible but with the right state of mind, in the absence of success, and in the rewards of failure, the world is upside down but to me right side up.

"Reindeer Dreams" Watercolor. 18 by 24

Where I go from here is a choice to be the best person I can be. I
am continuing to look for my dream job as a game designer and for

positions with my experience to open up. I'm using my story, my art and my knowledge to start my life. I'm ready for the long-awaited opportunity that will relieve me from my burdens to live the life I deserve.

The passion dragon that was once a metaphor and lived inside of me is now a physical form of art on my flesh. My tattooed right arm bears the battle marks of a dragon I designed unlike any seen. The abstract marks of purple, green, black, red, with some yellow create a passion dragon clawing two thorny roses. It bleeds because my heart is an open wound and I constantly heal myself with love, ability, friendship, understanding and an open heart and mind. The dragon's head lies on my shoulder. It's hard to find those things that heal my heart. Love is what heals me most when making love, if it doesn't tear me open. My art, passion, abilities and life-long aspirations have come to a point that does not stop. Inside of me is endless love and drive for discovery. As the ink settles in my skin, my hair has highlighted red through it, all because my mind wants to believe what my heart feels. To be free to express and make the world laugh at the challenge at hand, even though my hands don't work. I have shown that ability and passion can take form and bring meaning to life.

I like to say to those who are going through the most difficult time in their life that you have choices, beliefs, vices or whatever it is that you hold onto for strength. I am only an example, but if human life is as precious as we all hold it to be, we must hold an open mind and an open heart so that when all else fails, your faith, your belief, your vice or versa, is in yourself you will become strong again.

Self-empowerment is a must for survival because no matter what we have faith in, unless it is a physical form that actually is producing something that is giving you life sustaining quality and positive reinforcement, you ultimately will be let down and faced with a choice. When I chose to find that strength and confidence in myself first, it was very difficult not to pray for something as I have every night. My body and my spirit have been pulled so many different directions, and in assessing my life and where I am today and how I got through all of it. It was always my choice.

"Halloween" Watercolor. 18 by 24

I chose to think positive and I chose to follow my dreams and not let anyone or anything tell me I couldn't do what I love. Because of holding onto faith so single-handedly, I began to feel insecure and uncertain of who I was and started to judge myself and others. The true test of any belief or faith is whether or not it is acceptable in your mind without a doubt that it's okay to not believe or believe something else. Accepting others for who they are and not judging them--If I can do all that, with a higher power promising everything but never delivering, not becoming weak, or fearful then I'll be just fine. I finally see what I have been missing, the ability to think freely, relying on myself and accepting the fact that I will never know the answers to most of life's questions.

I've discovered that the universe is larger and full of endless possibilities, more than anyone ever told me and more than people even knew was possible. As recent as 2005, using the Hubble telescope, looking into a dark empty part of space, scientists discovered millions of galaxies clustered tight together. In one little spot of sky finding millions of galaxies, knowing our own galaxy contains two hundred billion stars, means the universe is filled with billions of galaxies and teaming with life. Scientists are now scouring the skies for stars that have orbiting planets the same size and distance from the sun as our planet. With that discovery, I don't doubt whatsoever that life exists throughout the entire universe. I only hope the emergence of intelligence does not inherently mean that humanoids, no matter where they're from, are inevitably fragile and stupid. It's funny to me that humans are so intelligent, and so stupid; naïve, heart stricken, with endless potential, yet riddled with passion and disaster. It's a simple truth. The evidence of intelligence is to do something stupid.

"Phelps Glorification" Watercolor. 18 by 24

"Yes We Can" President Obama. Watercolor. 18 by 24

Life should be enjoyed to its fullest. I can appreciate everything because of my loss, but physically I can't do everything that I understand and appreciate. It's a stupid truth. The evidence of stupidity is to do something intelligent. I've been heart-stricken and motivated by passion and I refuse to give up, even though odds are always against me. It's stupid not to give up, but if I give up, I'll never accomplish my dreams that prove my intelligence. If our existence is proof of what life would look like in a planetary system, then there are endless possibilities for life. We are the evidence that life is and can be produced in this exact biosphere. We only need to accept that we are the blueprint. It has already been done. We are the proof of life. Stars in our own galaxy have revolving planetary systems around them and that begs the question, maybe I'll see that alien who visited me when I was a child? If Jesus does return one day on his space ship I hope he takes me with him. I call shotgun. I look at my faith. I look at myself, and then I look up at the sky at night and I know I'm part of something great.

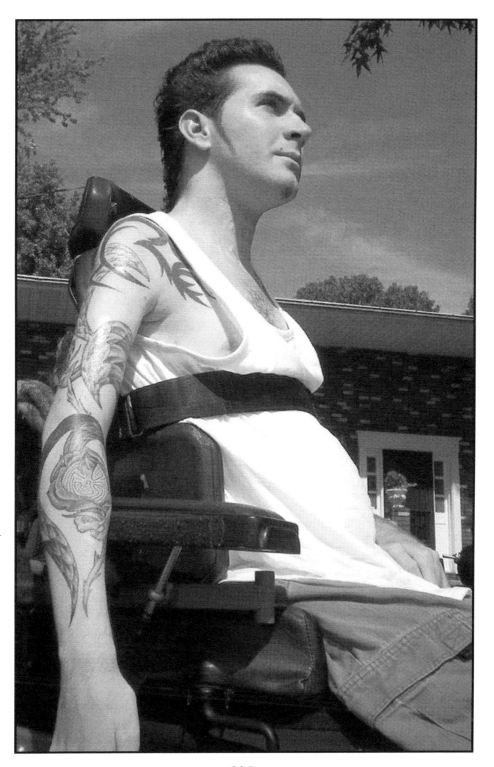

My conscience is a spark, just like the birth of a star through the fire and ignition and abuse I have gone through, that someday all my efforts will mean something. I feel that energy every warm summer day when I lay back and feel the sun on my face. It's one of my favorite things to do. The existence of the sun, the universe of living creatures on this planet tells me that there's something more, but it is my physical proof. I must be honest with myself. It's not like any person has ever gone to heaven and come back with proof and a detailed report. Considering billions of people have come and gone, and not one of them has ever come back, tells me there might be something not right with this idea. To those reading my story countless years from now I say, at least I'm alive at the beginning of what I call a people's awakening of consciousness and endless discoveries. For God's sake, if you have a time machine in the future, I could really use one about now. That way I can retain what I know and go to the future and get the best spinal cord treatment then come back. I hope we continue exploring human potential and if there are any quadriplegics still in the future, find a hot nurse for him and give him some loving.

I will focus now on the things I know I have control over like my talent, my attitude, my actions and how I interact with the people I love. After all, isn't that the basis of God's grand theory? We must live, love, laugh and everything in-between. I don't hold a higher power responsible for my life anymore. I have come through the process and at the end I do see light at the end of the tunnel. In this life, on this planet, and the way our physical form allows us to interact with everything, maybe the light at the end of the dark tunnel is actually dangling and attached to a huge rod. When illuminated it is a huge trap gaping mouth promising everything to survive, but ready to eat me alive.

I will no longer walk aimlessly into the dark believing that the path will be magically lit up for me, instead, when the light goes out, I carry my own energy and lantern to light the way. It's OK to make mistakes. It's not like I ever physically heard a voice shouting when I was all alone, *I am here with you*, when believing so many years that the basis of existence all came down to one individual. Except the difference is that one individual turns out to be myself. Perhaps the meaning of all religion is not a single impossible human, alien or god sacrificing themselves, but a metaphor for every person to find the strength in our selves.

"Vision of Hope" President Obama. Watercolor. 11 by 15

This realization is not easy for everyone to grasp onto and understand fully. I see it in the eyes of people who have lived very hard lives. They don't go to church every Sunday or pretend to go to church every once in awhile. A lot of people are suffering and it just isn't fair to look up to anyone anymore and offer a piece of hope, something written on a piece of paper, and tell them to believe what man himself has created. I respect all beliefs and all personal discoveries. I only speak for myself after witnessing what I have, on the journey I've been on, the roads I have taken, that who I am is a warrior of laughter.

Genesis teaches people that an entity not from this world, "God", put two people, "Adam and Eve", on this planet where human beings never existed before. The entire world accepts this as, "fact". It should not be a shock if in fact another unidentified entity thousands of years older than our oldest beginnings are responsible for everything. It's the same theory as, "God" did it, because we already believe in a transplantation theory. What I really want to know is, how can people accept the condemnation faith demands for immorality and sexual depravity when in fact we believe this is how life began. Follow me with this logic if you will please. "God" created "Adam and Eve" and

338

no one else. "Adam and Eve" have children. There are no other people around whatsoever. Now what I want to know is, in order to create a population like we see today, who is sleeping with the children? Don't tell me "God" will destroy an entire civilization as punishment for doing the exact same acts that must be required to create life in the beginning. "God" cannot make an exception otherwise he can not be a "God". He must do what He says He will do. My father always says to me "maybe" or "we'll see" and even "one of these days". Not "God".

Noah's Ark is the symbol of God's punishment for sin. An entire civilization wiped off the face of the earth. No more human beings were left on earth except for Noah, his wife, his son's and their wives. Now the only solution for repopulation must be to recommit the exact same sexually unacceptable sinful acts that "God" eradicated the human race for committing.

The only solution is to one day look up into the skies once again for salvation. The circular logic faith assumes will always create a flaw called, "the human condition". People will always ask the question, why? We are like a planet of children. We should not survive only to be controlled by our fears.

I laugh in the face of adversity because I've been forced so low I've always been looking up. There's never been any room for me to look down any further. I was at the bottom of every pit imaginable. When I reached that bottom there was nowhere to go but up. The upside down frown is a reflection in a mirror because it never lies it only shows me what is right in front of my face. To be human is to be truthful by realizing and completely accepting the flaws in myself, that I have become stronger, better, faster and free from anything that could ever hold me down again. I work hard every day for what I want to accomplish. I might be the most passionate guy in the world, but who will ever discover that unless I can find someone special to stick with me no matter what? I long every day for a beautiful woman with a beautiful mind and spirit, a wonderful sense of humor and smarts to share my life with.

I have not found a way to walk again, but I have found a way to love again. I don't know why these two things have always been the hardest for me to accomplish. Maybe it is because I want those things the most. Every day I struggle, I tear myself up inside and have to rebuild my happiness when I feel loss or pain. I admit these truths about life. I have moved on. I have found my happiness. Have you found your happiness? Do you have hap-piness?

This life is a sacrifice and I know that better than anyone. I am the real survivor man versus the wild. I have lived in the wilderness and I have survived. Everyday I think about the one that I love, the one I have not met yet, or the one I am in love with and cannot have. I know that when I am forged all alone in one of the best survival techniques is to think of the one I love. I will carry that hope every day as my story reaches the hearts and minds of the people who need it the most, that I will find love. I will use this story to help fund my journey to have stem cell therapy and to afford a better quality of life.

No Fear!
By Robert Florio

No fear!
It's all I hear.
The child inside with fearful hands he steers.
Away from pride the fear is inside.
While God stands by to save his pride.
Children grow with fear and lies.
No fear!
It's all I hear.
I lie awake in floating tears.
Paralyzed! I waited for fourteen years.
Waiting for God to look inside.
I found my fate between the lies.
No fear!
It's all I hear.
My childhood instincts made it clear.
All along I had no fear.
In laughter and talent I've opened my eyes.
So now I think before I lie.
No fear!
It's all I hear.
Thou shalt not fear.
I will not be controlled by my fear.
My hat stood by while I've been blind.
The truth has always been in mind.
No fear!
It's all I hear.
A woman's breath fills my atmosphere.
With a pounding heart I steer clear.
Of her hands covering my eyes.
To simplify and be the strongest in the pride.
No fear!
It's all I hear.

Laughter is the best medicine. Sometimes the world just doesn't make any sense. It is at that precise moment in a life when desperation and frustration become the actual antidote for happiness. I laugh in the face of adversity because sometimes the one person I need to make fun of the most is myself. The mind is a powerful tool and I have used it well. It is hard to stay confident and positive, but because I have chosen to be self-empowered I am finally free. I know my heart will always be in the right direction and the simplest truths in life will set me free, and because I can finally understand what it means to live, love, laugh and everything in-between. In life the things I need the most are always just a out of reach. No matter where I go I'm absolutely convinced of that even on a different planet, in a different solar system or a different galaxy. I hope intelligent life or humanoids evolving somewhere else are not as stupid as humans.

The giraffe is a beautiful animal and has the world's longest neck. In the giraffes natural habitat its only source of vegetation and food is at the very top of a tall tree that only the giraffe can reach. However, the more the giraffe eats from the tree, the further the tree grows away from it... I should have the world's longest tongue because; I love to eat bush, but it's always just out of reach! Life is what you make it, no matter how cold hearted and misunderstood it can be. Sometimes a hero is made in a spark like the connection being in love creates. The spark becomes a fire inside, and that is what I live with everyday. Life is a practical joke, but my life is hardly practical. I have to laugh at life to survive, because I'm staying alive but burning up inside, with a broken extinguisher, and that's when I realized; - if it's about life, it must be a comedy.

"...but I believe what I see!"
(Robert Florio)

I am thankful for my mother and father, because of you all things are possible.

Memorial

This book is dedicated to the loving memory of Robert Joseph Cherry.

Robert Joseph Cherry

You may be gone, but never forgotten. You'll always be in our
thoughts. We'll miss ya Rob!

September 3, 1985 ~ March 28, 2006

Special Thanks

A special thank you to my Artworx Tattoo gang from top left to right;
Carrol, Robert Florio, Crystal, Joe, Jon, and Kirsten.

Robert Florio's Biography

A standup comic with a rock star sensibility and insightfully charming personality has propelled himself as an amazing artist and inspiration. Robert's past experiences, one of which injured his spinal cord at the age of fourteen diving into a swimming pool, has given a new outlook and a path to Robert's life. Robert Florio is one of the most entertaining comedians in a wheelchair. Robert is twenty eight years old, when his first book is published, and is a phenomenal artist not just on stage speaking but using his mouth to create strikingly realistic artwork and expressions. Robert's shows are let up with artwork, music sung by Robert, poems, all in hysterical tone and sarcastic wit of insight and passion. Robert translates and captivates the frustrations of everyday life for him living with a paralysis. Moving forward and not looking back is how Robert maintains a positive message.

Robert has created a documentary called *Robert Florio: A New Way to Live*, completed in 2008, spanning the course of his life up on to the most recent present, where Robert's experience and passion for reaching out to others has led to a discovery in the videogame industry for people with disabilities. Robert received a scholarship to the game design conference in San Jose, California in 2006. Fair play and a chance for success for anyone no matter what their ability or disability is the driving power behind Robert's message. Robert has reached out to athletes by painting their realistic portraits expanding Robert's outreach grabbing the attention of the Baltimore Orioles former outfielder Jay Gibbons. Robert has captured the likeness of Denison Cabral of the Baltimore Blast, Cal Ripken Jr. formally of the Baltimore Orioles, and Baltimore Ravens, including a ghostly remnant of Babe Ruth, and President Obama, just to name a few. Robert is an artist for higher and revered for his realistic paintings of animals like dogs.

Robert's story has received Emmy nomination recognition and Associated Press award in 2005. Robert received a Citizen Award. Robert graduated from the Art Institute of Pittsburgh online division in 2007 with a bachelor's degree in Game Art and Design. The art Institute awarded Robert with the first ever Dean's Merit Award upon graduation. Robert's lifelong mission to create success and motivation through videogames for the disabled is a course in Robert's life that has impacted him tremendously and personally. Robert is one of twenty-two finalists out of 60,000 volunteers to be awarded during the development and creation of the Project Top-Secret videogame awarded in 2008. The game is developed by Acclaim Games and directed by David Perry.

Robert's experience and insight is brought to the entertainment forefront when speaking and creating art spanning, history, science, art, health care, politics, religion, relationships, rock 'n roll, to say the least, and all comically delivered with the intention to inspire and motivate success. Robert's last project is the long waited self publication of his autobiography, illustrating a children's book, while recording his day-to-day life in the efforts to create another documentary in the near future. Robert is currently booking to go out and tell his story. To see Robert's work, get your copy of Robert's documentary, and get your own personal Robert Florio artwork or portrait and autobiography you can visit his personal web site www.RobertFlorio.com.

Associated Press Award

Outstanding Sports Feature

2005

WBAL

Robert Florio

Anne Kramer   *President*

The White House Letter

THE WHITE HOUSE

WASHINGTON

December 9, 2003

Mr. Robert Florio
████████████
████████████████

Dear Robert:

Congratulations on the recent exhibition of your art at the Arundel Center.

Your determination to overcome difficult circumstances and to focus on the positive is an inspiration to all. By setting high goals and working hard to achieve them, you demonstrate the spirit of our Nation.

Laura and I send you and your family our best wishes for a joyous holiday season.

Sincerely,

George W. Bush

David Perry Recommended

August 8, 2008

To Whom It May Concern:

Please accept this letter as a recommendation for Rob Florio.

In 2007 Acclaim Games ran the biggest user-generated development project in the history of the video game industry. Over 60,000 people signed up into one team to work on developing a game project together. The result was an incredibly innovative game design never seen before.

On June 28, 2008 we announced the finalists in the project, the people that stood out above all others. As you would expect, only a handful really had the determination, skills and sustained commitment to complete all the tasks at hand, so if you are looking for someone that's been pre-tested, that ended up a finalist from such a huge amount of people, then please consider Rob Florio.

Rob Florio is an artist and a true student of game design. He brought his considerable talents fully to bear in the Top Secret project, providing art and design concepts at every stage. He was always an outspoken leader who would challenge the status quo and demand innovative solutions. He co-developed an innovative and original user interface designed to make games accessible to players with physical, visual, audio and cognitive impairments, produced a full "project risk analysis" and worked to bring people together in common visions. Robert was, from the very beginning, one of the most dedicated members of the community, showing his passion, creativity and will to succeed at every step. Rob Florio is quadriplegic, and I only mention that because, based on his contributions to the project, you would never have guessed that. Highly recommended.

If you have a question, contact me at dp@acclaim.com. You can also contact my Assistant Director, Rusel DeMaria at demaria@demaria.com. Rusel worked closely with each of these project members.

White Rhino Production
A Robert Florio Trade Mark TM
"The crap you actually want to buy."

FIRST EDITION, 2010

$17.99 USA

Life! It Must Be a Comedy
An Autobiography by Robert Florio

Quotation: Robert Frost
Quotation: Linkin Park

Cover design: by Robert Florio

Photos: Personal

ISBN-1452833508
EAN-13 9781452833507

Manufactured in the United States of America

Made in the USA
Charleston, SC
26 September 2010